WITHDRAWN FROM CANISIUS COLLEGE LIBRARY

Saying and Meaning

Saying and Meaning

A MAIN THEME IN J. L. AUSTIN'S PHILOSOPHY

MATS FURBERG

'I dreamt a line that would make a motto for a sober philosophy: *Neither a be-all nor an end-all be.*'
       J. L. AUSTIN

Rowman and Littlefield Publishers
REFERENCE AND SCHOLARLY BOOKS
Totowa, New Jersey

FIRST PUBLISHED IN THE UNITED STATES 1971
by Rowman and Littlefield, Totowa, New Jersey

ISBN 0-87471-065-0

© Mats Furberg, 1963 and 1971

Printed in Great Britain

TO THE MEMORY OF MARGARETHA

Preface

John Langshaw Austin was born in 1911. He was educated at Shrewsbury School (Classical Sch.) and then at Balliol College (Classical Sch.). At Oxford he remained, first as a Fellow of All Souls College, then as an Official Fellow and Tutor in Philosophy at Magdalen College. In 1952, he was appointed White's Professor of Moral Philosophy in the University of Oxford, and Fellow of Corpus Christi College. He died in 1960.*

Like Moore in an earlier generation, Austin was a philosophers' philosopher and exerted an immense influence. According to G. J. Warnock, as reported in *The New Yorker*, Dec. 9, 1961,

he did succeed in haunting most of the philosophers in England, and to his colleagues it seemed that his terrifying intelligence was never at rest. Many of them used to wake up in the night with a vision of the stringy, wiry Austin standing over their pillow like a bird of prey. Their daylight hours were no better. They would write some philosophical sentences and then read them over as Austin might, in an expressionless, frigid voice, and their blood would run cold. Some of them were so intimidated by the mere fact of his existence that they weren't able to publish a single article during his lifetime.

It was a sorrow for Austin that he was unable to write much. Although such papers as 'Other minds', 'A plea for excuses' and 'Ifs and cans' were recognized as outstanding examples of 'Oxford philosophy', they did not for a long time provoke much discussion in philosophical periodicals. His reputation rested mainly on the spoken word. His lectures and classes gathered scholars from many parts of the world. In meetings each week of the terms from 1947 to 1959, he led discussions among younger teachers of

*[For biographical information, see G. J. Warnock's excellent paper 'J. L. Austin, a biographical sketch' in *Symposium on J. L. Austin*, ed. K. T. Fann (London, 1969). —I shall henceforward use *Symp* as an abbreviation of the title of Fann's anthology.]

philosophy at the university. Perhaps because of his literary unproductivity, he took a great pride in teaching.* When he felt he had reached the summit of his influence at Oxford, he thought about going to the University of California in Berkeley, where he thought he would be more influential as a teacher. He died of cancer before the step had been taken.

Most of Austin's production has now been published. *Philosophical Papers* contains all his mature essays.† Three of them, 'The meaning of a word', 'Unfair to facts' and 'Performative utterances', had not been published during his lifetime.—From Austin's manuscript notes, G. J. Warnock has 'reconstructed' *Sense and Sensibilia*, a famous series of lectures on some problems of perception. Austin wrote sets of notes for these lectures in 1947, 1948, 1949, 1955 and 1958.—J. O. Urmson has edited a still better known series of lectures on performatives and illocutionary acts. These lectures were delivered at Oxford from 1952. Austin prepared a new set of notes for the William James Lectures in Harvard in 1955. He also gave the lectures a new title under which they have been printed, *How to do things with Words*.

Besides these three books, there exists a tape-recorded lecture of Austin's, called 'What I do as a philosopher' and delivered at Gothenburg in 1959. Its main parts consist of the programmatic passages of 'A plea for excuses' and 'Ifs and cans'.‡

Austin's intellect was mainly critical and negative. His positive suggestions are mostly concerned with moral philosophy. But he also offered a doctrine of different kinds of speech acts, and that tenet will occupy us in the present book. In references to his works, *S&S* will stand for *Sense and Sensibilia*, and *Words* for *How to do things with Words*. The essays of *Philosophical Papers* are indicated by the year when they were written:

*[Once he remarked, 'I had to decide early on whether I was going to write books or to teach people how to do philosophy usefully'. (S. Cavell: 'Austin at criticism', *Symp*, p. 75.]

†[This is incorrect. It does not include '*Agathon* and *Eudaimonia* in the *Ethics* of Aristotle' (*Aristotle*, ed. J. M. E. Moravcsik); 'Three ways of spilling ink' (*Ph. R.* 75, 1966); and 'Performative—Constative' (*Philosophy and Ordinary Language*, ed. Ch. E. Caton). Nor does it include Austin's lectures on the *Nicomachean Ethics*.]

‡[In *Symp* there is a contribution to 'A Symposium on Austin's Method' by J. O. Urmson (pp. 76–86). It contains, among other things, quotations from Austin, entitled 'Something about one way of possibly doing one part of philosophy'. The quotations seem to be from the remainder of 'What I do as a philosopher'.]

1939: 'Are there *a priori* concepts?'
1940: 'The meaning of a word'
1946: 'Other minds'
1950: 'Truth'
1953: 'How to talk'
1954: 'Unfair to facts'
1956a: 'A plea for excuses'
1956b: 'Ifs and cans'
1956c: 'Performative utterances'
1958: 'Pretending'.

Page-references to the essays are to *Philosophical Papers*. '1945. 56' is thus to be read '"Other minds", p. 56 in *Philosophical Papers*'.—In all quotations, the italics are those of the author of the passage.

As a British Council scholar at Oxford, I attended Austin's lectures and classes in 1956/57. Travelling scholarships, granted by the Faculty of Arts at the University of Gothenburg, enabled me to spend the summer terms of 1959 and 1961 at Oxford and enlarge my knowledge of his philosophy. During the last of these stays, Messrs G. J. Warnock and J. O. Urmson kindly gave me access to then unpublished writings by Austin.

Apart from the subject of this book, three teachers of philosophy have influenced me profoundly: Mr H. P. Grice who in tutorials stressed the importance of many and closely studied examples; Mr Sören Halldén who patiently has tried to make my ideas clearer and more coherent; and Professor Ivar Segelberg who has forced me to withdraw from a greater number of philosophically untenable positions than I care to remember.

I also owe a debt of gratitude to Mr Tore Nordenstam and the participants in Professor Segelberg's classes. Mr Jan Andersson has discussed practically every point in the book with me and considerably improved it. He has also helped me with more tedious aspects of book-production.

Mrs M.-Z. Rinman has checked my English.

To these institutions and persons I tender my sincere thanks. My remaining—and immense—debt of gratitude is to my wife, without whom I should not have had the leisure to write this book.

Preface to the Second Edition

My doctor's dissertation *Locutionary and Illocutionary Acts*—henceforward called *LIA*—appeared in May 1963. Professor G. H. von Wright made me aware that at a few but important points it conflated the locutionary act with the constative illocutionary one. I spent the better part of the summer trying to delete this bad mistake. At the same time I reorganized the book by splitting its second chapter into two, the second half of which was enlarged with material from the first section of Ch. 4 together with new ideas on 'practical' and 'theoretical' discourse and new attempts to define a performative.

The first edition of *LIA* is unfit to be reprinted because of the conflation. What is published here is the 1963 Summer version with additional notes in square brackets discussing some later papers on Austin's philosophy. The newly-written postscript will perhaps make it clear that if I had written the book today, it would have been different.

Among the participants in my classes who have positively and negatively helped me to form the ideas of the postscript I would like to mention Dick A. R. Haglund, Per Lindström—who brought a decisive objection to the idea behind my earliest new attempt to account for the locutionary/illocutionary distinction—Beata Agrell-Lindström and Thomas Wetterström.

The name of Jan Andersson occurs only once in the text. It ought to have appeared on nearly every page of the postscript. He has forced me to rethink and amend almost all its main points.

Gunnilse,   M.F.
February, 1967.

Contents

Preface	vii
Preface to the Second Edition	xi

Chapter 1. Austin's Approach — 1

I. THE INHERITANCE FROM MOORE — 2
1. A tenet of Moore's — 2
2. 'Analysis' as distinction — 6
3. Similarities between Moore and Austin — 7
4. Austin's criticism of analysis — 9
5. One task of philosophy: the elucidation of speech acts — 28
6. Summary — 30

II. SOME MAIN CHARACTERISTICS OF AUSTIN'S APPROACH — 31
7. Austin's 'linguistic phenomenology' — 31
8. The 'science of language' — 47

III. WITTGENSTEIN AND AUSTIN — 50

Chapter 2. The Locutionary Act: Speech and Language — 56

I. LANGUAGE — 58

A. VOCABULARY — 58
1. The vocabulary of speech situation S_0 — 58
2. The vocabulary of S_1 — 59
3. Adapter-words — 60
4. Entailment — 70
5. Open texture — 71

B. SYNTAX 75
6. The syntax of the primitive speech acts 75
7. Syntax and other speech acts 75
II. LANGUAGE AND SPEECH 76
A. 'INTERNAL SEMANTICS' 76
8. Misreferring and misclassifying 76
B. 'EXTERNAL SEMANTICS' 80
9. Fitting and matching 81

Chapter 3. The Illocutionary Act 89
I. TWO PRINCIPLES OF SERIOUS SPEECH 89
1. The principle of the speaker's trustworthiness 90
2. Trustworthiness and the demands of a common language 92
3. The principle of relevance to the addressee 93
4. Pragmatic implication 94
5. Violations of the two principles 96
II. PRAGMATIC IMPLICATION AND DISCOURSE IMPLICATION 98
6. Discourse implication 98
7. 'Practical' and 'theoretical' discourse 103
8. Performatoriness and implications of trustworthiness 106
III. THE ILLOCUTIONARY ACT 107
9. Serious speech and the new 'science of language' 107
10. Illocutionary and perlocutionary acts 108
11. The locutionary and the illocutionary act 111
12. Locutionary act/illocutionary act versus phrastic/neustic 113

Chapter 4. Unguarded Constatives: Truth and Knowledge 116
I. TRUTH 117
1. The use of the phrase 'is true' 117
1.1. Is 'It is true that p' a statement about a statement? 121
1.11. Are 'is true'-utterances not about statements? 123

1.12. Are 'is true'-utterances always about statements?	126
1.13. Are 'is true'-utterances themselves statements?	127
1.2. The traditional problems of truth and Strawson's problem	129
2. The Correspondence Theory of truth	130
2.0. Austin's 1950 account of the felicity-conditions of statements	133
2.1. Strawson's objections	139
2.11. Facts as quasi-objects	139
2.12. The status of facts	142
2.13. Facts as true statements	147
2.2. A digression: Austin's model of truth and Strawson's 'presuppositions'	155
3. The constative discourse	158
3.1. The criteria of a statement	160
3.2. The ideally true statement	162
3.3. The ideally true statement and actual statements	171
II. KNOWLEDGE	173
4. Sufficiency of backing	174
5. Reliability of backing	182
6. Our knowledge of other minds	185
Chapter 5. The Performative Thesis and the Force Thesis	192
I. PERFORMATIVES AND THEIR FUNCTIONS	193
1. Performatives	193
2. The Performative Thesis	200
2.1. Connexions between performatives and constatives	202
2.2. Are performative true and false?	203
3. The Force Thesis	206
4. 'Illocutions'	212
5. Constating, performing, and degree-showing	217
II. TWO KINDS OF FORCE-SHOWING	219
6. Discourse-marking expressions	219

6.1. Promising	219
6.11. The performatoriness of saying 'I promise'	219
6.12. The force-showing function of saying 'I promise'	223
6.13. The interplay between the two functions	225
6.2. Fact-stating	226
7. A new type of force-showing expressions	229
8. Degree-showing devices	229
8.1. 'I believe'	231
8.2. 'Problematic' devices	244
8.3. The scale of degree-showing devices	245
8.4. 'I know'	247
9. Austin on 'I know'	252

Postscript 256

I. A Reconsideration of the Locutionary/Illocutionary Distinction 256

1. Nonnatural meaning introduced	256
2. The vehicle of meaning $_{NN}$	257
2.1. Meaning $_{NN}$ in a preverbal language	258
2.2. Meaning $_{NN}$ in a budding language	262
2.3. Meaning $_{NN}$ in an established language	265
3. Meaning $_{NN}$ and the locutionary/illocutionary distinction	269
4. Illocutionary devices	275

II. ARCHETYPICAL PERFORMATIVES 279

5. Archetypical performatives	279
5.1. Archetypical performatives are accomplished	280
5.2. Archetypical performatives are alinguistic	281
5.3. Archetypical performatives are essentially neither locutionary nor illocutionary	285
6. Archetypical performatives and promises	286

Index

CHAPTER 1

Austin's Approach

From the end of World War II till his death in 1960, J. L. Austin was the intellectual leader of the most 'linguistic'-minded of all the heterogenous groups of thinkers labelled 'Oxford philosophers'. The 'linguistic' philosophers have often been charged with being engrossed in purely linguistic problems, or at least with showing no interest in perennial philosophical questions. Thus it has been said that they are occupied with linguistic distinctions, whether these have any 'therapeutic' value or not; that they confer a quite unwarranted philosophical authority to dictionaries and grammars; that they hold that a fine ear for linguistic nuances is a pre-requisite for their variety of investigations; and that in their opinion 'it is not the world that we are to try to understand but only sentences'.[1] Were these allegations right, they would go some way to show that the proponents of the 'linguistic movement' are really engaged in doing linguistics, not philosophy.

On other occasions, critics have conceded that, after all, the 'linguistic' philosophers are philosophers, though pretty poor at their business: they believe that *all* philosophical problems arise from misuse of language and can be remedied by careful attention to the nuances of ordinary language; they believe that language in its ordinary use is endowed with a kind of superior genius or hidden intelligence; they believe that all knowledge is of a verbal sort; and they do not see that philosophical problems are more concerned with how a word *ought* to be used than with its ordinary usage.

These accusations are fairly common and are sometimes voiced by influential thinkers. So let us scrutinize the technique and aims of Austin's philosophy. I shall first sketch the assumptions from which he starts his investigations, and then essay an account of

[1] Bertrand Russell, *My Philosophical Development*, p. 217.

his usual approach and what he claimed and did not claim on its behalf. Finally, I shall compare his technique to Wittgenstein's.

I. THE INHERITANCE FROM MOORE

1. A tenet of Moore's

In 'A defence of common sense' G. E. Moore maintains that there are a lot of propositions of a certain type which are part of the common sense view of the world. Examples are that there exists a body which is mine; that it was born at a certain time in the past and that it has existed continuously ever since; that there are other human bodies which have also been born at a certain time in the past and have existed continuously for some time; that I have perceived things and been aware of my perceiving them; that I have been aware of facts which I was not at the time observing; that I have had expectations, and thought of imaginary things, and dreamt; and that very many, though not all, human beings have frequently known, with regard to themselves and their bodies, the truth of a proposition corresponding to each of the propositions about myself and my body.[2]

Moore maintains that all these propositions are wholly true and literally true. Each of them is unambiguous; we all understand its meaning. Each of them is wholly true and known to be wholly true. So what puzzles philosophers cannot reasonably be what their truth-value is; for we all know it. Nor can it be what their meaning is; for we all understand them. Moore suggests that what troubles us is their analysis. Before we turn to his account of the nature of philosophical analysis, we had better see why he thought that his propositions were (a) true and (b) unambiguous.

(a) It seems to me that his reasons for holding them true are of two kinds. In the first sort of case, they cannot be denied without absurdity, since the objector either presupposes their truth or the truth of a proposition of the same type as the one he rejects, or he relies on more uncertain propositions than the ones he objects to. In the second kind of case, the propositions cannot be rejected since they are obviously true.[3] In *Some Main Problems of Philo-*

[2] G. E. Moore, *Philosophical Papers*, p. 34f.
[3] Cf Alan R. White, *G. E. Moore*, Ch. II, (b).

sophy, p. 122, Moore argues that there have to be such propositions if we are ever to know that any proposition is true.

For if I cannot know any proposition whatever to be . . . true . . ., unless I have first known some other proposition, from which it follows, to be so; then, of course, I cannot have known this other proposition, unless I have first known some third proposition, before *it;* nor this third proposition, unless I have first known a fourth before it; and so on *ad infinitum.*

He hesitates whether to assign 'I do not know that this pencil exists' to the first or the second kind; but it is nevertheless much more certain that any premiss which could be used to prove it false, and also much more certain than any other premiss which could be used to prove it true.[4]

(*b*) Moore's reason for thinking that his propositions are unambiguous seems to be simply that none of them (or rather none of the sentences expressing them) could be misunderstood by anybody who knows English.

Moore's notion of analysis. Now, what does Moore mean by 'analysis'? He gives no good explanation in 'A defence of common sense'; but in 'A reply to my critics' he lays down that his analysis is an analysis of concepts, and that the following conditions have to hold good:

That if in making a given statement one is to be properly said to be 'giving an analysis' of a *concept,* then (*a*) both *analysandum* and *analysans* must be *concepts,* and, if the analysis is a *correct* one, must, in some sense, be *the same concept,* and (*b*) that the *expression* used for the *analysandum* must be a different *expression* from that used for the *analysans.*

Finally,

(*c*) . . . the *expression* used for the *analysandum* must not only be *different* from that used for the *analysans,* but . . . they must differ in this way, namely, . . . the expression used for the *analysans* must *explicitly mention* concepts which are not explicitly mentioned by the expression used for the *analysandum.* Thus the expression '*x* is a male sibling' *explicitly mentions* the concepts 'male' and 'sibling', whereas the expression '*x* is a brother' does not. It is true, of course, that the former expression not only *mentions* these concepts, but also

[4] *Some Main Problems of Philosophy,* p. 125.

mentions the *way in which they are combined* in the concept 'brother', which is, in this case, the way of mere conjunction, but in other cases may be very different from mere conjunction. And that the *method of combination* should be explicitly mentioned by the expression used for the *analysans* is, I think, also a necessary condition for the giving of an analysis.

Moore admits that he does not know clearly what he means by saying that two concepts are, or are not, identical; but he tries to illustrate it by saying that 'in a sense, the expression "*x* is a brother" is *not* synonymous with, has *not the same meaning as*, "*x* is a male sibling", since if you were to translate the French word *frère* by the expression "male sibling", your translation would be *incorrect*, whereas if you were to translate it by "brother", it would not.'[5]

Moore's account fosters a well-known paradox. For the analysans either has the same sense as the analysandum, in which case the analysis tells us nothing new; or it has a different sense from the analysandum, and then the analysis is wrong. So an analysis either tells us nothing new or tells us something wrong. Moore attempts to avoid the horns of the dilemma by his stipulation that the analysans must explicitly mention something which is only implicit in the analysandum; but this is hardly of any avail until we know what it is for the analysandum and the analysans to be the same, or for the analysandum implicitly to contain something which is explicitly mentioned in the analysans.

An important feature of Moore's account is that he thinks of analysis as the splitting up of something into something; he thinks of analysis as division. But, as Alan White has argued,[6] his practice sometimes betrays that he uses another method which White baptizes (rather unhappily, I think) 'analysis as distinction'. There are two sub-classes of this kind of 'analysis'. First, there is discriminative distinction which consists in 'drawing attention to, pin-pointing, and enumerating the various meanings of a given ambiguous expression and of other expressions considered relevant to it'.[7] Secondly, there is analytic distinction which consists in 'saying, or describing, how one particular meaning of an expression which interests us is to be distinguished

---

[5] *The Philosophy of G. E. Moore*, p. 666f.
[6] White, *op. cit.*, Ch. V.   [7] *Op. cit.*, 74f.

from and related to other meanings both of the same expression and of other expressions'.[8] White is, on good grounds, hesitant to ascribe to Moore the view that any of the two methods of distinction is to be called analysis; but there is no doubt that Moore often uses them in his philosophical work.

Moore's famous paper 'Is existence a predicate?' is, I think, an example of how a philosopher can do his task without splitting anything up into anything. Moore first uses discriminative distinction in order to pick out the sense in which he uses the word 'predicate'; then he selects a few examples where something is predicated of x, e.g. 'x growls' and 'x scratches'; and finally he raises the question 'Is "exist" in "x exists" used in a way which closely resembles the way in which "growl" and "scratch" are used in "x growls" and "x scratches"?' And he points out several great differences between the behaviour of 'exist' on the one hand and 'growl' and 'scratch' on the other.

Moore would probably claim that this is *not* a philological study.[9] His denial is tied up with his notion of meaning. In *Some Main Problems of Philosophy*, pp. 206f, he maintains that

> no discussion about the meaning of a word is *merely* about the meaning of a word. It always involves some discussion as to the way in which the things or notions, for which the word may stand, are distinguished from or related to one another. And every new discovery of this nature which we may make, for instance, about the notion which is conveyed by such a word as 'real' or 'true' is, you see, a new discovery which applies to the whole range of things which *are* real or true: it is, in that sense, a new discovery about properties which would belong to the Universe, even if there were no such things as words at all, and properties which are exceedingly general—which belong to an enormous number, if not to the whole, of the important constituents of the Universe.

He did not doubt that lots and lots of words 'stand for' or are names of something, and his interest was given to what the name named and not to the name itself. When later philosophers found radical faults in the name theory of meaning, his simple account would no longer do as an explanation of how the methods of distinction tell us something about the world.

[8] *Op. cit.*, p. 75.
[9] Cf 'A reply to my critics', *The Philosophy of G. E. Moore*, p. 661.

2. 'Analysis' as distinction

Moore stressed, then, that there are utterances which puzzle us although we know perfectly well both what they mean and what their truth-value is. He suggested that our bewilderment is due to our ignorance of their correct analysis—that we want to know how the concepts expressed by the utterance are to be split up into other concepts. But in practice he sometimes did not analyse anything but tried to make something plain by means of the methods of distinction.

As these methods became more and more common, some factors which had been neglected earlier were spotlit. In the first place, the methods of distinction suggested that the elucidation which Moore desired might be brought about by unearthing the rules governing the employment of philosophically controversial words. The words themselves, regarded as a string of sounds or letters, are not essential to the philosopher; it does not matter whether we compare the statements made by using 'x exists' and 'x growls' or the statements made by saying 'x existerar' and 'x morrar'. What worries us is that we do not clearly see how the rules governing the words resemble and diverge from each other.

The methods of distinction also strongly suggest that we cannot profitably discuss the employment of a certain word *in vacuo*; we have to insert it into whole utterances and even into non-linguistic contexts. This had already been stressed by Frege for philosophical reasons and by Sir Alan Gardiner for linguistic ones; but when philosophers more habitually used the methods of distinction, it became increasingly difficult to neglect the context.

When a word is placed into a whole utterance and that utterance into a non-linguistic context, we cannot fail to observe that the utterance is spoken by somebody and, in general, addressed to somebody. May it not be worth our while to pay heed to the relations between the utterance, its utterer, and the addressee? That question became pressing for logical positivists who held that non-formal utterances which were not even in principle verifiable or falsifiable were nonsense. It was agreed that e.g. genuine ethical utterances could not be verified or falsified and hence were nonsense. Since they did not express any 'proposition', they could not profitably be analysed. Nevertheless, they could not be just discarded; they obviously had an important job to do. According to logical positivists, the moral philosopher had to elucidate neither the ('cognitive') meaning nor the truth-value but the function of ethical utterances: he had to show that their standard function was to express and/or evoke emotions.

As soon as the utterance is considered in its context, other problems crop up, e.g. that of telling what those features are which in a certain situation make an utterance suitable, true, appropriate, etc. or unsuitable, false, inappropriate and so on; and that of telling how the force of an utterance is conveyed, i.e., how the addressee is given to understand that the utterance is (say) a piece of information and not a tentative opinion or a guess. The former of these tasks is clearly a traditionally philosophical one, whereas questions of function and force have hardly received serious attention in the past.

In this way several factors have contributed to a general drift away from philosophy as analysis—philosophy as splitting something up into something—to philosophy as distinction.

3. *Similarities between Moore and Austin*

There are at least two main respects in which Austin takes Moore's position as his point of departure.

(1) Like Moore, Austin accepts a large part of the common sense view as undoubtedly true. Sometimes I know that another person is happy, or moody, or angry; sometimes I look at a cat; sometimes I could have done something which I in fact did not do; I have at various times in the past promised somebody something, apologized, regretted things I have done, and so on. All these things are also true about a great number of other people.

As a rule, Austin gives no arguments in favour of this common sense view. He simply assumes that its truth is obvious as soon as it is pointed out: I *do* sometimes know, without any possibility of doubt, that my wife is very angry indeed. (Cf, for example, point 1 of the Final Note of 1946.83.) The only place where he has defended common sense explicitly and at length is in *S&S*. But even there he does not argue certain things, presumably because he thinks that any argument for them would rely on more dubious premisses than they themselves do. Thus he quotes Ayer as making the 'assumptions' that a stick does not change its shape when placed in water and that it cannot be both crooked and straight; and he remarks that it is both strange and important that Ayer speaks of 'assumptions' here, for it makes it possible for him to 'take seriously the notion of denying at least one of them, which he could hardly do if he had recognized them . . . as the plain and incontestable facts that they are' (*S&S*, 21n).

When Austin argues for a common sense view, his arguments have a typically Moorean form: again and again he points out that philosophers in rejecting the common sense view have fallen back on tenets which at crucial points assume something much less likely to be true than what we ordinarily say. It is much more probable that we really see a straight stick that looks crooked than that we don't see a stick at all but only a sense-datum or a construct of sense-data. In fact (and this is an argument which is reminiscent of some of Moore's in 'A defence of common sense'), the philosophers he is concerned with contradict themselves, since their conclusion denies what they took for granted when setting out their argument, viz. that we do see a straight stick half immersed in water. Very often our common sense statement is not only *much more likely* to be true than philosophical counter-assertions; it *is* true. We all know it is; so the philosophical task cannot, in this case, be to find out its truth-value.

(2) Austin undoubtedly follows Moore in regarding such common sense utterances as the ones I have mentioned as unambiguous. They are 'the very type of . . . unambiguous expression[s], the meaning of which we all understand', as Moore says (*Philosophical Papers*, p. 37). But if everyone who knows English understands what they mean, the philosophical task cannot be to elucidate their meaning—it is perfectly clear already.

These are the two main respects in which Moore and Austin agree: certain common sense utterances are perfectly clear, and we know that they are true; so the philosopher has no business to tell us what they mean or what their truth-value is. But Austin could not accept Moore's view that the reason why philosophers are troubled by these utterances is that they don't know the analysis of the concepts by which the meaning of the utterances is expressed.

4. Austin's criticism of analysis

Moore did not hold that analysis is the only legitimate business of philosophy (cf 'A reply to my critics' in *The Philosophy of G. E. Moore*, pp. 675–6); but he did not doubt that the splitting up of concepts formed an essential part of his task. Austin had to reject this view since, as he said as late as in his 1959 lecture 'What I do as a philosopher', 'I do not really believe there are any concepts'. His case against them is stated in 1939 and 1940; and a few relevant remarks on propositions are to be found in 1950 and 1954.

Why did he disbelieve in concepts? I shall treat his main types of reasons under different headings.

The criticism of universals (1939.1–9). It is, says Austin, a common view that concepts can be explained only in terms of universals; but what is a universal? It is emphatically not anything we stumble across in any familiar way. It was 'calculated into existence' 'not so very long' ago—a pretty surprising statement in view of the medieval struggles between nominalists and realists over universals. What brought universals into being was, he tells us, transcendental arguments explaining how certain practices are possible. A universal is what provides the solution of a certain problem. If the arguments are sound, they prove *that* there are universals but not *what* they are.

There are several transcendental arguments for the existence of universals, says Austin. He gives us two of them without telling us by whom they have been employed. The first of them introduces universals to answer the question 'How is it possible to call numerically different sensa by the same single name—that two different sensa both can be called "grey"?' If the answer is that this is possible because the same universal is 'there' in each case, it is nonsense to ask e.g. 'How is the universal related to the particular?' or 'Could there be universals without instances?' Since a universal *by definition* is related to certain sensa in a certain way, we 'might as well worry about what is the relation between a man and his aunt, and as to whether there can be aunts without nephews (or nieces)'.

The other transcendental argument runs in Austin's words like this: 'A true statement is one which corresponds with reality: the statements of the scientist are true: therefore there are realities which correspond to those statements. Sensa do not correspond to the statements of the scientist . . . : therefore there must exist other objects, real but not sensible, which do correspond to the statements of the scientist. Let these be called "universals".' Having given a sample of the questions this argument begs, Austin stresses that it, too, is transcendental. 'The "universal" is an x, which is to solve our problem for us: we know only that it is non-sensible, and in addition must possess certain characters, the lack of which prohibits sensa from corresponding to the statements of the scientist. But we do not stumble across these "universals": though, needless to say, philosophers soon take to talking as though they did.'

The two arguments do not, he holds, establish the existence of the same sort of universals. 'Except that both are non-sensible nothing more is known in which they are alike.' It is odd to speak of 'arguments for the existence of universals'; for 'no two of these arguments are known to be arguments for the existence of the same thing', and the phrase 'suggests that we know what a "universal" is quite apart from the arguments for its existence—whereas, in fact, "universal" *means*, in each case, simply "the entity which this argument proves to exist".' Austin even claims to be able to prove indirectly that the two arguments, if sound, prove the existence of different sorts of universals. For (i) whilst the former of them proves that there is a universal corresponding to every general name, 'the latter only does so when the name is that of an object studied by the scientist', and (ii) if such universals as 'circularity' and 'straightness' are proved to exist by the first argument, they *must* be applicable to sensa, whereas they *cannot* be thus applicable according to the second argument. When 'universal' is used as in the latter, the question 'How are universals related to particulars?' makes sense; and the question 'Are there universals without instances?' is now absurd, for the new reason that a universal in the sense of the second argument 'is not the sort of thing which "has instances" at all'.

This is a devastating criticism—if anyone ever accepted the two arguments, and accepted them simultaneously. Let us, however, shelve the question of Austin's historical accuracy and turn to his consideration of the first argument (the other he quietly drops).

THE INHERITANCE FROM MOORE

(i) In a more elaborate form the first argument for the existence of universals runs thus: We 'sense' things and call many numerically different sensa by the same name. The transcendental argument to save this practice has two steps:

(a) If the same single name is correctly used, there must be a single identical bearer 'there' for the name to be a name of. That bearer, whatever it may be, is a universal.

(b) *Ex hypothesi* the things we sense are many or different. Consequently the universal is not sensed.

Austin insists that if the argument holds in (a), it also holds in (b). We cannot accept the former and reject the latter: 'the whole point of the argument is that there must exist something of a kind quite different from sensa'. He also points out that (a) depends on the suppressed premiss that words are essentially names.

He finds two faults with the argument: 'there is no reason whatever' to accept the view that words are essentially names; and, quite independent of that criticism, the argument involves a *petitio principii*. At this point I shall only consider the latter objection. It goes like this:

The transcendental argument takes it for granted that the *same* single word is used for different sensa. But '"grey" and "grey" are *not* the same, they are two similar symbols (tokens), just as the things denoted by "this" and by "that" are similar things. In this matter, the "words" are in a position precisely analogous to that of the objects denoted by them.' It is no use objecting that the words 'same single' do not mean 'numerically identical' in this context. If they mean 'qualitatively identical', 'then it is clear that the sense in which there is an identical "type" of the tokens is just like the sense in which the sensa share in an identical common character: hence the former cannot be taken as self-explanatory while the latter is admitted obscure'. If on the other hand 'the same single word' means that all these tokens 'have the same meaning', 'then we cannot *assume* that it is the business of similar tokens to "mean" something which is numerically self-identical, without begging the whole question'. And if I nevertheless assert that I do *sense* something identical in different sensa, I have given up the whole transcendental argument, since the identical something cannot then be an entity different in kind from sensa.

I find the rejoinder convincing; but has any famous philosopher ever held the argument criticized? I shall leave my text in order to claim that both Russell and Moore seem to be sinners in this respect. (There is, however, more to be said on behalf of universals than Austin has allowed for. Cf (iv) and (v) below.)

A digression: Russell and Moore on universals. Consider first Russell's introduction of universals in *The Problems of Philosophy*, p. 89f:

> The fact seems to be that all our *a priori* knowledge is concerned with entities which do not, properly speaking, *exist*, either in the mental or in the physical world. These entities are such as can be named by parts of speech which are not substantives; they are such entities as qualities and relations. Suppose, for instance, that I am in my room. I exist, and my room exists; but does 'in' exist? Yet obviously the word 'in' has a meaning; it denotes a relation which holds between me and my room. This relation is something, although we cannot say that it exists *in the same sense* in which I and my room exist.— Thus relations . . . must be placed in a world which is neither mental nor physical,

viz., as the next chapter tells us, 'the world of universals'. On p. 98 of the same work he says, discussing the universal 'north of' as instanced by 'Edinburgh is north of London', that

> the relation 'north of' does not seem to *exist* in the same sense in which Edinburgh and London exist. If we ask 'Where and when does this relation exist?' the answer must be 'Nowhere and nowhen'. There is no place or time where we can find the relation 'north of'. It does not exist in Edinburgh any more than in London, for it relates the two and is neutral as between them. Nor can we say that it exists at any particular time. Now everything that can be apprehended by the senses or by introspection exists at some particular time. Hence the relation 'north of' is radically different from such things. It is neither material nor mental; yet it is something.

From these passages I infer that according to Russell
(1) the meaning of 'in' or 'to the north of' is an entity;
(2) that entity exists neither in time nor in space and cannot be perceived;
(3) consequently, it must subsist in the realm of universals.

Inference (1) may seem too rash. After all, Russell does not say that 'in' has a relation as its meaning but only that it denotes a relation. But the only reason given for his claim that the relation subsists in a realm of universals is that 'in' has a sense. If the meaningfulness of a word is enough to guarantee that there is something it denotes, its meaning must include its denotation. Russell is, I think, a clear example of a philosopher who accepts the transcendental argument just criticized.[10]

I am inclined to think that even Moore accepted it for at least some words. One example must suffice. In *Some Main Problems of Philosophy*, p. 304, he points out that 'being near' has the same meaning in three situations though the space between the things said to be near each other varies. From this he concludes that there is a universal of *being near*. He offers this as a fulfilment of his promise to 'point out what kind of things "universals" are and that there are such things—that they are not pure fictions, like chimaeras and griffins' (p. 303).

It has been suggested to me that if Russell and Moore assumed that the meaning of some words is an entity, they thought of that entity as a theoretical construct. Perhaps they did, but I have found no evidence for it either in *The Problems of Philosophy* or in *Some Main Problems of Philosophy*. If Russell had believed that what such words as 'in', 'north of' and 'being near' stand for is only a logical construct, he would surely have taken back his claim on p. 51f that we are acquainted with universals, and instead maintained that we know them by description; whilst Moore, with his meticulous habits, certainly would have qualified his claim that there are universals and that they are not fictitious. Nor do I see that a doctrine of logical constructs avoids Austin's *petitio principii* objection.

The criticism of universals (continued). (ii) The passages quoted from Russell contain another argument for the existence of universals, which may be paraphrased thus: This sense-datum is to the right of that sense-datum. But *being to the right of* cannot be apprehended by the senses and does not exist in time or space. Yet it must *be*, if our first statement is true. Hence it subsists.

The argument contains the dogma that relations cannot be seen, heard, etc. and therefore have another mode of being.

---

[10] That Russell still holds that the sense of some words is their referent has, I think, been neatly proved by Alan R. White in his note 'The "meaning" of Russell's Theory of Descriptions'. *Analysis* 20, 1959/60.

Austin delivers a criticism of that dogma in the course of a scrutiny of another argument which we shall consider later.

The dogma, says Austin (1939.18), is exceedingly strange.

If I say 'this dot is to the right of that dot', is it not quaint to say that I am sensing the two dots but not sensing the to the right of? It is true that I cannot say I *do* sense the to the right of: that is not good English—but then nor is it good English to say that I do not sense it, or that I intuit it. I sense what in English is described by means of two demonstrative pronouns and an adverbial phrase. To look for an isolable entity corresponding to the latter is a bad habit encouraged by talk about 'concepts'.

He points out the queerness of assuming (as Russell does) that I see the (sense-data) dots but not the to the right of: it is given me by acquaintance of another kind. For if we can be acquainted with relations thus, why should we not be acquainted with them in sensation? Now we have a mysterious separation of the to the right of and the dots: 'we have a sensing and simultaneously an intuiting, as we might feel a stab of jealousy while tasting porridge. Even if one is never found without the other, what has the one to do with the other?' (1939.19). Finally, we do say that we feel this to the right of that, that you see me in my room, and that A is sensibly near B. What reasons are there for not accepting these statements at their face-value? (1939.21f.) The sting of the question is, I think, a Moorean one, viz. Are there any reasons for the philosophical view that we do not and cannot sense any relations which are better than, or even as good as, the ones we have for our everyday assertions that we do sense them?

(iii) There is a very common argument to the effect that any attempt to explain why the same word is applicable to more than one thing must admit at least one sort of universals. Once again I quote Russell's *Problems of Philosophy* (p. 96):

If we wish to avoid the universals *whiteness* and *triangularity*, we shall choose some particular patch of white or some particular triangle, and say that anything is white or a triangle if it has the right sort of resemblance to our chosen particular. But then the resemblance required will have to be a universal. Since there are many white things, the resemblance must hold between many pairs of particular white things; and this is the characteristic of a universal. It will be useless to say that there is a different resemblance for each pair, for then we shall have to say that these resemblances resemble each other, and thus at last we shall be forced to admit resemblance as a universal . . . And having been forced to admit this universal, we find that it is no longer worth while to invent difficult and unplausible theories to avoid the admission of such universals as whiteness and triangularity.

From the context it is clear that Russell intends to show more than the futility of attempts to avoid universals in explanations of why two things both can be called triangles or both can be called white; his point is that *any* explanation of why the same word is applicable to two different things must admit at least that this is so because they are *alike in a certain respect* which, in turn, is to be accounted for only by means of universals. In 1940 Austin attacks this wider assumption—he tries to show that in a good many cases the same word is for good reasons applicable to different things, although they are not in any ordinary sense similar. He mentions seven types of case (pp. 39–42):

1. It is not easy to find any respect in which a healthy body is similar both to a healthy complexion and a healthy exercise; but the adjective is not equivocal. We find a connexion between the three employments if the first is taken as a nuclear one which is, as it were, contained in the other two—'productive of healthy bodies' and 'resulting from healthy bodies'. Following Aristotle, Austin calls this a case of paronymity.

2. 'When A:B :: X:Y then A and X are often called by the same name, e.g. the foot of a mountain and the foot of a list. . . . We may say that the relations in which they stand to B and Y respectively are similar relations. Well and good: but A and X are not the relations in which they stand: and anyone simply told that, in calling A and X both "feet" I was calling attention to a "similarity" in them, would probably be misled.' How far is it true that qualitative change, change of position, of place, etc., are 'similar'?

3. 'I call B by the same name as A, because it resembles A, C by the same name because it resembles B, D . . . and so on. But ultimately A and, say, D do not resemble each other in any recognizable sense at all.' (This is, of course, the sort of case for which Wittgenstein coined the term 'family resemblance'* and which he showed to be at the root of many philosophical troubles.)

*[Wittgenstein did not coin it; Schopenhauer speaks of 'Familienähnlichkeiten' in *Die Welt als Wille und Vorstellung*.]

4. Some words, e.g. 'fascist', originally connoted a great many characteristics at once. Subsequently they are used of things possessing only one of these characteristics. 'This often puzzles us most of all when the original "complete" sense has been forgotten: compare the various meanings of "cynicism": we should be puzzled to find the "similarity" there!'

5. Determinates and determinables provide notorious difficulties for similarity theorists. The relationship is in Austin's opinion too often overlooked. 'A striking example is the case of "pleasure": pleasures we may say not merely resemble each other in being pleasant, but also *differ* precisely in the way in which they are pleasant. No greater mistake could be made than the hedonist mistake (copied by non-hedonists) of thinking that pleasure is always a single similar feeling, somehow isolable from the various activities which "give rise" to it.'

6. A word like 'love' is used sometimes of the passion, sometimes of the object of the passion. And in discussions of truth, disagreements have largely turned on whether 'truth' is the name of a substance, of a quality, or of a relation.

7. Different objects, such as a cricket ball, a cricket bat and a cricket umpire, may be called by the same name because each of them has its own special part to play in the activity called cricket. It

is no good to say that cricket *simply* means 'used in cricket': for we cannot explain what we mean by 'cricket' *except* by explaining the special parts played in cricketing by the bat, ball, &c. Aristotle's suggestion was that the word 'good' might be used in such a way: in which case it is obvious how far astray we should go if we look for a 'definition' of the word 'good' in any ordinary simple sense: or look for the way in which 'good' things are similar to each other, in any ordinary sense. If we tried to find out by such methods what 'cricket' meant, we should very likely conclude that it too was a simple unanalysable supersensible quality.

This ends his 1940 list of troublesome cases for the similarity theorist. Later on he could have added to it his adapter-words (discussed in ch. II below). In 'The meaning of a word' he concludes that it is

essential ... to have a thorough knowledge of the different reasons for which we call different things by the same name, before we can embark confidently on an enquiry. If we rush up with a demand for a definition in the simple manner of Plato or many other philosophers . . . we shall simply make hashes of things. . . . All that 'similarity' theorists manage to say is that all things called by some one name are similar to some one pattern, or are all more similar to each other than any of them is to anything else; which is *obviously* untrue.

So Austin has found reasons to reject three well-known arguments for the existence of universals: he holds that (i) the suggestion that some words are names of universals involves a *petitio principii*; (ii) the argument from the impossibility of perceiving relations goes against common sense and has nothing to be said for it; and (iii) it is false that all accounts of how the same word collects different things must admit at least the universal of resemblance in some respect. If 'universal' is defined as what solves certain problems, Austin is right in claiming that if the solution is wrong, we do not know what a universal is. And if it is impossible to explain what a concept is without dragging in universals, it follows that we do not know what a concept is either.

(iv) Now one may very well accept Austin's criticisms and yet feel that there is more to the craving for universals than he has allowed for. Let us concentrate on sensible things that are similar to each other in the sense that they are indistinguishable from each other except for position in space and time. Then both Russell and Moore would claim that there is a property or set of properties common to them all. It is then an example of a universal; for a universal, says Moore, 'is so called, because it is a property which can be (and is) *common*' to many things.[11] And Russell chimes in, '[A] *universal* will be anything which may be shared by many particulars'.[12]

The problem of universals is in this version more of an ontological than of a semantical question. Whether there is a word for the common property is inessential; what is at issue is whether there is, in the nature of some things, a basis for collecting them. A defender of universals need not hold any doctrine of natural kinds, if that is the crude view that things come down to us somehow already sorted. *We* classify things, and classify them according to our desires and interests, and consequently different

---

[11] *Some Main Problems of Philosophy*, p. 304.
[12] *The Problems of Philosophy*, p. 93.

people and different languages may sort things up in different ways—all this may be conceded without detriment to the tenet that when things are sorted together it is sometimes, usually or always done (not arbitrarily, but) because they exhibit some common and peculiar feature or set of features: we only seize upon different features according to our different interests.

It is probable that this was the conclusion Russell wished to establish in his argument about whiteness and triangularity. But two problems are conflated here. There is no inconsistency in holding that red things are classified together because they are red, but that they nevertheless do not instantiate (or whatnot) one and the same timeless entity. It is up to the defenders of universals to prove the validity of the inference from 'These things are indistinguishable from each other except for spatiotemporal position' to 'There is some entity common to them all'; for from the days of Plato's *Parmenides* it has been notoriously difficult to give sense to—let alone give support for the truth of—claims that different particulars share or partake in or instantiate or have a property in common.

It may be because of this well-known difficulty that Austin does not even mention the argument in 1939. '"The same" does not always mean the same', he remarks in 1950.88n2; and a sorting out of various uses of 'same', 'identical' and so forth is certainly needed before the argument can be tested. But from a cryptic saying in *S&S*.4n it is evident that he found fault with one of the pillars of the argument, viz. the distinction universal/particular. For he gives this antithesis as an illustration of the moral that in philosophy 'it is often good policy, where one member of a putative pair falls under suspicion, to view the more innocent-seeming party suspiciously as well'. I have no idea of what he thought wrong with it;* in 1953 he was ready to handle the term 'item' in a way which to me is indistinguishable from philosophers' customary operations with 'particular' and 'individual'. Whatever his doubts were about universals and particulars, we shall soon see that he was convinced that we very, very often in our classifications of things seize upon features which are given in nature; our words and our classificatory enterprises are

---

*[Sect. 253 of Wittgenstein's *Philosophical Investigations* may suggest an answer. Cf. J. W. Cook: 'Wittgenstein on privacy', Sect. IV, *Ph. R.* 74 (1965).]

very seldom arbitrary in the sense that there is no basis for them in the nature of things.

What matters at present is, however, that the new argument for the existence of universals hardly helps us to see what concepts are. Since it makes doubtful sense to say that a universal is what different particulars share (etc.) when they have something in common, any attempt to elucidate concepts by this type of universal would be a case of *obscurum per obscurius*.

(v) It is possible that semantical considerations are not fundamental to most problems about universals. We sometimes think that this dot is the same red as that. It may indeed be doubted whether this belief is correct; but it is certain that we sometimes entertain it. That we think of the colours of the two patches as not two but one may be the reason why the same colour-name is applied in the two cases.* The semantical considerations which occupy Austin may thus be subordinated to questions which concern operations in our minds. What mechanisms are at work when two different things are conceived of as exhibiting the same property? No discussion of universals which omits such inquiries is trenchant.

Austin has, however, also objections which are not founded on the troubles with universals.

'*Possessing a concept*' (*1939.9–17*). Austin maintains that when asked whether someone possesses the concept of redness, we usually take the question to mean something roughly like 'Does he know the meaning of "red"?' But not exactly like; for we may very well admit that he possesses the concept of redness even if he uses another word, e.g. 'rouge' or even 'green', according to the rules governing most Englishmen's use of 'red'.

Perhaps we should say he 'possesses the concept of redness' if he has paid attention to certain features in that with which he is acquainted, to call attention to which most Englishmen would use the words 'red', 'redness', &c., and has adopted some symbolism to call attention to them, and has not 'forgotten' either the features or the symbolism. This is still only one of the things which might be meant, and is still not precise enough: and all the difficulties arise

*[This may be wrong. 'This dot is the same red as that dot' does not necessarily entail 'Their colours are not two but one'. See references in the preceding footnote.]

with which we are even more familiar in the puzzles about material objects—surely he might do all you say and yet *still not* possess the concept?

Rough as it is, this interpretation of 'Does he know the meaning of "red"?' remains, in Austin's opinion, more plausible than two more philosophical ones:

(*a*) The question 'Do we possess the concept of so-and-so?' is sometimes taken to mean not 'Do you and I possess it?' but 'Does anyone possess it?' But that question makes doubtful sense; for the step from the meaningfulness of 'Do you possess the concept?' to the meaningfulness of 'Does anyone possess the concept?' is illegitimate, much as the step from 'Does he understand the word?' to 'Does anyone understand the word?' 'For, in the former [of the second pair of questions] . . , to "understand" means, speaking roughly, to use as we, or as most Englishmen, or as some other assignable persons use: or again, the features of *his* experience, about which it is asked whether he has or has not paid attention to them, require to be indicated by referring to certain definite experiences of *other* persons. Clearly nothing of the kind is possible in the case of the second question.'

From this Austin concludes that 'to ask "whether we possess a certain concept?" is the same as to ask whether a certain word—or rather, sentences in which it occurs—has any meaning'. But then he is too rash. By taking it for granted that 'possessing the concept of *x*' is handled in a way that is in relevant respects similar to that of 'understanding the word "*x*"' he begs the question at issue.

(*b*) Philosophers have also held that the question whether we possess such-and-such a concept must be kept distinct from the question how we come to possess it. Yet they connect them very intimately when trying to get rid of an alleged concept. Since we can hardly claim that a given concept does not exist, it is often rejected on the ground that it *cannot* exist. The reason is sometimes that it is self-contradictory; but when the alleged concept is a simple idea—like 'necessity' for Hume—we have to try other methods. One is to show the *causal* impossibility for anyone to possess such a concept. 'We construct a theory about the condition or conditions under which alone we can "acquire" concepts: and then we claim that, in the case of certain alleged concepts, these conditions are not satisfied in the case of any man: therefore *no one* possesses them, i.e. they do not exist.' But if we try induction to establish these conditions for the acquisition of concepts, we must know whether we have the concept before we can even begin to prove that we cannot have it; and our means for making sure whether we possess it must be distinct from the as yet unformulated theory of how we got it. Why don't philosophers then use induction when they create their theories of the origin of our concepts? Is it not possible that it is because the question they are concerned with is not 'How do we come to possess such-and-such a concept?' but 'How do words mean?' 'Hume's theory about the "derivation of our ideas" really amounts to the theory that a word, x, can only have meaning provided that I can know, on at least one occasion, that "this is an x", where "this" denotes something *sensible*. And most other theories about this subject, are really theories of a very similar sort'. Thus the question of innate ideas 'seems very commonly to be simply the question: whether a word can have a meaning even though I never know "this is an x"?' Then it is dubious whether 'Do we possess that concept?' is distinguishable from 'How do we come to possess it?': 'surely it will be very difficult indeed to keep the two questions: "Has x a meaning?" and "How do words mean?" apart. It would appear that to ask the latter is to ask "What is meant by 'having a meaning'?"' Now, *if* either of these questions can be treated independent of each other, it seems clear that it is this latter . . . ; unless the question, whether a certain word has a meaning, is to be taken as absolutely unanalysable, and to be answered by means of some sort of direct inspection.'

Austin no doubt thinks that the intelligent discussions of the possession and acquisition of concepts at bottom have been about whether a word is meaningful and how it means. Serious discussions of the apparent issues do, he suspects, always tell us 'either nothing or nonsense'. Such phrases as 'origin', 'source', and 'how we acquire' may mean many things: our theories about the acquisition of concepts may be about the *agents* responsible for my possession of them, about the *operations* forming them, about the *materials* of the operations, about the *sources* from which concepts are drawn, and about the times or *occasions* on which the concepts are acquired, and so on—most of them questions which he refuses to take seriously.

He has now argued, plausibly, though far from conclusively,

that, according to ordinary language, possessing a concept of so-and-so and knowing how it is acquired go together with understanding a word and how it means. There is, however, a well-known objection to this line of argument which Austin considers only by implication. I now turn to this objection.

A digression: non-verbal concepts. In *Some Main Problems of Philosophy* Moore stresses that in some cases we 'apprehend a proposition, which we desire to express, before we are able to think of any sentence which would express it'—'none of the words we can think of will express exactly *the* proposition we are apprehending and desiring to convey' (p. 61). I suppose that he is not interested in aphasia where the patients have had a word for something but 'lost' it; what he is concerned with are situations where we know what we want to say but there is no word for it in the language—i.e., where our failure is due not to defaults on our knowledge of its vocabulary but to the insufficiency of its vocabulary. If we sometimes suffer such a failure, cannot a plea be entered that we then have a concept for which there is no word—a non-verbal concept which cannot be explained as a truncated verbal one? (That a concept is non-verbal means here that there is no word for it; that it is verbal that there is a word for it.)

Can Austin accept this? His claim, that to ask whether someone possesses a concept is to ask whether a certain word is meaningful, is only supported by a stipulation: the question about somebody's possession of a concept can, he says, be unpacked into something like the conjunction of the questions 'Has he paid attention to a certain feature in that with which he is acquainted? Has he adopted some symbolism to call attention to that feature? Has he not forgotten the feature or the symbolism?' Since the middle question makes a symbol an essential element of a concept, there is small wonder that his conclusion is that concepts are tied up with words. But in the first of the unpacked questions he seems to allow that we can e.g. single out and re-identify a feature without having a word for it; and I think that this ability is, for many philosophers, a sufficient (and necessary) condition for saying that someone possesses a non-verbal concept. It may be this Austin has in mind when he grudgingly admits that it 'perhaps is *sometimes* not harmful to talk about . . . "concepts"' (1939.8).

He admits and indeed stresses (e.g. in 1940.36 and 1946.56) that there are, and that we can imagine, situations for which there are no words. Presumably Moore would maintain that they exemplify cases where we know what we want to say although we have no words for it. And then there is no disagreement between Moore and Austin on this issue.

Although Austin admits classifications which are not marked out by verbal means, he nevertheless tends to overlook them in his investigations. Miss Anscombe has in my opinion managed to show this very clearly in her criticism of his paper on 'Pretending'.[13] His 'linguistic phenomenology' (described in section II of this chapter) is liable to make him err in that way if he is not constantly on his guard.

The meaning of a word. Behind all these prickings at traditional theories of universals and concepts lies the conviction that talk about concepts almost forces us to give a caricature of what understanding is. In 1940 Austin tells us that most ordinary words can be explained by giving an account of their syntactics and/or semantics. To explain the syntactics of 'racy' is to describe in words what raciness is and what it is not, and to give examples of sentences in which 'racy' can be used and of sentences in which it is impossible. To demonstrate the semantics of 'racy' is to get the questioner 'to *imagine*, or even actually to *experience*, situations which we should describe correctly by means of sentences containing the words "racy" "raciness", &c., and again other situations where we should *not* use these words'. (1940.25.)

From this position, talk of concepts must be abominable.

(i) The concept is often said to be the meaning of the word and that which the word is the name of. Austin does not mention the criticism of the name theory of meaning that not even in the paradigmatic case of proper names the nominee is their meaning: if 'Winston S. Churchill' has a meaning at all, that meaning has not been Prime Minister of Great Britain and does not smoke cigars, though these things are true of one nominee of the name. This kind of criticism is due to Wittgenstein[14] and Ryle.[15] Austin

---

[13] G. E. M. Anscombe, 'Pretending'. *PASS 32* (1958).
[14] L. Wittgenstein, *Philosophical Investigations*, §§1–118; *The Brown and the Blue Books*, passim.
[15] G. Ryle, 'Meaning and Necessity', *Ph.* 24 (1949) and 'The Theory of Meaning', *British Philosophy in the Mid-Century* (ed. C. A. Mace).

is content with pointing out that it is absurd to answer a man who asks us what 'muggy' means, 'The idea or concept of "mugginess"', but that this is what we are bound to answer if the meaning of a certain word is a certain concept (1940.27).

Some philosophers have taken 'Concepts' to be the answer of two questions, which Austin rejects as nonsensical. The first of them is 'What is the meaning of a word?' in the sense of 'What is the meaning of any word (not any word you like to choose but rather no particular word at all)?'* Recognizing this as a nonsense question, 'we transform it in a curious and noteworthy manner. Up to now, we had been asking . . . "*What-is-the-meaning-of a word?*" But now, being baffled, we change so to speak, the hyphenation, and ask "What is *the-meaning-of-a-word?*" . . . At once a crowd of traditional and reassuring answers present themselves: "a concept", "an idea", "an image", "a class of similar sensa", &c. All of which are equally spurious answers to pseudo-questions.' (1940.26f.)

(ii) If we say that the meaning of a word 'x' is a concept, we are tempted to think of it as a thing—something with parts, etc. If it has parts, then it seems platitudinous to say that one concept either is or is not (part of) another concept. This is the basis of the analytic/synthetic dichotomy. But

if 'explaining the meaning of a word' is really the complicated sort of affair that we have seen it to be, and *if* there is really nothing to call 'the meaning of a word'—*then* phrases like 'part of the meaning of the word *x*' are completely undefined; it is left hanging in the air, we do not know what it means at all. *We are using a working-model which fails to fit the facts that we really wish to talk about.* When we consider what we really do want to talk about, and not the working-model, what would really be meant at all by a judgment being 'analytic or synthetic'? We simply do not know. . . . [When] we are

---

*[In her article 'Austin's Philosophical Papers', *Ph*. 38 (1963), A. Ambrose remarks on this rejection: 'This is rather different from Wittgenstein's procedure of dealing with the question, "What is the meaning of a word?", by asking another question, "What is the explanation of the meaning of a word?" The effect is much the same, since what the explanation explains will in each case be the meaning of a *particular* word. And in addition it diverts one from a search for a *something* which is the meaning even of a particular word.' (P. 205).

Her remark goes some way to support my claim in Sect III of this chapter that Austin was not a disciple of Wittgenstein's, and a longer way to show that I exaggerate the difference in result between Austin and Wittgenstein.]

required to give a *general definition* of what we mean by 'analytic' or 'synthetic', and when we are required to justify our dogma that *every* judgment is either analytic or synthetic, . . . we find we have, in fact, nothing to fall back upon *except our working-model*—

a model that fails to do justice to the distinction between syntactics and semantics. (1940.30f.)

It is important to notice that Austin's attack is launched against the analytic/synthetic *dichotomy*, not the analytic/synthetic *distinction*. There are no doubt very many cases where we can and ought to distinguish between analytic and synthetic 'judgments'; but not every 'judgment' is either analytic or synthetic. (Of course you can stipulate that no utterance that is neither analytic nor synthetic is to be called a judgment; but such a definitional stop rules out a great many philosophically interesting utterances.)

Examples of utterances that hardly fit into the analytic/synthetic pidgeon-holes are, says Austin, 'I think x good, but I don't approve of it', 'This noise exists' and 'What is good ought to exist'. In 1940 he does not yet know how such utterances are to be treated; he only advises us to throw away the old analytic/synthetic model in favour of the syntactics/semantics one, but at the same time he warns us that an actual, in contradistinction to an ideal, language 'has few, if any, explicit conventions, no sharp limits to the spheres of operation of rules, no rigid separation of what is syntactical and what semantical' (1940.35).

That the breaking away from the analytic/synthetic dichotomy has been beneficial is by now evident. I only need to mention some works in moral philosophy: J. O. Urmson's 'On grading', R. M. Hare's *The Language of Morals*, S. Toulmin's *The Place of Reason in Ethics*, and P. H. Nowell-Smith's *Ethics*.

(iii) Talk about concepts does not only tempt us to take an absurd view of meaning and to accept a rigid and unwarranted dichotomy of 'judgments' into analytic and synthetic ones; it also makes us take a philosophically dangerous view of translation. Ryle tells us that to say that Hume was concerned with the *concept* of cause emphasizes that he was not interested in the *word* 'cause' but rather in the *use* of 'cause' and similar words.

Hume's question was not a question about a bit of the English language in any way in which it was not a question about a bit of the

German language.—[The philosophical] enquiry is an enquiry not into the other features or properties of the word . . ., but only into what is done with it, or with anything else with which we do the same thing.[16]

Couldn't we then continue to use the word 'concept' in order to keep the language-neutrality in mind, although we must be careful not to accept the doctrine of universals, or the name theory of meaning, or the consequences of an acceptance of these doctrines? In later years Ryle seems inclined to a positive answer —cf e.g. the title of *The Concept of Mind*.

This use of 'concept' seems innocent; but I think Austin would consider it dangerous.* For it leads us to think of translation as producing a word governed by the very same rule as a given word. Thus Ryle says, without qualifications, that 'the use of "cause" is the same as the use of "Ursache", though "cause" is not the same word as "Ursache"' (*op. cit.*, p. 171). With his philological leanings Austin is almost bound to question this. For

a word never—well, hardly ever—shakes off its etymology and its formation. In spite of all changes in and extensions of and additions to its meanings, and indeed rather pervading and governing these, there will still persist the old idea. In an *accident* something befalls: by *mistake* you take the wrong one: in *error* you stray: when you act *deliberately* you act after weighing it up

(1956a.149f). And when we go into the history of a word, we also

come back pretty commonly to pictures or *models* of how things happen or are done. These models may be fairly sophisticated and recent . . ., but one of the commonest and most primitive types of model is one which is apt to baffle us through its very naturalness and simplicity. We take *some very simple action*, like shoving a stone, usually as done by and viewed by oneself, and use *this*, with the features distinguishable in it, as our model in terms of which to talk about other actions and events: and we continue to do so, scarcely realizing it, even when these other actions are pretty remote and perhaps much more interesting to us in their own right than the act originally used in constructing the model ever were, and even when

---

[16] G. Ryle, 'Ordinary language'. *Ph.R. 62* (1953), pp. 171-2.
*[But, as A. R. White points out in his review of *LIA* (*Mind* 74, 1965), he does not seriously consider Ryle's language–neutrality view of concepts. He tends to blur 'word investigations' with Rylean 'concept investigations'. And so do I.]

the model is really distorting the facts rather than helping us to observe them.

(1956a.150.) Acting on these principles Austin would have to ask whether 'cause' and 'Ursache' have the same etymology, and, if the answer is No, whether it is not somewhat rash to assume that a German speaking of 'Ursache' really uses the word in exactly the way an Englishman employs 'cause'.[17] Austin was well aware of the Sapir-Whorf hypothesis, and he thought that there may be relevant differences in the 'conceptual systems' even within the group which Whorf in *Language, Thought and Reality* is content to bundle together as 'standard average European' ones. I remember Austin stressing that other languages within that group ought to be investigated in order to see whether different language communities really structure their experiences in exactly the same way.*

So besides his objections to explaining concepts in terms of universals, Austin has now argued that some traditional discussions of our possession and acquisition of concepts are really about understanding a word and how it means; that the meaning of a word cannot be a concept; that this fallacious belief is responsible for the untenable dichotomy—not the untenable distinction!—between analytic and synthetic judgments; and finally that to speak as if philosophers are concerned with language-neutral entities (rules of meaning or what not) is very rash. As late as in his lecture in Göteborg in 1959, he maintained that it is only obfuscating to drag in the term 'concept': we can, he said, say what we want to say without using that troublesome and bewildering word.

Objections to propositions. Moore speaks roughly as if concepts are what detached words express, and propositions what whole

---

[17] Cf Axel Hägerström, *Religionsfilosofi*, p. 15: 'Det som kraften är kraft till måste ju på något sätt finnas hos den. Det vill säga, det enligt sin natur i tiden efterföljande skall existera innan det existerar'. [That which the power is a power to do must in some sense exist in it. I.e., that which in its essence is temporally subsequent must exist before it exists.] Isn't this idea that we usually think of a cause as something which, as it were, is pregnant with its effect due to the fact that Hägerström is thinking of the Swedish 'orsak' or the German 'Ursache'—words with quite another etymology than 'cause'? Is his idea likely to occur to an Englishman?

*[For criticisms of Austin's etymological bias, see Ch. 4:2.12 and C. G. New: 'A plea for linguistics', *Symp.*]

sentences express[18] (or, as Austin has it in 1950.87, '"the meaning or sense of a sentence or family of sentences"'). It is clear that the faults Austin finds with concepts also effect propositions. There is also another and less important objection, viz. that outside philosophy a proposition is 'something portentous, usually a generalization, that we are invited to accept and that has to be recommended by argument' (1950.87), whereas in philosophy it has come to be used as an umbrella term for lots of utterances which have totally different functions but which, on account of their indicative form, have been confused with statements: formulae in a calculus, performatives, value-judgments, definitions, utterances in works of fiction, and so forth (1950.99.)

5. *One task of philosophy: the elucidation of speech acts*

The next main difference between Moore and Austin concerns the philosophical task in the case of utterances that are obviously true and unambiguous. Moore said that he was puzzled about their analysis; Austin maintained that *he* tried to make explicit 'the total speech act in the total speech-situation'.[19] What does that mean?

Take an utterance which is unambiguous and which is quite certainly true. Then, in what circumstances is such an utterance true? To answer the question we have to investigate in how many ways and dimensions that sort of utterance can go wrong; for this is often fairly easy to detect and, as Ryle puts it, the 'boundaries of a right of way are also boundaries of forbidden ground'.[20] Thus, we sometimes do know that there is a bittern in the garden or that Tom is very angry indeed—no doubt about it. But one philosophical task is to sift out *how* we know it; and this is done at great length in 'Other minds' by considerations of how our claim to know can go wrong. Again, there are no doubt utterances that sometimes are true. But in what circumstances are they issued when they are so, and in what manners can they go wrong? This is a dominating question in the 1950, 1953 and

---

[18] With qualifications: since a proposition is true or false, some of its words must have reference and not (only) meaning. But more of this in a later chapter.

[19] His set phrase at his informal instruction, also occurring frequently in *Words*.

[20] 'Philosophical arguments', Inaugural lecture 1945, p. 14.

1954 papers and even in *Words*, and it is thrashed out with regard to perceptual utterances in *S&S*, with regard to different excuses in 1956, with regard to 'I can if I choose' in 1956b, and with regard to pretending in the 1958 essay.

But it would be singularly inept to say that Austin's preoccupation was to investigate when an utterance is *true*. For he is perhaps best known for his view that there are utterances which, although grammatically very like statements, are not intended to be true or false; and in his writings there is a steadily growing conviction that, in fact, very few utterances are true without qualifications. It is more correct to say that his aim was to investigate in what situations utterances are in order which obviously sometimes *are* in order. What does 'being in order' mean here? The best answer is perhaps that an utterance is in order if it is issued in a situation where it performs its normal job faultlessly. The normal job as well as the faults varies from utterance-type to utterance-type. The normal job of 'The cat is on the mat' is to say something true or false; the normal job of 'I promise' is to promise; the normal job of 'This is good' is (perhaps) to commend it, etc. The statement can go wrong in ways which at least *prima facie* differ from the ways in which the performative can; and so on.

So the first task Austin sets himself is to investigate in what ways different types of utterances can be in order. This is not an investigation of their meaning, if that is an inquiry into the (philosophical) syntax of the utterances. It is a study of the relations which have to hold between the utterance and the world, if the former is to do its usual job. This is one reason why it will not do to include Austin in the group of (largely mythical) linguistic philosophers who, according to Russell,[21] devote all their interest to what a question means and none to what its correct answer would be.

A second task which fairly naturally springs from the first one is a classification of the utterances according to the ways in which they can be in order, i.e., according to their job. Austin scorns people who like Wittgenstein[22] speak about the infinite uses of

---

[21] In e.g. 'The cult of ordinary language', reprinted in *Portraits from Memory*.

[22] Cf *Philosophical Investigations*, §23: 'But how many kinds of sentences are there? Say assertion, question, and command?—There are *countless* kinds: countless different kinds of use of what we call "symbols", "words",

language. 'Philosophers will do this when they have listed as many, let us say, as seventeen; but even if there were something like ten thousand uses of language, surely we could list them all in time. This, after all, is no larger than the number of species of beetle that entomologists have taken the pains to list.' (1956c.221.) In contrast to Wittgenstein he was a systematizer, not at all adversed to the aim of grammarians; indeed he hoped, as we shall see, that his branch of philosophy would merge into a new science of language.

Austin did not deny that many other types of problems are worth a philosopher's while; but he himself spent most of his time on the two tasks I have mentioned, or rather on studies of certain smaller questions pertaining to these general tasks. He was well aware that he was laying down a programme whose realization would demand the work of many generations.

The two tasks cannot easily be fitted into Moore's conception of analysis. It goes against the grain to say, for instance, that in investigating the ways in which an utterance is in order, Austin is splitting something up into something; and in 'What I do as a philosopher' he denied that he was doing anything of the sort. Of course he quite often uses what White calls analytic distinction: he studies how one particular meaning of an expression is distinguished from and related to other meanings both of the same expression and of different expressions. But this is not analysis in the traditional sense.

6. *Summary*

Moore and Austin agree that sometimes persons make true and unambiguous utterances. They disagree about what to do philosophically with these utterances. Moore wants to analyse them; and an analysis involves, according to his theory though not always to his practice, the existence of concepts or propositions which are split up into smaller units. This makes him neglect the particular situation in which the utterance is issued, since a proposition is a logical construct. It also makes him concentrate too

"sentences". And this multiplicity is not something fixed, given once for all; but new types of language . . . come into existence, and others become obsolete and get forgotten.'—In the same paragraph Wittgenstein supports his claim that there are countless uses by mentioning about twenty employments . . .

exclusively on truth and falsehood (even in ethics), propositions being either true or false.

Austin denies that there are concepts or propositions, and he does not split anything up into anything. What he tries to do is to detect in what situations utterances of a certain kind which are sometimes in order (this including but not being confined to their being true) actually are in order, and to classify them according to their ways of being so. This involves taking account of linguistic and, above all, non-linguistic *contexts* in a way foreign to Moore.

II. SOME MAIN CHARACTERISTICS OF AUSTIN'S APPROACH*

7. *Austin's 'linguistic phenomenology'*

By training a classical scholar, Austin had the linguist's liking for tracking down exactly what words people use in what situations, how they construe their sentences grammatically, what the truest rendering of a certain utterance would be in another language, and what the etymology of the words is. He thought that such inquiries had an intrinsic value, apart from philosophical considerations; but in this section I shall consider how he used them for furthering traditionally philosophical ends.

In 1956a.129–30 Austin gives three reasons for examining what we should say when:

> First, words are our tools . . .: we should know what we mean and what we do not, and we must forearm ourselves against the traps that language sets us. Secondly, words are not (except in their own little corner) facts or things: we need therefore to prise them off the world, to hold them apart from and against it, so that we can realize their inadequacies and arbitrariness, and can relook at the world without blinkers. Thirdly, and more hopefully, our common stock of words embodies all the distinctions men have found worth drawing, and the connexions they have found worth marking, in the lifetimes of many generations: these surely are likely to be more numerous, more sound, since they have stood up to the long test of the survival of the fittest, and more subtle, at least in all ordinary and reasonably

*[Cf the contributions by J. O. Urmson and Stuart Hampshire to the symposium on Austin's method (*Symp*.). A. Ambrose's 'Austin's Philosophical Papers' and S. Cavell's 'Austin at criticism' also contain pertinent observations.]

practical matters, than any that you or I are likely to think up in our arm-chairs of an afternoon—the most favoured alternative method.

The first of his reasons, then, is that we put our problems and our arguments in words and that we then run certain risks. The pursuit of truth demands accuracy. If our premisses are only half-true, or obscure, or nonsensical, our conclusion is liable to be so too. Arguments to this effect are scattered all over Austin's works. A few examples will be enough. The bulk of *S&S* tries to show that if we state uncontroversial facts about perception accurately, there is no need to assume that there are such things as sense-data: they are, according to Austin, introduced by much too facile dichotomies, and the famous 'arguments from illusion' do not prove the existence of sense-data when stated with due attention to facts.

If we don't pay heed to our words, we may mislead others and even ourselves by them: Taking the phrase 'the evidence of my senses' literally and not as an understatement, I may think that in order to be sure of the existence of x, I must have *more* than 'the evidence of my senses'. For 'evidence of the existence of x' suggests that the question whether x exists is not yet settled. Thus pig-food, pig-like marks on the ground and pig-like noises from the sty are evidence that there is a pig about. But if the beast itself comes into view, that is not one more piece of evidence of its existence: the question is settled. Again, if I see a man shoot another, I may *give* evidence but I don't *have* evidence—although the *jury* after listening to me will have some evidence as to what happened. The point of the metaphor 'the evidence of my eyes' is that I *don't* have evidence in the ordinary sense, I have *more* than mere evidence. (*S&S*. 115–16.)

Even in his second argument for studying what we say when, Austin stresses that language sets traps for us. Words may be inadequate and arbitrary; they may blinker us. This comes out strongly in 1940.36f where he reminds us that

we can only describe what it is we are trying to imagine, by means of words which precisely describe and evoke the *ordinary* case, which we are trying to think away. Ordinary language *blinkers* the already feeble imagination. It would be difficult . . . if I were to say 'Can I think of a case where a man would be neither at home nor not at home?' This is inhibiting, because I think of the *ordinary* case where I ask 'Is he at home?' and get the answer, 'No': when certainly he is not at home. But supposing I happen *first* to think of the situation when I call on him just after he has died: then I see at once it would be wrong to say either. So... the only thing to do is to imagine or experience all kinds of odd situations, and then suddenly round on oneself and ask: there, *now* would I say that being extended it must be shaped? A new idiom might in odd cases be demanded.

Austin often stresses that our words are few, compared to the different types of phenomena they are used to classify and describe; and that we therefore often have to rely upon the context to get their meaning aright in a particular situation. In *S&S*.41 he says that 'it is not enough simply to examine the words themselves; just what is meant and what can be inferred (if anything) can be decided only by examining the full circumstances in which the words are used'. Thus, 'when we say of the stick partly immersed in water that it "looks bent", it has to be remembered what sort of situation we are dealing with; it certainly can't be assumed that, when we use that expression in that situation, we mean that the stick really looks exactly like, might well be mistaken for, a stick that was actually bent' (*S&S*.42; he gives evidence for his point of view on p. 30f and 53f). Again, 'descriptions of dreams, for example, plainly can't be taken to have exactly the same force and implications as the same words would have, if used in the description of ordinary waking experiences. In fact, it is just because we all know that dreams are *throughout un*like waking experiences that we can safely use ordinary expressions in the narration of them; the peculiarity of the dream-context is sufficiently well known for nobody to be misled by the fact that we speak in ordinary terms.' (*S&S*.42; he elaborates the point on pp. 48–9.)

Since language evokes the ordinary cases although it also has to cater for phenomena that are far from the paradigms, it makes us blind to the open texture[23] of a good many words (1940.35f; 1946.56f; *S&S, passim*). Lots of our words are governed by vertical rules, rules tying a certain vocable to items of a certain sort. When philosophizing, we are apt to think that these rules are fairly strict, so that we in most cases know, without cudgelling our brains, whether this thing satisfies them or not: a cat has these-and-these characteristics, a goldfinch those-and-those, and

[23] This is the term F. Waismann coined in 'Verifiability' (*L&L* I) for a phenomenon well-known already to Kant. Austin does not give it a name.

so on. Suppose that something which for years has looked and behaved as a cat all of a sudden delivers a philippic. Is it then a cat or not? We feel sure, at our philosophical moments, that it must be one of the two; and pretty often we wager that it is *not* a cat. Since it is always logically possible that a cat takes to talking, we can never be sure that Pussy is a cat: we can in fact never know that *anything* is a cat.—This reason for epistemological scepticism is, in Austin's opinion, fostered by insufficient attention to how such words are related to the world. How he dealt with the problem will be discussed in later chapters.

In arguing for his approach to philosophy Austin has now given us two defensive reasons: we have to know how to handle our linguistic tools, and we have to beware of linguistic blinkers. These two pieces of advice do not bring anything new into philosophy. The first has been given—without much effect—from the dawn of thought, and the second dominated the later philosophy of Wittgenstein.[24] But Austin's third reason is, I think, new and remarkable.* For here he suggests that in ordinary language we find recorded all the distinctions past generations have found worth drawing and all the connexions they have found worth marking. That is, he suggests (i) that language is influenced by what its speakers believe the world to be like, and (ii) that *whenever* (a sufficient number of) people think they have detected an important difference or connexion between things in the world, they mark the difference or connexion in their language. Hence, a study of the variety of different expressions and constructions our language has for a given field of phenomena will tell us (not necessarily something about the world, but) at least what phenomena generations of men have thought that they discerned.

Now (i) is surely enormously plausible. We certainly use our language to speak about the world, and then our vocabulary has to be adapted to that task. So if there is a difference which seems to us very important, it is almost certain that we shall design words or constructions of words to mark it.

It is a corollary of this point that our language is tied to this world as we see it. This supports Austin's remarks on the open texture of terms; but it also makes a study of language a study of

---

[24] This is not to say that Austin has taken it over from Wittgenstein. Cf section III of this chapter.

*[Remarkable, but not new. I had not read Thomas Reid.]

how its speakers look at the world.²⁵ A man who wishes to study a language in a thorough manner has to consider what people who use it want to do with it, what sorts of things they want to record, etc. A philosophical inquiry into promises has to take into account why we have the institution of promising, in what situations a form of word is a promise and in what situations it isn't, etc. Thus the border between linguistics, philosophy and social anthropology vanishes. Much spite is required to turn this into something favouring 'a lack of historical and social awareness'.²⁶

If there is an interplay of the sort suggested between language and a view of the world (a *Weltanschauung* if that word is freed from its suggestion of a *philosophical* and *integrated* view of the world), then a person who takes delight in words may, by making a patient investigation of what people say in various situations, hit upon distinctions which are made in ordinary language but have been neglected by philosophers. He is then 'using a sharpened awareness of words to sharpen [his] perception of, though not as the final arbiter of, the phenomena' (1956a.130). Austin thought that 'linguistic philosophy' or 'philosophy of language' is a misnomer for this kind of activity which had better be called 'linguistic phenomenology'—'only that is rather a mouthful' (*loc. cit.*). An investigation of this kind he often called a study of what we (you, etc.) 'say when' (sc. confronted with such-and-such a situation).

I don't think that (ii)—the suggestion that *whenever* a sufficient number of people think they have found an important connexion or distinction between things in the world they also mark it out in their language—is at all as plausible as (i). Nor is it as essential. Whether or not we accept Austin's claim that our common stock of words embodies *all* the distinctions men have found worth drawing, we must surely think it probable that our words take care of at least *some* of them; and then it might be worth our while to try and sift them out. It seems to me that this is all that can be plausibly claimed; and since I don't think that any of Austin's arguments rely on (ii), I shall henceforward disregard it.

²⁵ Cf Wittgenstein, *Ph.I.* §19: 'It is easy to imagine a language consisting only of orders and reports in battle.—Or a language consisting only of questions and expressions for answering yes and no. And innumerable others.— And *to imagine a language means to imagine a form of life.*' (My italics.)
²⁶ E. Gellner, *Words and Things*, p. 214.

Misunderstandings of 'linguistic phenomenology'. What did Austin *not* claim on behalf of his 'linguistic phenomenology'?

(1) He did not think that it was the only way of philosophizing. There are many others—he was not at all dogmatic about it. He held Frege in high regard, I am told; and he translated his *Grundlagen der Arithmetik* (under the title *The Foundations of Arithmetic*).[27] But he certainly thought that the study of what we say when is *one* way of doing philosophy, and one which suited his bent for exact observation of linguistic usage.

(2) He did not think that it can solve all philosophical problems. I see no reason whatever to accept Hampshire's view that Austin held the 'strong thesis' that

> the multiplicity of fine distinctions [in ordinary language], which such a study would disclose, would by itself answer philosophical questions about free-will, perception, naming and describing, conditional statements.[28]

It is belied in 1940.37 where Austin claims that it 'will not do, having discovered the facts about "ordinary usage" *to rest content* with that, as though there were nothing more to be discussed and discovered. There may be plenty that might happen and does happen which would need new and better language to describe it in. Very often philosophers are only engaged on this task, when they seem to be perversely using words in a way which makes no sense according to "ordinary usage". There may be extraordinary facts, even about our everyday experience, which plain men and plain language overlook.' That he did not recoil later on is shown by the fact that he maintains (*a*) with regard to questions about free-will, that we have to take care of cases which crop up in the law and in psychology, and that psychology has a special and constant need (to which he raises no objections) 'to supplement, to revise and to supersede the classifications of both ordinary life and the law' (1956a.133–4, cf also *op. cit.*, pp. 151–2); and (*b*) with regard to perception, that philosophers have neglected that a great quantity of psychological investigations

---

[27] Although the book contains a good many observations in descriptive semantics, e.g. the principle not to ask for the meaning of a word except in its context, and the remarks on the difference between 'wise' and 'one' (G. Frege, *The Foundations of Arithmetic*, pp. 39–40), the bulk of the book is obviously written in a spirit very remote from Austin's.

[28] S. Hampshire, 'J. L. Austin', *Symp*, p. 41. Cf J. O. Urmson's and G. J. Warnock's rejoinder in the same anthology.

(not investigations of common usage!) has shown that discrimination between two things frequently depends on more or less extraneous concomitants which might not have been consciously noticed (*S&S*.52–4), and that it is possible that something is seen in different ways and not just described in different ways (*S&S*.100–2).

I have found no such explicit disclaimer with regard to conditional statements; but he certainly did not hold that a scrutiny of the fine distinctions clustering around naming and describing would *by itself* answer philosophical questions, for he writes in the introduction of the very paper devoted to these issues (1953.181) that 'essential though it is as a preliminary to track down the detail of our ordinary uses of words, it seems that we shall in the end always be compelled to straighten them out to some extent'.

Nor does Hampshire's alternative version of the alleged 'strong thesis' (*op. cit.*, p. 35f) come much closer to the mark:

For every distinction of word and idiom that we find in common speech, there is a reason to be found, if we look far enough, to explain why this distinction exists. The investigation will always show that the greatest possible number of distinctions have been obtained by the most economical linguistic means. If, as philosophers, we try to introduce an altogether new distinction, we shall find that we are disturbing the economy of the language by blurring elsewhere some useful distinctions that are already recognized.

Since Austin had admitted that superstition and error can be embodied in our language (1956a.133), the reason for a distinction cannot always be a good one, if that equals an acceptable one. Probably he would, as Urmson and Warnock stress (*op. cit.*, p. 47), have regarded the notion of 'the greatest possible number of . . .' as incoherent; and the quotations I have given show that he emphatically denied that the distinctions recognized in ordinary language are all the distinctions there are to be drawn. Finally, he himself introduced 'altogether new distinctions', e.g. that between a constative and a performative.

I conclude, then, that Austin did not think of his 'linguistic phenomenology' as something leading to the solution of all philosophical problems. In *S&S* he even says that all his discussion of sense-data theories in a sense leaves us where we began—'but actually we may hope to learn something positive in the way of a technique for dissolving philosophical worries (*some kinds of philosophical worry, not the whole of philosophy*)' (p. 5). He probably believed that no *single* method for solving philosophical problems will ever be found;* but he certainly hoped that his own approach not only dissolved certain puzzles but also made the remaining questions clearer. 'Clarity, . . . I know, has been said to be not enough: but perhaps it will be time to go into that when we are within measurable distance of achieving clarity on some matter' (1956a.137).

(3) In 'What I do as a philosopher' he stressed that he did not think that his study of what we should say when is an investigation of what we *ought* to say when: he wanted to know what we *in fact* say when. There are at least two apparent exceptions to this. When Moore writes 'I could, for all anyone could know for certain beforehand, have done something different', Austin objects that 'could have' in this context is a '*vulgarism*, "could" being used *incorrectly* for "might"' (1956b.155; my italics). And in *S&S*.34–5 he maintains that although we perhaps sometimes say, in colloquial language, 'It looks to expand', 'He looks to like her', 'It looks as a dark speck on the horizon' or 'It looks that they've all been eaten', we are then speaking loosely; and that if we know English and are at all sensitive to it, we know that we are speaking loosely. In these two cases he certainly seems to appeal to what we *ought* to say, not to what we in fact do say. But he may mean either that if the speaker considers his words, he will reformulate his utterance; or that most Englishmen in fact choose other words; or that the speaker's deviating use blurs a distinction that is in fact marked out in English. That he means at least the last of these alternatives comes out in 1956a.132: 'If the usage is loose, we can understand the temptation that leads to it, and the distinctions that it blurs'.

(4) He did not think that all of us say the same things in the same situations. He certainly believed, and showed in practice (perpetually at his informal instruction and sometimes in his

*[This is an understatement, if Urmson is right in claiming that Austin 'thought that those inquiries which had continued to be called philosophical and had not hived off under some special name (as have, for example, physics, biology, psychology, and mathematics) were precisely those for the solution of whose problems no standard methods had yet been found' (*Symp*, p. 76). Austin could hardly have imagined that there is one single method to solve *all* unsolved problems.]

writings, e.g. in 1956a.148–9), that when people do not say the same thing it *very often* depends on the fact that they do not envisage exactly the same situation: when asked to amplify their description of it, one of them will often mention features which the other has not observed, or one will count as one action what the other counts as two, etc. Further, different people's different classifications of something will sometimes depend on what theories they hold of how certain phenomena are to be explained. A may think of seeing ghosts as a case of something being conjured up, perhaps by the disordered nervous system of the victim; and then he will count seeing ghosts as a case of delusion. But B may maintain that seeing ghosts is a case of being taken in by shadows, reflections, or a trick of light, and hence he will call seeing ghosts a case of not delusion but illusion. (*S&S*.24.) The point is, however, that although two people do not agree on what to say of something, both of them will, very often, concede that *if* the other's account of the situation is accepted, then they both will react verbally in the way he did.

But although this is very often the case, it is not always so. Disagreement in verbal behaviour is, however, not fatal to 'linguistic phenomenology'. For an eccentric speaker may be as valuable as or more valuable than normal ones: his form of words may draw our attention to features in the situation which otherwise may be neglected (perhaps because of their very obviousness), or he may teach us to look at the situation in new ways.[29] This is valuable, since our inquiry is not primarily an inquiry into what we say but into how we conceive the world. 'A disagreement as to what we should say is not to be shied off, but to be pounced upon: for the explanation of it can hardly fail to be illuminating. If we light on an electron that rotates the wrong way, that is a discovery, a portent to be followed up, not a reason for chucking physics: and by the same token, a genuinely loose or eccentric talker is a rare specimen to be prized.' (1956a.132.)

(5) He did not think that 'we' in the formula 'what we say when' refers just to 'plain men' or to 'Oxford philosophers' or to

---

[29] Austin touches the immensely important problem of 'seeing in another way' in 1940.37, 1956a.135 and *S&S*.100–2. The *locus classicus* is, however, Wittgenstein's *Ph.I.*, II:xi. The problem has been discussed at length in N. R. Hanson's *Patterns of Discovery*, Ch.1. It has also given rise to a series of essays about the philosophy of religion, starting from John Wisdom's 'Gods' (*L&L* I; also reprinted in *Philosophy and Psycho-Analysis*).

'Oxford philosophers masquerading as plain men'. In investigating perception, we have to take into account what psychologists say, and in investigating responsibility what jurists say. 'We' refers simply to the group of men whose usage of words is under investigation.

(6) He did not think that his 'linguistic phenomenology' is likely to yield result except where language is 'rich and subtle' (1956a.130); that is, I suppose, where something matters in practice for a group of people and they therefore have found it necessary to make fine discriminations and to adapt their language to convey these with precision. What matters for one group of people may, of course, be of no interest at all for another. The plain man gets along without rich and subtle discriminations with respect to time (*loc. cit.*), although such distinctions are very important for the physicist: 'In ordinary life we dismiss the puzzles that crop up about time, but we cannot do that indefinitely in physics' (1956a.134). In 'What I do as a philosopher' Austin suggested that something might be learnt about time by studying what physicists say. At least, he claimed, we have to try it before we assert that the approach *cannot* yield any results in this area.

(7) He did not think that his 'linguistic phenomenology' would show that language is in order as it is. At least he doubted that language forms a consistent and interlocking system. This may be all that the following quotation from 1956a.151n shows; but he *seems* to leave open the possibility that our terms are not only disparate but also incompatible:

It seems to be too readily assumed that if we can only discover the true meanings of each of a cluster of key terms, usually historic terms, that we use in some particular field . . ., then it must without question transpire that each will fit into place in some single, interlocking, consistent, conceptual scheme. Not only is there no reason to assume this, but all historical probability is against it, especially in the case of a language derived from such various civilizations as ours is. We may cheerfully use, and with weight, terms which are not so much head-on incompatible as simply disparate, which just do not fit in or even on.

If Austin's suggestion is true, it strengthens point (2): an examination of what we say when will not solve all philosophical problems. For I take it that one task which some moral philosophers have set themselves *is* to give us an *explication* of our moral terms such that they fit into a single, interlocking and consistent system.

This ends my list of claims which Austin did *not* make on behalf of his approach, although they have sometimes been ascribed to him.

The nature of 'linguistic phenomenology'. Let us remind ourselves what sort of investigations Austin was typically concerned with. As we have seen, there are some common sense views which no sane man doubts and which are such that anyone who doubts them either has no reasons for doing so or has reasons which are much weaker than those produced or producible for the common sense view. Take one of these tenets, e.g. that I have sometimes apologized, said something true, or known that someone has been very depressed. Then the typical task Austin undertakes is to tell *in what type(s) of situation* I manage to apologize, say something true, or know something about other minds. His technique is to list possible sources of error and try to eliminate them.

Bearing this technique in mind we can now start to list the claims Austin made on behalf of his 'linguistic phenomenology'.

(1) The approach provides us with a great number of distinctions and connexions which tell us how people have conceived the world. This may suggest new possibilities and hence help us to keep an open mind. It also gives us more numerous, and probably sounder, distinctions 'than any that you or I are likely to think up in our armchairs of an afternoon' (1956a.130). It also helps us to avoid certain oversimplifications to which philosophers are prone. Austin never ceases to bring home the artificiality and crudeness of philosophers' use of dichotomies: the analytic/synthetic dichotomy makes us disregard other clashes between utterances than contradictions (1940); attempts to divide perception into two sorts, veridical and non-veridical, blur lots of important distinctions (*S&S*); and so on and so forth. His credo was that it 'is essential . . . to abandon old habits of *Gleichschaltung*, the deeply ingrained worship of tidy-looking dichotomies' (*S&S*.3).

His objection was to dichotomies, not to distinctions. For all I know, he may have regarded the analytic/synthetic distinction as useful within its proper field and for certain purposes. But as a dichotomy it had nothing to be said for it. Most dichotomies are much too simple. The dichotomy between perceiving material things and perceiving sense-data is too simple, since there is 'no *one* kind of thing that we "perceive" but many *different* kinds, the number being reducible if at all by scientific investigation and not by philosophy' (*S&S*.4). The effect of a dichotomy is, in most cases, that we think that all phenomena brought under the same name are alike, or have one respect in which they are alike; and so we do not pay attention to the individual cases but pre-judge and neglect them. (Cf *S&S*.14n.)—If his technique is the one I have outlined, his distrust of dichotomies is indeed only to be expected; for they slur over just what he finds important—the *variances*, the *different* ways in which phenomena can be, and fail to be, a so-and-so. The sources of error have to be detected before we can hope for a successful campaign to eliminate them.

Akin to the philosopher's reliance on dichotomies is his belief that verbal negation and verbal opposites mark real negations and opposites: that e.g. (*a*) any action *must* be done either voluntarily or involuntarily, and (*b*) the opposite of an action done involuntarily is one done voluntarily. 'Linguistic phenomenology' reveals that these beliefs are mistaken. As to (*a*): 'It is bedtime, I am alone, I yawn: but I do not yawn involuntarily (or voluntarily!) . . . To yawn in any such peculiar way is just not to just yawn.' (1956a.138.) As to (*b*): 'The "opposite", or rather "opposites", of "voluntarily" might be "under constraint" of some sort, duress or obligation or influence: the opposite of "involuntarily" might be "deliberately" or "on purpose" or the like. Such divergences in opposites indicate that "voluntarily" and "involuntarily", in spite of their apparent connexion, are fish from very different kettles.' (1956a.139.)—The importance of these observations is, I take it, that there are different and not complementary sets of conditions which have to be satisfied when something is done voluntarily and when it is done involuntarily— an act that fails to be voluntary does not *ipso facto* qualify as involuntarily, or *vice versa*. Being aware of the failure of complementarity is not merely being aware of a linguistic (and possibly logical) rule; it is also an awareness of factors in the world.

But although the investigation of what we say when may in this way make us feel 'that initial trepidation, experienced when the firm ground of prejudice begins to slip away beneath the feet' (1940.33), it may have disastrous effect if we allow it to blinker our imagination (1940.36). The risk is especially great if we investigate only one language or only languages within the same family. Austin sometimes considers how a phrase would be rendered in Latin (e.g. 1946.64, 1956b.163-4) and what the etymology is of certain words of Latin derivation (e.g. 1954.112, 1956a.149f, 1958.208). He also makes a few references to Greek (e.g. in his 1940 paper). They were languages of which he had first-hand knowledge. But I think he would have preferred to consider languages which are not Indo-European.

(2) We are fairly often unaware of the subtlety of our own language, although we master it in practice: in spite of the fact that we use a great many words and constructions that cannot be substituted for each other when we refer to roughly the same phenomena, and in spite of the fact that we use them according to fairly strict rules, we do not recognize their variety until we begin to study what we actually say when. This is hardly surprising: so much of our talk is, by now, automatic. But it explains how it can come about that an investigation of what we say brings us to pay heed to factors which we have earlier seen but not noticed. It also explains how Austin could think that there is a possibility, however faint, that an inquiry into the *language* of physics can tell us something about time.

(3) Where something has been an important matter for a group of people, so that their language is rich and subtle on that point, it is unlikely that its distinctions and connexions are totally wrong—mark nothing. It is unlikely that generations of people are misled in matters of practical urgency to a great number of them; though their distinctions are 'likely enough to be not the best way of arranging things if our interests are more extensive or intellectual than the ordinary' (1956a.133).

Gellner remarks:

> The objections one can, decisively, oppose to this are: what survives in one set of conditions may be far from ideal for a radically new environment, and the environment of man—technologically, socially, intellectually—has changed and is changing so radically and fast that past survival creates but a feeble presumption of fitness—and indeed, can sometimes be an index of unfitness. Past usages are often based on currently rejected presuppositions.[30]

[30] E. Gellner, *Words and Things*, p. 54.

I cannot see that the criticism is at all decisive. Is it true that the environment of man has changed and is changing so radically that the survival *of the terms Austin is interested in* creates but a feeble presumption of fitness? Do we for instance perceive things in another manner than our grandfathers did? Do we name and describe things in radically new ways? If this were so, the sense of such terms would, as far as they are ostensively defined, be one thing for our ancestors and another for us. That is of course true for many of our terms, especially the ones tied to outmoded institutions and things belonging to past cultures. But is it true of perception? or naming? or truth?

Is it likely that terms which *all* of us use in the practical business of life are based on currently rejected presuppositions? The terms that seem most liable to that failure are *theory-laden* words; but do the ordinary perceptual terms carry any cargo of the sort? Even if a term sets out with it, must it still retain it when it has come into the mouth of everyman (who knows next to nothing of scientific theories)? Can't I give someone a piece of information, although the notion of information was originally tied up with Aristotle's doctrine of form and materia which I reject? Suppose that the term 'essence' was introduced as a technical term for Aristotle's *ousia*.[31] Does it follow that it must occur in that sense now? Even if most words never shake off their etymology altogether, can't their meaning shift e.g. in the way Austin illustrated in the case of 'fascist' (1940.40)? Would Gellner say that since depression is not caused by a predominance of black bile, nobody can be melancholic? If not, in what way are the terms of perception, naming, describing, stating, promising, apologizing, etc., worse off than 'melancholic', 'humourous' and the other words once laden with the theory of temperaments?

My objections are, of course, not designed to show that Gellner is wrong but only that he is very far indeed from having proved his case. Austin admits that in fields 'trodden into bogs or tracks by traditional philosophy' 'even "ordinary" language will often become infected with the jargon of extinct theories' (1956a.130), and that 'superstition and error and fantasy of all kinds do be-

---

[31] Cf my paper 'Mr Halldén on essence statements' and S. Halldén's reply (*Theoria 27*, 1961). Halldén says that utterances containing the word 'essence' are 'the remains of an already obsolete way of speaking and thinking' (p. 186). Is there any reason to accept this for (say) 'The essence of what I have said ...'?

come incorporated in ordinary language and even sometimes stand up to the survival test' (1956a.133). But he adds, '(only, when they do, why should we not detect it?)' The suggestion that investigations of what we say when can give us reliable distinctions and connexions does not entail that they always do. We have to look and see in every particular case whether they yield anything worthwhile or not.

Suppose that we have found that we say sometimes that someone did something by mistake, sometimes that he did it by accident. How are we to prove that the verbal difference is connected with a difference on a non-verbal level—that 'by mistake' is tied to another type of situation than the phrase 'by accident'? I think that it can be done by a Moorean argument.

It is quite certain (*a*) that sometimes someone does something by accident and not by mistake, and (*b*) that sometimes someone does something by mistake and not by accident. These things are quite certain, either in the sense that they are *obviously* true or in the sense that they have immensely much stronger support than any that an argument against them has at its disposal. But if both (*a*) and (*b*) are true, the distinction 'by mistake'/'by accident' marks out two different types of situations: it cannot be true *both* that the distinction is not tied to two different types of situations *and* that a man sometimes does something by mistake and not by accident and at other times does something by accident and not by mistake. The distinction may be a merely syntactical one—as it would e.g. if a language had two verbs for sleeping, one of which was used of the king and the other of all other persons: there is, I daresay, no feature of the sleep (as distinct from the status of the sleeper) which characterizes the sleep of a king and is lacking in the sleep of his subjects, or *vice versa*. There is, however, a decisive reason for ruling out this possibility in our particular case, namely that it is perfectly certain that (*a*) would not be true unless certain features *in the situation*—in the world—are different from what they are when (*b*) is true, and the other way round. Hence, the distinction is not a merely syntactical one but marks out two different types of states of affairs in the world.

I believe that whenever we wonder whether a verbal distinction really marks out a difference in the world, the question can be settled by an argument of this sort. The truth-value of the premises of a particular application of this sort of argument cannot be determined *a priori*. But that people, within a field that really matters to them, use a word in certain situations and withhold it in situations which *prima facie* are similar to the first ones is (so Austin maintains) a good, though not a decisive, reason for believing that the situations are of different types.

(4) Since 'linguistic phenomenology' turns out to be an investigation of in what situations certain utterances are in order, it is about the valid use of these utterances. Austin might, I think, very well have agreed with Gellner's words: 'A question becomes philosophical when it is about the valid use of a term. This is what philosophy has always meant, and the only thing it sensibly can mean'.[32] But he would have been amused at Gellner's idea that this is an objection to his approach ('*this is precisely why past philosophers were not tempted to be philologists or lexicographers*').[33]

To sum up: On behalf of his 'linguistic phenomenology' Austin claimed, explicitly or implicitly, that it (1) stimulates our imagination and makes us aware of some important ways in which our language traps our thinking; (2) sharpens our awareness of how people conceive the world; (3) suggests distinctions and connexions which are likely to correspond to differences and connexions in the world and which also are important for some purposes; and (4) is an investigation of the valid employment of words.—He did not claim that his approach even if carefully executed is infallible, always leads to the truth of the matter under investigation, and so on. It does, he thought, give us a valuable help in certain philosophical inquiries; but he was probably of the opinion that there is no method with which *all* philosophical questions can be tackled, nor that there is any hope for it in the future. At all events, he felt no need for it.[34]

Practical advice. Suppose that we want to use Austin's approach. How are we to go about it? In 'A plea for excuses' he gives us a few pieces of advice (which, however, are designed only to help us to learn something from our own language or a language which is almost our mother tongue).

First, we ought to employ the dictionary. What he thinks of is clearly a book of the Oxford Dictionary type; English-French

[32] Gellner, *op. cit.*, p. 38.   [33] *Loc.cit.*
[34] Cf Hampshire, *op. cit.*, p. 34.

ones, etc., are not hinted at. He recommends us either to read the book through, listing all the relevant words; or to start with a wide selection of obviously relevant terms, widen it with new words in the dictionary explanations of our first list, and then add the new words which crop up in the dictionary explanations of these terms in their turn, and so forth till we come upon only repetitions.

We also ought to use the manuals of the sciences that are relevant to the matter under investigation. (1956a.134–7.)

The next step is to study in what circumstances our words can be used, in the usual manner of 'linguistic phenomenology'.

This ends his advice; but he himself often tried to break out of the 'conceptual schema' of his own language by using foreign grammars and dictionaries. And of course he used an etymological dictionary.

8. The 'science of language'

I have been at pains to stress that 'linguistic phenomenology' is an inquiry not just into what we say, but into what we say *when* —that it is an inquiry into language *and* into the world. It is misleading to say e.g. that Austin's 'How to talk'

> wholly consists in a careful distinction between different types of speech-act—'*describing* X as Y', '*calling* X, Y', '*stating that* X is Y' —an inquiry ... primarily an example of what one can properly call linguistic analysis, with no obvious therapeutic moral.[35]

For although it is true that Austin did not have any obviously therapeutic intentions, it is not true that his paper is merely an attempt to keep distinct the *phrases* 'describing X as Y', 'stating that X is Y', and so on. It is an attempt to tell in what situations we say that an utterance 'X is Y' is a description, in what situations we say it is a statement, and so forth: it is an attempt to tell *how the situations differ*—in what respects something in the world is otherwise—when one expression is appropriate, and when the other is.

Still, 'linguistic phenomenology' has a very pronounced linguistic side. Austin's approach is designed to be used by people willing to pay close attention to what exactly is said in what

[35] J. Passmore, *A Hundred Years of Philosophy*, p. 449.

situations: what words are used, in what constructions, with what stress and intonation? And although Austin in his published writings pursued such questions for traditional philosophical ends (to a lower degree in 'How to talk' than in his other papers), he also thought them worth pursuing for their own sake. He even thought that his 'linguistic phenomenology', *with* its non-linguistic side, might enter a new science of language. Of this new science he did not say much. The most explicit passage is 1956b.179–80. There he suggests that his arguments in 'Ifs and cans' might be assigned to grammar as well as to philosophy. He goes on,

> There are constant references in contemporary philosophy, which notoriously is much concerned with language, to a 'logical grammar' and a 'logical syntax' as though these were things distinct from ordinary grammarian's grammar and syntax: and certainly they do seem, whatever exactly they may be, different from traditional grammar. But grammar today is itself in a state of flux; for fifty years or more it has been questioned on all hands and counts whether what Dionysius Thrax once thought was the truth about Greek is the truth and the whole truth about all language and all languages. Do we know, then, that there will prove to be any ultimate boundary between 'logical grammar' and a revised and enlarged *Grammar*? In the history of human inquiry, philosophy has the place of the initial central sun, seminal and tumultuous: from time to time it throws off some portion of itself to take station as a science, a planet, cool and well regulated, progressing steadily towards a distant final state. This happened long ago at the birth of mathematics, and again at the birth of physics: only in the last century we have witnessed the same process once again, slow and at the time almost imperceptible, in the birth of the science of mathematical logic, through the joint labours of philosophers and mathematicians. Is it not possible that the next century may see the birth, through the joint labours of philosophers, grammarians, and numerous other students of language, of a true and comprehensive *science of language*? Then we shall have rid ourselves of one more part of philosophy (there will still be plenty left) in the only way we ever can get rid of philosophy, by kicking it upstairs.

This programmatic passage does not tell how much he wanted the new science to include. I gather that the new grammar will embody *explicit* semantic considerations and in this respect differ from the traditional one. The distinction between language and languages further suggests that it would be concerned not only

MAIN CHARACTERISTICS OF AUSTIN'S APPROACH 49

with the syntax, semantics, etc., of different languages but also with questions clustering around the problems of linguistic communication in general. But perhaps Austin had no definite views of what the new science would look like, and perhaps he would have regarded such speculations as premature—he might have been struck just by the fact that linguistic inquiries sometimes are pertinent to philosophy and that philosophical inquiries (of the sort brought into vogue by Wittgenstein) sometimes are pertinent to linguistics. He certainly claimed that the discovery of performatives demanded alterations in our ordinary grammar.*

But if the philosopher demands that linguists ought to pay attention to what he says, he has to forsake his amateur attitude to linguistic investigations; he has to become an artisan.—This must have been a factor to which the linguistic flavour of Austin's writings may be attributed to a considerable degree.

It is evident, from the passage quoted, that Austin thought that a new type of grammar is or will soon be within reach. The work of constructing it, or of constructing any other part of the science of language, may plausibly be considered a piece of teamwork; and he also 'privately expressed the belief that a large, co-operative, centrally directed project of linguistic analysis might indeed lead to solidly based results, and that uncontrolled private enterprise could accomplish very little'.[36]

Suppose, then, that the philosopher may do something useful even within the field of linguistics. This forces him to tackle linguistic phenomena in a more thorough way than earlier. Does it also force him to go round with questionnaires and makes statistics in order to check what people really say when? Austin seemed to think that it was not necessary; at least he thought that the philosopher's armchair method has something to be said for it. For (a) there are checks on the philosopher's claims. In the first place he can—and has to—watch what people actually say in certain situations; and although such a watching will not, perhaps, suffice to verify his claims, it can at least falsify them. In the second place, he has cantankerous colleagues who are not slow to point out the mistakes he commits. And (b) asking the

*[I now think that he had fairly definite ideas about at least part of the new science. See Ch. 3:9.]
[36] Hampshire, *op. cit.*, p. 40. Hampshire leaves it unclear whether 'linguistic analysis' refers to the linguistic side of the 'linguistic phenomenology', or to its non-linguistic side, or to both.

man in the street what he would say when, is just another, and less careful, version of the armchair method. For since the plain man cannot, as a rule, be placed in the situation envisaged, he will have to imagine that he is faced with it; and here there are stumbling-blocks of which he, but not the philosopher, is ignorant. He does not know how essential it is for the answer that the situation be imagined in a great many details. Nor does he, perhaps, consider the consequences of his reply in the careful way he would if he had actually been in the situation in question. But then his answer is likely to be *less* reliable than the philosopher's.[37] It is really no more scientific to ascertain what people say when by means of questionnaires and interviews with the man in the street, than to ascertain it by means of asking what I myself and my philosophical friends say; rather the other way round. But if such snags of the Oslo method[38] can be removed, statistics and questionnaires will, of course, be very relevant.

III. WITTGENSTEIN AND AUSTIN

Since Austin is sometimes counted among the group of philosophers vaguely labelled 'Wittgensteinians', I shall briefly set out my reasons for doubting that Austin was ever under Wittgenstein's influence.

Austin's knowledge of Wittgenstein's philosophy

The first question is whether there really is any reason to think that Austin knew much about Wittgenstein's philosophy. Hampshire denies he did;[39] and there are, so far as I am aware, only two references to Wittgenstein in Austin's works, both of them in writings which appeared after the publication of *Philosophical Investigations*.[40] Moreover, in his 1939 and 1940 attacks on the name theory of meaning Austin seems ignorant of the type of

[37] 'What I do as a philosopher.'
[38] Cf e.g. A. Naess, 'Towards a theory of interpretation and preciseness', *Semantics and the Philosophy of Language* (ed. L. Linsky); and *Interpretation and Preciseness*.
[39] Hampshire, *op.cit.*, p. 44.
[40] Wittgenstein's name occurs in *S&S*.100. In other references (1956c.221) Wittgenstein is not mentioned but probably intended (cf. p. 29f and note 22 of this chapter).

criticism launched against it in Wittgenstein's *Blue Book* (1933–1934) and *Brown Book* (1934–35).[41] In view of the space Wittgenstein gives to the issue, it is reasonable to infer that if Austin was ignorant of the criticism in question, he did not then know much about Wittgenstein's ideas.

In Wittgenstein's lifetime, *The Blue Book* and *The Brown Book* existed only in a few typed or stencilled copies which circulated among his students. Philosophers outside Cambridge learnt about the new ideas mostly through the essays by John Wisdom. These were, however, almost exclusively concerned with one aspect of Wittgenstein's philosophy, the 'therapeutic' one. In the most important of these papers, 'Philosophical Perplexity' and 'Metaphysics and Verification' (reprinted in Wisdom's *Philosophy and Psycho-Analysis*), two tenets are propagated: Philosophical problems are to be dissolved rather than solved; and philosophical assertions often resemble epigrams—the statement 'In contradistinction to deductive conclusions, inductive ones are never really justified' and the saying 'The thoroughbred is a neurotic woman on four legs' are alike in the respect that they, although literally false or even nonsensical, force us to regard things in a new way by spotlighting important similarities and dissimilarities. The former tenet comes from Wittgenstein; the latter is Wisdom's own contribution. Neither of them is taken up by Austin. Wisdom's papers do, however, also contain two Wittgensteinian suggestions which are important in Austin's philosophy, viz. that the same word is sometimes applied to things which do not have any property in common but are kept together by family resemblances; and the closely related contention that some words are criteria-delimited (see §5 of the next chapter). The latter of these ideas goes, however, back *via* Wittgenstein to C. D. Broad—cf *Philosophy and Psycho-Analysis*, p. 82.

What has earned Austin the epithet 'Wittgensteinian' is clearly his regard for what we ordinarily say. But his insistence on a close attention to ordinary language may as well be within an old Oxford (and Aristotelian) tradition. Philosophers such as J. Cook Wilson and his pupil H. Prichard had accustomed Oxford students to the ideas that distinctions marked in common language

[41] Now published together as *Preliminary studies for the 'Philosophical Investigations'*, generally known as *The Blue & Brown Books*.

cannot safely be neglected, and that at least some philosophical problems can be solved by paying earnest regard to *what* we ordinarily say, *how* we say it, and *when* we say it. There are amusing connexions between Austin's 'How to talk' and passages in Cook Wilson's *Statement and Inference* (e.g. Pt. II, Ch. IV, Vol. I); and in spite of the enormous difference in conclusions, it is rewarding to compare *S&S* to Prichard's 'Perception' (in *Knowledge and Perception*), or what Austin has to say on promises and the situations in which they originate, to Prichard's attacks on the same problem in *Moral Obligation*, especially in the paper 'On the obligation to keep a promise'. I do not know whether Austin ever read Cook Wilson, but a link between them is formed by Prichard whose lectures and classes Austin attended,[42] and with whom he corresponded regarding promises in the beginning of the '40's.[43]

Also Oxford scholars of a younger generation than Prichard's kept alive a philosophical interest in linguistic investigations. In 1932, Gilbert Ryle published 'Systematically misleading expressions' (reprinted in *L&L*, I). Independent of Wittgenstein, he claimed that one philosophical task is 'the detection of the sources in linguistic idioms of recurrent misconstructions and absurd theories'. The same year, the philologist Alan H. Gardiner gave a first sketch of the distinction between locutionary and illocutionary aspects of a speech-act. (See Part II of *A Theory of Speech and Language*.) His remarks on 'sentence-qualificators' (§§ 61 and 68) are clearly relevant to such philosophical puzzles as why it is odd to say 'S is P, but I don't believe it'.

There is, then, no need and no reason to suppose that Austin formed his basic ideas under Wittgenstein's influence.

Similarities between Wittgenstein's and Austin's philosophies

More important than this question of philosophical originality is, however, the fact that Wittgenstein's and Austin's philosophies differ in several central respects. But first for the similarities.

One respect in which Wittgenstein and Austin resemble each other is, of course, their belief that we are liable to be misled by

---

[42] Hampshire, p. 43.
[43] A fragmentary and unpublished preface in Austin's hand-writing to *Words*.

the fact that the verbal or grammatical forms of our language are less various than the actual uses they can be put to—that, e.g., we are tempted to think that feeling that there is a flaw in your argument is like feeling a coin in my pocket,[44] or that since 'real' is an adjective it must stand for a property like other adjectives. For this reason, Wittgenstein and Austin agree that it is necessary that we learn to command a clear view of the uses of words.

Another point of resemblance is their belief that we are liable to be swayed or even held captive by what Wittgenstein calls 'pictures' and Austin (semantic) 'models'. Austin's complaint that the analytic/synthetic dichotomy is due to our employment of a too simple working-model is of course of the same type as the one Wittgenstein gives vent to in his discussions of e.g. 'following a rule' (*Philosophical Investigations*, e.g. §§348–53, 422–6).

A third similarity is their discovery that in the case of some verbs there is an asymmetry between their use in the first person present indicative and their use in other persons and tenses (*Investigations* II:x; *Words*).

Differences between Wittgenstein's and Austin's philosophies*

The differences are, however, still more striking. Both *Tractatus* 6.53 and *Investigations*, the paragraphs around §123, make it fairly clear that Wittgenstein thought that *all* philosophy is therapeutic. Austin did *not* think so—he had not the slightest inclination to believe that the (only) 'work of the philosopher consists in assembling reminders for a particular purpose' (*Ph. I.* §127), or that philosophy 'may in no way interfere with the actual use of language; it can in the end only describe it. . . . It leaves everything as it is' (§124). Nor did he reject classification of the functions of language in the way Wittgenstein did. And whereas Wittgenstein held that an investigation of our language is in place exactly where the philosophical problems cluster because these *must* be 'one or another piece of plain nonsense

---

[44] G. Ryle, 'Feelings'. *Aesthetics and Language* (ed. W. Elton).

*[This section is poor. Wittgenstein did not think that all philosophy or even his own brand of philosophy is necessarily therapeutic. Nor was he concerned with merely conceptual matters. The *Investigations* is, I think, a kind of philosophical anthropology. I try to argue my case in a book called *This Language-Game Is Played* (not yet published).]

and of bumps that the understanding has got by running its head up against the limits of language' (§119), Austin claimed, as we have seen, that his 'linguistic phenomenology' is to be preferred in fields where (*a*) ordinary language is rich and subtle and (*b*) traditional philosophy has not been too much. The reason for (*b*) is that philosophy often infects ordinary language 'with the jargon of extinct theories, and our own prejudices too, as the upholders or imbibers of theoretical views, will be too readily, and often insensibly, engaged' (1930a.130f). I.e., Austin relied on an investigation of what we say when in the very situations where we are *not* philosophically puzzled and hence there is no need of philosophical therapy.

The difference is, however, less than it might appear. Austin is of course concerned with philosophical problems, but he thought that we see them clearer when we attack not the rubric words 'knowledge', 'truth', 'freedom', 'beauty' but more neglected words that are 'neighbouring, analogous or germane in some way to some notorious centre of philosophical trouble'—we ought to 'forget for a while about the beautiful and get down instead to the dainty and the dumpy' (1956a.131). If this is done in order to show where philosophers have erred, we seem to be back again at something like a therapeutic view.

But there still remains an important difference in attitude. Wittgenstein never abandoned the doctrine of *Tractatus* 4.111 that philosophy is not concerned with facts but only with conceptual matters. Its concern with these matters is 'therapeutic'— it eases our mental cramp and even causes it to disappear by a new arrangement of what we already know; but it does not, according to Wittgenstein, enlarge our knowledge and does not even attempt to. Austin, on the other hand, held that philosophy is not merely concerned with 'conceptual' matters: We have the words we have and speak as we do because we conceive of the world in a certain way. Had the world been different, we should probably have spoken differently. He was interested in what people say, because he thought that their ways of speaking both reveal how they structure a certain situation and also often spotlight different features in the situation—tell us something about the world. For this reason he studied how we all speak, or how certain specialists speak when dealing with their particular field, even when there is no suggestion that these ways of speaking lead to conceptual tangles and 'mental cramps'. His 'linguistic phenomenology' is among other things a method for bringing out how a small change of factors in a situation makes speakers change their words. One task of philosophy is, he thought, to elucidate what these factors are; for very often we know that this is a good way of putting something in a certain situation and that way of putting it is bad, although we cannot put our finger on the difference. In this way, philosophy strives to increase our knowledge of the world, and not only—in a Wittgensteinian manner—to make our conceptual system (our rules of language, etc.) more perspicuous.

In my eyes this is enough to make the similarities between Wittgenstein and Austin superficial. Austin has no therapeutic conception of philosophy. For him—as, I think, for Moore—there were no problems which were distinctly philosophical and could be solved by a certain method. But most problems needed to be clarified; and when that had been done, some of them might be answered even by people who, like most philosophers, do not work in laboratories, or assemble statistics, or prepare questionnaires.

CHAPTER 2

The Locutionary Act: Speech and Language

Austin was, I think, sincere in his declaration that he did 'not altogether like . . . producing a programme, that is, saying what ought to be done rather than doing something' (*Words*.163). He was more interested in studying how we talk in particular speech situations than in evolving a general theory of how language is used. Nonetheless he presents rudiments of such a theory in his 1953 paper and in *Words*. Although he was profoundly dissatisfied with the former,[1] it deserves careful consideration since it is his most explicit inquiry into what he in *Words* calls the locutionary act. Together with the 1950 and the 1954 essay, 'How to talk' is also the most rewarding of his studies of another notion, which he in *Words* dubbed the constative utterance.

This chapter discusses some aspects of the locutionary act. This act is not, however, wholly intelligible until contrasted with the illocutionary act, which is introduced in the next chapter. Ch. 4 deals with the constative utterance, i.e., with the locutionary act when performed with a certain force. The final chapter considers other kinds of (illocutionary and performatory) forces.

When someone says something to someone else in the 'full normal sense', he performs a speech act. Austin segments it into different 'acts'. This segmentation into other 'acts' is not to be taken at its face-value; there is just one speech act. The locutionary act and its sub-acts, as well as the illocutionary act, the perlocutionary act, and the enigmatic act *C.b* (*Words*.102), are different dimensions of this single act.

The locutionary act—i.e., the locutionary dimension of a speech act—is sketched in the following way (*Words*. 92–8):

To say something is always to perform the *phonetic* act of uttering some noises, and what we utter is a *phone*. To say something always also involves the *phatic* act of uttering noises that

[1] Hampshire, *op. cit.*, p. 39.

are words and are produced as words of a certain language with a certain grammar and a certain intonation, etc.; and what we utter is then a *pheme*. To say something is, further, in most cases to use the pheme with a certain sense and a certain reference. That is a *rhetic* act, and what we utter is a *rheme*. (The notions of sense and reference are here taken 'on the strength of current views' (*Words*.148).)

A phatic act, says Austin, involves a phonetic act but not the converse: 'if a monkey makes a noise indistinguishable from "go" it is still not a phatic act'. Both these kinds of acts are, however, mimicable down to intonation, winks, and gestures. Reports of someone's words in direct speech are reports of his phatic act ('He said, "I shall be there"'). Reports of someone's words in indirect speech are reports of his rhetic act ('He said he would be there'). A pheme is a unit of language, its typical fault being lack of meaning. A rheme is a unit of speech, its typical faults being vagueness, obscurity, etc. The same type-pheme may be used on different occasions with a different sense or reference; and then different type-rhemes arise. When different type-phemes have the same sense and the same reference they are rhetically equivalent acts, i.e., they make the same statement. Certain rhemes are in order although they lack reference, e.g. 'All triangles have three sides'. (I fail to see why that is to count as a rheme. According to the accepted view, 'All triangles have three sides' is 'true in virtue of its meaning'. Why should we not make all questions of sense questions of phemes? Traditional tautologies and contradictions are phemes but not rhemes—units of language, not of speech. We do speak of analytic *sentences* but empirical *statements*.)

The act of performing the phonetic, phatic, and rhetic acts simultaneously is a *locutionary* act, and 'the study of utterances thus far and in these respects [is] the study of locutions, or the full units of speech'.*

In 'What I do as a philosopher' Austin stressed that if one accepts de Saussure's and Gardiner's distinction between speech and language,[2] he and his colleagues were more interested in the

---

*[For a discussion of problems merely hinted at here, see Leslie Griffiths. 'The logic of Austin's locutionary subdivision', *Theoria* 35 (1969).]

[2] F. de Saussure, *Cours de linguistique générale*; A. H. Gardiner, *A Theory of Speech and Language*.

former than in the latter. But he did not deny that he was concerned with language too; and certain important stretches of his writings are investigations of our implements for saying something and not studies of how these implements are wielded. I propose therefore to begin our study of the locutionary act by considering the 'acts' on the language side. Since speaking of 'acts' is a little bewildering, we may perhaps rephrase my first task—it is to study those aspects of a fully fledged locution that belong to language.

I. LANGUAGE

A. VOCABULARY

1. The vocabulary of speech-situation S_0

In 'How to talk' Austin considers only rudimentary languages in worlds which are, or are conceived to be, very simple and homogeneous. In his simplest example, speech-situation S_0, the world consists of

numerous individual *items*, each of one and only one definite *type*. Each type is totally and equally different from every other type: each item is totally and equally distinct from every other item. Numerous items may be of the same type, but no item is of more than one type. Item and type are . . . apprehended by inspection merely

(1953.182). The vocabulary of the language of S_0 consists of noises and/or marks, etc., governed by certain conventions. The noises, etc., considered apart from the conventions governing them, are called *vocables*. In S_0 a vocable becomes a word by being tied with a convention to an item. I shall call conventions tying a vocable to something in the world *vertical* conventions. In S_0 they are of two kinds. Austin gives them different names in different papers, and his choice of labels in 'How to talk' is indeed unhappy, as D. R. Cousin has brought out in 'How *not* to talk' (*Analysis* 15, 1954/55). I shall call them *individuating* and *classificatory* conventions. The former serve to refer to an item, the latter to say something about that item. (Both the noun and the adjective 'square' are, according to this terminology, governed by classificatory rules. There is, of course, an important difference between them; but it will not be in point in this book.)

Austin takes it for granted that there are classificatory and individuating words, and he does not discuss how they acquire meaning. In 1953.183 he says rather awkwardly that a classificatory word is associated with an item-type, one to one. This sounds as if he thought that not only the items but also the item-types are some sort of entities, and as if he held that the name theory of meaning can explain how a vocable becomes a classificatory word. But on the next page he declares that the item-type probably is a construction. He asks us to think of the items as a number of specimens of colours, the 'types' as patterns of colours, and the act whereby a vocable acquires meaning as the selection of a specimen as a standard pattern. In the new account the 'types' are no longer a sort of Platonic idea named by classificatory names; and in view of his 1940 criticisms he can hardly have held that a classificatory word is a name.* He was thinking of an 'ostensive definition', and although such a 'definition' of, say, squares introduces us to something which—especially in S_0—very well may be called an item-type, it does not introduce us to an entity.—He does not say anything about how a vocable becomes an individuating word. He only tells us that it fixes the item that it refers to 'on each . . . occasion of the uttering (assertive) of a sentence containing it'; and that this individuation is not the one consisting in picking out an item as the same item again, is not a form of reidentification.

2. *The vocabulary of* S_1

Suppose that we have the same language as in S_0 but that the world is more complex. It contains 'items of types which do not exactly match any of the patterns in our stock (the sense of any of our names [= classificatory words]), though they may be more or less similar to one or more than one of those patterns' (1953.193). How are we to speak to one another about the new sorts of things? We can, of course, assign a new label to a new type as soon as it crops up; but that is often unpractical. We can, however, proceed in two other ways.

*[It is difficult to reconcile 'How to talk' with Austin's early papers. R. M. Chisholm is, I think, right in his comment: 'Had he tried to justify his remark [in 1953.184] that "sense" might appear as a construction', then . . . he would have found himself dealing with "the so-called problem of universals".' ('J. L. Austin's Philosophical Papers,' *Symp*, p. 105.)]

(i) The first of them is to make shift with our old vocabulary without adding anything to it. Although one of the items we come across in S_1 deviates from the pattern of squares we had in S_0, the differences are so small that we decide to call it, too, a square. This stretching of the meaning of a word is the possibility discussed in 1953.194.

(ii) Linguistic parsimony may, however, make us unable to express certain distinctions. Suppose, for example, that we want to keep apart squares in the S_0 sense and the deviations which only by courtesy are called squares. How are we to distinguish them verbally without introducing a new label for the latter? Well, we may try an *adapter-word*: we may say that the new things are *like* squares, or that they are *quasi-squares*, or that they are *of square-type*, or that they are *squarish*. Or we may tackle the question from another side and say that although the new things are squares, they are not *real* or *genuine* or *true* or *proper* squares. A few of these adapter-words are mentioned in 1953.196–7, but only in passing. There is also a reference to them in 1950.88. More is said about them in 1946.57 and *S&S*. Ch. VII, esp. 73–7. So let us turn to these sources.

3. Adapter-words*

An adapter-word is a device to make our limited vocabulary more flexible. It is 'part of our apparatus *in* words for fixing and adjusting the semantics *of* words' (1950.88). If we think of words as arrows, shot into the world, the function of an adapter-word is, according to Austin, that it enables us to hit targets which do not lie straight ahead—it enables to shoot in a curve. By its means we gain flexibility *without changing the sense of the term we apply it to*: 'if I can say "Not a real pig, but like a pig", I don't have to tamper with the meaning of "pig" itself' (*S&S*.74–5).

Since an adapter-word requires a term to adjust, it cannot by itself do duty as a predicative expression. There is no temptation to treat e.g. 'like' in that way; but the statements 'These diamonds are real' and 'These are real diamonds' certainly look grammatically like 'These diamonds are pink' and 'These are pink diamonds'. Austin stresses, however, how different they are:

*[For a forceful, influential but (I believe) exegetically dubious criticism of Austin's views, see Jonathan Bennett: 'Real'. (*Symp*.).]

I cannot *just* say of something 'This is real' and leave it at that—it is not a complete message in the way 'This is pink' (period) is. In the former case, but not in the latter, we 'must have an answer to the question "A real *what*?", if the question "Real or not?" is to have a definite sense' (*S&S*.68–9). The same remark applies to 'true', 'genuine', 'proper', and so forth.

Two ways of adjusting a term. Austin thought that 'like' is '*the* great adjuster-word, or, alternatively put, the main flexibility device by whose aid, in spite of the limited scope of our vocabulary, we can always avoid being left completely speechless' (*S&S*.74). It 'equips us *generally* to handle the unforeseen, in a way in which new words invented *ad hoc* don't, and can't' (*S&S*.75). Why do we then bother to have other adjuster-devices, such as 'real', 'true', 'genuine', 'proper', 'pink*ish*' and 'port-*type* wine'? He vouchsafes no answer but just asserts that if we knew why we sometimes say 'It's like a pig' and sometimes 'It isn't a real pig', we should have gone a long way towards elucidating the use of 'real'.

It is, in my opinion, false that 'like' is *the* adjuster-word in Austin's sense. There are at least two ways of adjusting the semantics of our words by adjuster-devices. I shall call them *quasi-extension* and *quasi-contraction*. Let the term be 'T'. In a quasi-extension we use an adapter-device to draw attention to the resemblances between the items falling within 'T':s range of application and an item *a* outside the range; in a quasi-contraction we indicate that within 'T':s range of application an item *a* is rather unlike the others. In neither case do we change 'T':s range of application; but quasi-extending devices imply that it could reasonably be extended to *a*, whilst quasi-contractive devices imply that it could reasonably be withheld from *a*.

Austin seems concerned exclusively with quasi-extensions. He pays heed merely to cases like speech-situation S_1, where the vocabulary appropriate to S_0 has to be stretched or quasi-stretched in order to cater for new types of phenomena.

In that sort of situation 'like' certainly is our main flexibility device. If I see a boar for the first time, I cannot afterwards describe it to you by saying 'I saw a pig which wasn't real (true, genuine, etc.)'. As the plain man revealingly remarks, that would not tell you what the animal I saw was like. My description naturally takes the form 'I saw something like a pig'. That gives you a rough idea of its visual appearance, and if I then tell in what ways it differed from normal pigs, you may get a fairly faithful picture of it.—Kindred expressions are 'quasi-', 'kind of', and the suffix '-ish' as it occurs in e.g. 'whitish', 'swinish', 'stiffish'.

Suppose now that a language more complex than S_0 has no separate word for 'pig' and none for 'boar'—the word 'gip' is applied indifferently to both. That natives grow tired of this linguistic poverty and try to find a cure for it. Being conservative they do not wish to coin a new term but prefer to make shift with their old vocabulary together with adjuster-words. They may then try 'real', 'true', or 'genuine': they point to pigs and say 'These are true (real, etc.) gips', and then they indicate boars and say 'Those are not true (etc.) gips'. They have then effected a quasi-contraction.

The disadvantage of this procedure is of course that our natives now will find it difficult to speak of boars. They may try 'gips but not true ones', and that may do for a time. But if they often need to speak about them, it is convenient to introduce a new term. To employ 'real', 'true', 'genuine', etc., is to take a first step towards restricting a term's range of application and hence a first step towards restricting its sense; but it is not yet to forbid its application to all the things it hitherto has ranged over. That is a later, legislative step.

Excluders. 'Real', 'true' and 'genuine' are what Austin in *S&S.* 70–1 calls *trouser-words*:

It is usually thought, and I dare say usually rightly thought, that what one might call the affirmative use of a term is basic—that, to understand '*x*', we need to know what it is to be *x*, or to be an *x*, and that knowing this apprises us of what it is *not* to be *x*, not to be an *x*. But with 'real' . . . it is the *negative* use that wears the trousers. That is, a definite sense attaches to the assertion that something is real, a real such-and-such, only in the light of a specific way in which it might be, or might have been, *not* real. 'A real duck' differs from the simple 'a duck' only in that it is used to exclude various ways of being not a real duck—but a dummy, a toy, a picture, a decoy, &c.; and moreover I don't know *just* how to take the assertion that it's a real duck unless I know *just* what, on

that particular occasion, the speaker had it in mind to exclude. . . .
[The] function of 'real' is not to contribute positively to the
characterization of anything, but to exclude possible ways of
being *not* real—and these ways are both numerous for particular
kinds of things, and liable to be quite different for things
of different kinds. It is this identity of general function combined
with immense diversity in specific applications which gives to the
word 'real' the, at first sight, baffling feature of having neither one
single 'meaning', nor yet ambiguity, a number of different meanings.

Further 'real' is a *dimension-word*, i.e.,

it is the most general and comprehensive term in a whole group of
terms of the same kind, terms that fulfil the same function. Other
members of this group . . . are, for example, 'proper', 'genuine',
'live', 'true', 'authentic', 'natural'.

So Austin's 'trouser-words' are words which, in virtue of the
rules of English, have it as their standard function to rule out
something. They are *excluders*, to adopt Roland Hall's handy
term.[3] An adjective is an excluder if it (*a*) is attributive as opposed
to predicative, (*b*) serves to rule out something without itself
adding anything, and (*c*) rules out different things according to
the context. It is *not* ambiguous, not even systematically (*S&S*.
64); it is an expression which as its standard function in *language*
rules out something or other—but what it rules out in a particular
situation is determined in *speech*, in ways which soon will be
described. Not all excluders are, however, adjectives. Austin
mentions 'dream', 'illusion', 'mirage', 'hallucination' (*S&S*.71)
and Hall (*op. cit.*, p. 7) 'chance', 'intuition', 'luck'. I shall not
discuss these exceptions.

Austin insists, then, that the expression 'a real (etc.) so-and-so'
is in place only where there is 'some "reason for suggesting" that
it [the so-and-so] isn't real, in the sense of some specific way, or
limited number of specific ways, in which it is suggested that this
experience or item may be phoney' (1946.55). 'Real' (etc.) must
whenever it is employed have a contrast which it is used to rule
out. That contrast is more specific than an *unreal* so-and-so: if I
wonder whether her pearls are real, I'm not asking myself whether

[3] Roland Hall, 'Excluders'. *Analysis* 20, 1959/60. As Hall mentions, the
discovery of excluders goes back to Plato who in *Politicus* 262d discusses one
of them, viz. 'barbarian'. For a short history of this type of linguistic devices,
see Hall, pp. 1–3.

they are unreal but e.g. whether they are paste. 'Sometimes (usually) the context makes it clear what the suggestion is: the goldfinch may be stuffed but there's no suggestion that it's a mirage, the oasis may be a mirage but there's no suggestion it might be stuffed' (1946.55). The contextual hints as to the contrast are often due to the fact that we 'have a well-founded antecedent idea in what respects the kind of thing mentioned could (and could not) be "not real". For instance, if you ask me "Is this real silk?" I shall tend to supply "as opposed to artificial", since I already know that silk is the kind of thing which can be very closely simulated by an artificial product. The notion of its being *toy* silk, for instance, will not occur to me.' (*S&S*.72.)

According to Austin, less general excluders than 'real' will often suggest 'more or less definitely what it is that is being excluded. . . . If I say that I wish the university had a proper theatre, this suggests that it has at present a *makeshift* theatre; pictures are genuine as opposed to *fake*, silk is natural as opposed to *artificial*, ammunition is live as opposed to *dummy*, and so on.' (*S&S*.71.)

But if neither the context nor the excluders make it clear what suggestion the speaker wants to rule out, 'then I am entitled to ask, "How do you mean? Do you mean it might be stuffed or what? *What are you suggesting?*" The wile of the metaphysician consists in asking "Is it a real table?" (a kind of object which has no obvious way of being phoney) and not specifying or limiting what may be wrong with it, so that I feel at a loss "how to prove" it *is* a real one.' (1946.55.)—That the table has no *obvious* way of being phoney does, of course, *not* imply that it cannot be phoney. All Austin has maintained is that the speaker has to make *explicit* what kinds of failures he envisages, whereas in the case of the oasis or the silk the context makes explicitness unnecessary.

If it is conceded that 'real', 'true', 'genuine', etc., are excluders, it must, I think, also be conceded that there is no reason to hold that a real duck, a real hiding, a real dream, and a real knife have anything in common except that in each case some suggestion is ruled out, different to each case. *Prima facie*, the real things mentioned seem to be very unlike each other; and what has encouraged philosophers to search for something common to them all is simply the belief that all words are names and hence that 'real' must be the name of something, e.g. of a property. (Moore's struggle with 'real' in Ch. XII of *Some Main Problems of Philosophy* is instructive in this respect.) The belief in the name theory of meaning leads thinkers to use 'a real so-and-so' without specifying what ills they want to exclude in the so-and-so. In its turn that philosophical (mis)use of 'real' 'leads us on to the supposition that "real" has a single meaning ("the real world" "material objects"), and that a highly profound and puzzling one. Instead, we should insist always on specifying with what "real" is being contrasted—"not what" I shall have to show it is, in order to show it is "real": and then usually we shall find some specific, less fatal, word, appropriate to the particular case, to substitute for "real"' (1946.55f). Of course philosophers may disregard the usual employment of a word. But then they have to pay a price: if they use a word such as 'real' or 'know' or 'certain' as Humpty-Dumpty used 'glory', their results will tell us nothing about reality, knowledge or certainty. (Cf *S&S.* 62–4.)

This is an argument of the type Moore employed in e.g. Ch. XI of *Some Main Problems of Philosophy*: the philosopher who tries to convince us that time is not real, either is using words as they are commonly employed, and then what he says is obviously false; or he uses them in some new sense, and then he is no longer speaking about what he seemed to be speaking about—and presumably himself thought he was speaking about.

The legislative function of 'real', 'true', etc. To say that x is not a real (true, genuine) T is usually a step towards putting x outside the range of application of the term 'T'. But our adapter-words may also have another related function. Suppose that we come across a type of phenomena very like but not exactly like those we have previously called 'T', and that we stretch 'T' to cover them also. We may then be in doubt as to whether the new items are Ts only by courtesy. 'Real' and its mates may be brought in to settle the question. They then lay down the ruling that henceforward the new items are to be treated as just as good examples of Ts as the old items are.

'True', 'real', etc., are also used to remind us that a linguistic legislation of a restrictive sort has already taken effect. It would, I think, be careless to say that the man who says that frogs are not true reptiles is excluding them from the group of reptiles and laying down the rule that they do not fall within the range of application of the term 'reptile'. Even if he is correcting someone who has given the term much too generous a scope, it would be natural to say that he is merely reminding or teaching him that the scope is thus restricted. It is, however, easy to see how it comes about that a word which usually does duty as an adapter and excluder is used also to point out a term's limit of application.

A digression: Are 'real', 'true', etc., always adapter-words? There are at least two sorts of cases which may make us doubt that 'real', 'true' and so forth in their attributive use always adapt another term.

(i) In *True love, true humour and true religion*, p. 56, Halldén introduces what he calls a paradoxical use. 'In *The Decay of Lying*, Wilde gives us an example of an employment of this kind when he asserts that "the only real people are the people who never existed" . . . Here, the sender distinguishes radically between the phenomena called "A" and the true As.'

The example seems difficult to explain by means of the notion of adjuster-words. But consider another case. A mathematician says 'Nobody can draw a real circle'. Are we to say of him that he distinguishes radically between the phenomena called 'circles' and real circles? Hardly. What he says is that no circle ever drawn in the past, present or future satisfies the definition of a circle, a definition which presumably was arrived at by extrapolation from drawn circles. His procedure is not in the least paradoxical: it is a case of *restricting* the range of application of 'circle', not of *shifting* it. If we come across a perfect circle it would indeed fall within the range of the everyday application of 'circle'. It seems to me that Wilde's use of 'real people' is exactly analogous.

The other examples adduced by Halldén also yield to the same treatment. A special case is when we 'count some Austrians, Dutchmen and Scandinavians as true Germans whilst excluding some German citizens of Jewish extraction from this group' (*loc. cit.*). It is obvious that the scope of the term has been shifted here, but this is, I think, done by means of adjuster-words: By means of 'not true (real, etc.) Germans', Jews are excluded from the group of Germans. Then 'like', etc., comes into play and makes 'German' shelter even Austrians and so on. Finally 'real' or 'true' is used to lay down that 'German' henceforward is to have the new range of application.

(ii) Can the theory of adjuster-words explain the use of 'true' in what Ch. L. Stevenson calls 'persuasive definitions'? In such a definition, he says (*Ethics and Language* Ch. IX), the definiendum is both descriptive and strongly emotive, while the definiens has retained the emotive meaning and changed the descriptive one. 'Persuasive definitions are often recognizable from the words "real" or "true" employed in a metaphorical way', he continues (p. 213f):

'Charity', in the true sense of the word, means the giving not merely of gold, but of understanding. True love is the communion between minds alone. Real courage is strength against adverse public opinion. Each of these statements ... is a way of redirecting attitudes, by leaving the emotive meaning of a word laudatory, and wedding it to a favored descriptive one. In the same way we may speak of the true or real meaning of 'sportsmanship', 'genius', 'beauty', and so on. Or we may speak of the true meaning of 'selfishness' or 'hypocrisy', using persuasive definitions of these derogatory terms to blame rather than to praise.

In Ch. 10 of *True love* Halldén attacks these ideas. He argues that Stevenson cannot explain three facts about our use of a phrase of the form 'true A': (1) The positive or negative 'emotive' meaning of statements about true A is usually more intensely positive or negative than it is if 'true' is dropped. (2) 'True A' ('True Andalusian') may be 'emotively' charged, although 'A' ('Andalusian') apparently is 'emotively' neutral. (3) 'A' may have an unequivocally negative 'emotive' meaning, as e.g. 'scoundrel' has, and yet when prefixed with 'true' turn into something with both positive and negative elements.

Halldén tries to account for these three phenomena. As to (1) he maintains that in 'true A' the word 'true' sharpens the already existing positive or negative 'emotive' edge. As to (2), 'A' is despite appearances partially governed by value criteria. Thus, a native Andalusian may forfeit the right to that appellative if he fails to come up to certain standards. And (3) is, according to Halldén, explained when we recognize that we have conflicting attitudes to scoundrels: we disapprove of them and yet reluctantly admire them. 'An extra complication is that the term "true" itself is positively coloured. The positive tone of the expression "true scoundrel" might to some extent depend upon the positive colouring of "true". There is of course something paradoxical in this use of a word as "true" to emphasize a negative evaluation.' (P. 87.)

It seems to me that neither (1) nor (3) is true unless certain qualifications are made. (i) When someone says 'A frog is not a true reptile' he neither commends nor takes exception to reptiles. So not all uses of the construction 'true *x*' are 'emotive'.—Halldén can, I think, counter the criticism by saying that 'true' only intensifies an *already existing* 'emotive' meaning but cannot create it.

(ii) A more serious objection is that if 'true' in conjunction with an 'emotively' charged word *always* is positively 'emotive', 'true scoundrel' ought to be more neutral than 'scoundrel' alone and not the other way round as Halldén maintains. We may try to escape this awkwardness in two ways. (*a*) The first is to say that in 'true scoundrel' the adjuster-word is as 'emotively' neutral as it apparently is in 'true frog'. (*b*) The other is more complex. Its first part is the concession that 'true' among other things serves to call forth the 'emotive' meaning (if any) of the word it is conjoined with. Its next part is that 'true' nevertheless also quasi-contracts the range of the term's application to only clear or even paradigmatical cases; i.e., 'true' has also an adjusting function. Its third part is that the positively 'emotive' load of 'true' never forces out the negatively 'emotive' load of 'scoundrel'—the words work, as it were, in different dimensions. I suggest, then, *both* that 'true' intensifies the positive or negative 'emotive' meaning (if any) of the word it adjusts, *and* that it quasi-contracts that word's scope of application, *and* that we use this particular adjuster in situations where we want to convey that we e.g. feel some form of admiration of the phenomenon at issue. According to this suggestion, one of the features of 'true' is to convey that the speaker *in fact* admires the person, whilst 'scoundrel' is used to tell us how we *ought* to react to him. 'He's a true scoundrel' then works something like 'Although I admire him, he is indeed a scoundrel'. That is not a self-stultifying form of expression: we are often uneasily aware that we have other feelings about something that we ought to have.

There is something to be said for this complex way of avoiding the awkwardness. For when we want not merely to call forth the negative 'emotive' meaning of the word adjusted but also to convey our own aversion to the thing in question, we do not employ 'true' but e.g. 'thorough-paced' or 'out-and-out'. The two new intensifiers are also adjusting the word they are attached to. They do so by quasi-contracting its range of application.

How do we go about the matter when we want just to intensify the dormant 'emotive' or rather prescriptive meaning of a word without telling our audience our own psychological attitude to it? It seems to me that 'real', perhaps because of its generality, suggests nothing about the speaker's own actual feelings as distinct from the attitude that in his opinion *ought* to be taken up. 'He is a real scoundrel' stands in this respect neutral, whilst 'He's a true scoundrel' and 'He's an out-and-out scoundrel' do not.

It is, I think, the adjusting function which brings the intensifying one into being. We have been brought up to have a 'con-attitude' to people who are properly called 'scoundrels'. Indeed, if we did not grasp that when Jones calls Smith a scoundrel he is denigrating him and conveying that we also ought to, we have not understood an essential part of the meaning of 'scoundrel'. But our reaction admits of degrees. A person who is almost a scoundrel is not as bad as one who certainly is. The effect of restricting the term's scope is that the clear cases, the people who certainly are scoundrels, come into the spotlight; and that naturally makes our con-attitudes more violent than they were when we e.g. thought of someone in the borderline region of the term. If this is so, the fact that 'real', 'true', etc., occur in persuasive definitions is indeed only to be expected.

Linguistic parsimony and adapter-words. We have found reasons for rejecting Austin's tenet that by means of 'like' 'we can *always* avoid being left ... speechless' (*S&S*.74; my italics). What he maintains is true only when we want to quasi-extend a term's range of application. When we want to quasi-contract it, such devices as 'real' and 'true' are in place. These remarks may be helpful in answering Austin's question 'Why exactly do we want to say, sometimes "It is like a pig", sometimes "It is not a real pig"?' (*S&S*.76).—A proper answer would, however, take us too far afield.

We may well wonder why we have all the adapter-words we have. Wouldn't it be more economical to have just one quasi-contractive and one quasi-extending device of this kind? Austin discusses why the other quasi-extending adapters cannot replace 'like' (S&S.75) but not why we bother to have them as well as 'like'. He has nothing to say about the variety of quasi-contractive adjuster-words. I shall concentrate on the latter set.

I have suggested that 'true' has three jobs simultaneously when conjoined with an 'emotively' charged word: it quasi-contracts its range of application, intensifies its 'emotive' part, and signals that the speaker admires (etc.) the item in question. In the same sort of situation, 'real' performs only the two former functions. That is surely one reason for keeping both 'true' and 'real'.

What about 'genuine'? We can say 'He may become a real (true) philosopher if he puts his shoulder to the wheel'; but there is an odd ring to 'He may become a genuine philosopher if he puts his shoulder to the wheel'. You cannot *become* a genuine philosopher; either you are or you are not; and if you are not, you can never turn into a genuine philosopher although you can turn into a real or true philosopher. What is genuine must be something we believe to be innate, something that you have 'by nature' and hence cannot create by any act of yours, although you can call it forth if dormant. When a term 'T' is adjusted by means of 'genuine', the speaker conveys that its range of application is restricted to the set of items that 'by nature', right from the very beginning of their existence, are Ts.

It seems, then, that although 'real', 'true' and 'genuine' all are quasi-contractive adjuster-words, the two less general of them also have other functions peculiar to them. Investigations of 'proper', 'accurate', 'correct', etc., confirm the impression. I feel less sure that this is true even of the quasi-extending adapter-devices. But this is a matter for future case-studies.

4. Entailment

Adapter-words are devices for adjusting our words so that they fit new types of items—they are devices for adjusting our vertical conventions. But another type of conventions is discernible even in the primitive speech-situation S_1. It may be called a *horizontal* convention. Its job is not to tie a vocable to something in the world, although it cannot work unless there already are vertical conventions. When two vocables have become classificatory words, we can establish conventions relating their senses in various ways. Entailment is an example of such a horizontal rule. Suppose that in speech-situation S_1 there crops up a colour which none of the colour-terms in S_0 fits. It is rather like the specific colour we have until now called 'red'; but we do not want to assimilate it to that colour. Instead we give it a name of its own, 'crimson'. We do not, however, want to keep the colours too far apart from each other. Therefore we also give the colour called 'red' in S_0 a new name and 'adopt the convention that *crimson is a sort of red*, thus giving the explicitness of statute law to the modification in the sense of the name "red" and recognizing "red" as the name of a multiform pattern, i.e. as a generic name. This legislation will show itself, in our restricted language, by the phenomenon of entailment between sentences of form S, which now appears for the first time: henceforward, "1228 is a crimson" will entail "1228 is a red".' (1953.196.)

5. Open texture

In the primitive speech-acts of the 1953 paper there are two phrases which do not conform to the conventions now discussed, viz. 'not' and what Austin calls the 'assertive link', 'is a'. Since he is not concerned with how words acquire their meaning, he says nothing of how we come to understand these two expressions.*

Austin stresses that S_0 and S_1 are artificially simple, since 'each item in the world is still being assumed to be of *one type only*—or to possess, we may say, one feature only, or to be assessable in one dimension only'. If we assume that the items are shades of colours, none of them 'must be conceived as having, for example, shape or size to be talked about as well as colour . . . It is only in some further model of the speech-situation, to be called say "S_2" but not here discussed, that we might introduce the complication that the *same* item may possess more than one feature or be of more than one type or be assessable in more than one dimension.' (1953.193.) This suggests that in S_2 classificatory words may acquire meaning by yet another type of vertical convention—a type which proves to be important in 'Other minds'.

*[The omission proves important for his theory of truth. See P. F. Strawson: 'Truth: a reconsideration of Austin's views'. *Ph.Q.* 15 (1965).]

Criteria-delimitation. In recognizing something as a lemon we go by a great many things which do not exactly enter the meaning of 'lemon', if that means that we, from the fact that something is a lemon, are entitled to infer that it has every one of these things. Yet they are tied up with it so closely that although the absence of a few of them does not matter, the absence of some of them would make it dubious whether the thing before us really is a lemon, and our hesitation would change into certainty that it is not a lemon if still more of them are absent. Something which does not fall within a certain range of sizes and is not green or yellow or greenish-yellow, does not have an oval shape and a waxy skin, does not contain pips and does not taste sour is certainly not a lemon, though every lemon may lack one or another of these properties. When being an F entails having a large number of the properties $P_1 \ldots P_n$, although it does not entail any of them in particular, these properties are, in Wittgenstein's terminology, *criteria* of F.[4] When $P_1 \ldots P_n$ are criteria of F, we can always from 'That's an F' infer 'That has a fair number of the properties $P_1 \ldots P_n$', but we are *not* entitled to infer 'That has (say) P_1'. So although no one of these properties is necessarily connected with F, its relation to it is not merely contingent. We can, e.g., explain the meaning of 'F' by giving a set of its criteria. I shall call such an account of the sense of 'F' a *criteria-delimitation*.

It is fairly clear that a great number of ostensive definitions are criteria-delimitations. When teaching a child the meaning of 'elephant' we point at Jumbo at the Zoo; but not all the things by which the child learns to tell elephants are necessary characteristics of those animals. Nor does the child normally think they are —if it has remembered its lesson, it cheerfully cries 'Elephant!' when looking at the next animal fairly like Jumbo, although the new specimen's skin has another nuance, its tusks look different or something of the sort. Since the set of criteria is often left fairly unspecified we cannot, without stipulation, list *all* the criteria there are for being an F—the set is indefinite. The indefiniteness

---

[4] Remarks on criteria are scattered all over Wittgenstein's writings from *The Blue Book* on. The most helpful single passage is perhaps *The Blue Book*, pp. 24–5. An abundance of references is given in N. Malcolm, 'Wittgenstein's *Philosophical Investigations*' (*Ph.R.* 63 (1954)) and R. Albritton, 'On Wittgenstein's use of the term "criterion"' (*J.Ph.* 56 (1959)). See also M. Scriven, 'The logic of criteria' in the same issue of *J.Ph.*

of a great number of words which have acquired their meaning by ostension is noteworthy: the fact that a vocable has become a word by being tied to a type of items by criteria-delimitation is an important feature of the open texture of such words, and it explains why some philosophers are unwilling to call the procedure of giving a vocable meaning by ostension a 'definition'—no *exact* limits of its range of application are laid down.

Presumptions. Suppose that there is an indefinite set of criteria by which we determine whether or not something is a goldfinch. All of us agree, however, that the bird over there certainly satisfies a sufficient number of them—it is a clear case. All of a sudden it quotes Virginia Woolf. Is it then a goldfinch?

According to P. Wilson, the bird has in the situation envisaged turned out to be something other than a goldfinch, and he sneers at Austin for not admitting this.[5] I find the complaint seriously misguided. (i) The freak is not a borderline case, something satisfying only a small number of our criteria. On the contrary we have assumed that we all agreed that it quite certainly was a goldfinch—until it spoke. (ii) And 'a speaking goldfinch' is no contradiction in terms, so there is at present no linguistic convention enjoining us to expel our *lusus naturae* from the rank of goldfinches. Nor does the fact that it spoke show us that we have misclassified it—that it had by mistake been put in the pidgeon-hole reserved for goldfinches instead of in the hole reserved for birds exactly like goldfinches except for the fact that they speak. For there is no such pidgeon-hole. (iii) It is of course true that if some goldfinches took to talking we should in all likelihood find the feat so startling that we should give them a new name—'N', say—in order to keep them apart from ordinary goldfinches. As soon as that had been done, we should certainly be wrong if we said of a temporarily silent N that it was a goldfinch. But until we have decided to make the distinction between goldfinches and Ns, everything satisfying a sufficient number of the criteria of the former goes as a goldfinch.

The fact is, of course, that if there occurs an outrage of nature of the sort imagined, we would stand crestfallen. Although it does not clash with any criterion or set of criteria in the indefinite set governing the application of the appellative, it violates something

[5] Patrick Wilson, 'Austin on knowing'. *Inquiry* 3 (1960), p. 51.

much deeper. It snatches away something we have all along taken for granted, something which because of its very obviousness is not consciously noted, viz. that goldfinches are not the sort of birds that can mimic a phonetic act of ours and still less speak in the more demanding sense of performing a locutionary act.

I suggest that our language contains a good many criteria-delimited words whose application is flawed unless two kinds of conditions are satisfied. Let 'T' be such a word. The first condition is then that a sufficient number of 'T':s criteria are satisfied. None of these criteria is *per se* necessary or *per se* sufficient; and they are factors we *consciously* take note of when settling whether 'T' is applicable. The second type of conditions I propose to call *presumptions*. A thing may satisfy a sufficient—and a more than sufficient—number of 'T':s criteria, yet if it does not satisfy one of the word's presumptions, there is *no answer* to the question whether it is a T.[6] If a goldfinch quotes Virginia Woolf, 'we don't say we were wrong to say it was a goldfinch, *we don't know what to say*' (1946.56). There is no answer to the question whether it is a goldfinch, since the presumption that goldfinches don't speak is satisfied in all ordinary cases, so that we are usually not aware that we make it. Hence we are not linguistically prepared for the advent of speaking goldfinches; we don't know whether to count them as goldfinches or not, and there is no convention we can appeal to. We have to make a *new* linguistic legislation in order to deal with utterly unexpected phenomena. Until it is made, there is *no* correct answer to the question whether they are Ts or not.

Waismann's 'open texture' covers both (*a*) the indefiniteness of the set of delimitating criteria, (*b*) the fact that none of these criteria is necessary, although a fair number of them has to be present if the word is correctly used, and (*c*) the fact that certain presumptions also have to be satisfied if our employment of the word is to be flawless—presumptions which we are not normally aware of and which are brought to our notice by considering miracles and other outrages of nature. When we come to Austin's account of knowledge in Ch. 4.4, we shall find it important to keep (*c*) distinct from (*a*) and (*b*).

---

[6] Cf. G. E. Moore, *The Commonplace Book*, p. 129.

B. SYNTAX

6. *The syntax of the primitive speech acts*

In Austin's models, the language permits of only two forms of sentences. Form S is presented by the schema

I is a T;

form SN by

I is not a T.

In both schemata 'I' does duty for an individuating word and 'T' for a classificatory word; and the link is used for asserting that I is, or is not, a T. In the models, *any* utterance of the form S is 'a sentence in the language' (1953.182). As we shall see when we come to the use of an utterance in actual speech, Austin claims that utterances of the form SN may be given nonsensical interpretations; so not even in the primitive speech acts will the form of an utterance be a guarantee that it is 'well-formed' in the sense of 'not nonsensical'. This means that Austin in 1953 thought that an irreproachable pheme, uttered with a certain sense and a certain reference, in certain cases turns into a nonsensical rheme; and that goes against his claim in *Words* that what is nonsensical is units of language and not units of speech.

The simple subject/predicate models are, I think, designed for investigations of the kind of utterances whose employment interested him above all in the 1946, 1950, and 1954 papers. They are models for investigating what he in *Words* dubs *constatives*—statements that are either true or false. With the possible exception of some dubiously constative utterances discussed in 'Ifs and cans', Austin's constatives are always of the subject/predicate form.

7. *Syntax and other speech acts*

Austin has little to say on the syntax of sentences outside the primitive speech-situations. Presumably he thought that there is not much we can say *a priori* about it, and that although grammar needs a revision, other parts of it are worse off than syntax is. He sometimes points out that philosophers have erred because they have not studied grammars closely enough: they have taken 'what' in 'knowing what I see' as a relative, whilst it is an interrogative (1946.64), and they believe that 'could' is a past subjunctive even in situations where it is a past indicative (1946b. 163f). In *Words*.96 he remarks in passing that his definition of the phatic act has lumped together vocabulary and grammar, and that we have to distinguish between the failure of such a pheme as 'cat thoroughly the if' and the failure of such a pheme as 'the slithy toves did gyre'. In this book we shall consider only simple subject-predicate utterances.

II. LANGUAGE AND SPEECH

A. 'INTERNAL SEMANTICS'

Suppose that the stage of linguistic legislation is over and that we begin to use our language to speak about the world. We have then proceeded from language to speech. The speech act is in order only if the parts of the utterance is in order, i.e. (in the simple speech-situations) only if (1) the individuating word used by the speaker really, according to the conventions of the language, refers to the item he intends to refer to; and (2) the classificatory word he uses really, according to the conventions of the language, signifies what he intends it to signify; and (3) the thing he refers to really has the characteristics signified with the classificatory word he uses. These are necessary though not sufficient conditions which his speech act has to satisfy if it is to be in order. For want of a better term I call them the 'internal semantics' of the speech act. Since we shall be concerned with (3) in Ch. 4, only (1) and (2) will be considered.

8. *Misreferring and misclassifying*

In the 1946 and 1953 papers as well as in *S&S*. Ch. X, Austin goes into the details of the 'internal semantics'. A sin against (1) he calls misreferring and a sin against (2) misnaming. The latter choice of label is unhappy, since what we typically name are things which we want to single out from other things like them. I shall therefore speak of misclassification. (Austin uses the term 'classify' in another way which will not concern us.)

The great point of having a language is to have a means of

communication. Hence, if I misrefer or misclassify, I tend *pro tanto* to mislead my audience. Austin says in 1953.185f:

> Misleading ... goes ... to the *meaning* of the utterance, not to the *facts*: whether or not I create additionally in those hearers, or more strictly tend to create in them, a *misapprehension* as to the facts depends *additionally* on whether or not I have been correct in matching sample to pattern (or conversely), a quite distinct consideration. I mislead (as to meaning) when, through my use of the wrong I-word or T-word, my hearers are caused, in assessing or relying on the justifiability of my assertion, to advert to a different sample or a different pattern from that which I, in making the assertion, was adverting to.

Misclassifying and misreferring alike can be either aberrational or idiosyncratic. In the former case they are a sin against the linguistic legislation I as well as other people accept; in the latter case I follow my own linguistic legislation, but it is not in accord with the one commonly accepted. An aberration and an idiosyncrasy can cancel each other; and so can a combination of other disorders. (1953.186.)

An idiosyncratic language is not a private language in the sense which Wittgenstein objected to in *Philosophical Investigations*, §243 *et seq.*: it is not a language which I alone can understand. Another person can detect my idiosyncrasies and take them into account, and then my words will not mislead him. Since we continually speak to each other and try to get across what we mean, it seems likely that grown-up people who speak their mother tongue have few idiosyncrasies left, though there may be a good many in a baby's prattle or a Swede's English.

At the first glance, aberrations seem unproblematic. My tongue or my pen slips, and although I may mislead you if I do not notice and correct it, there is nothing philosophically perplexing in it. But Austin thought the view that the only aberrations there are are slips of tongue or of pen was wrong, in a way which has contributed to the myth of basic propositions.

Aberrations and 'basic propositions' (*1946.58–65; S&S.112f*). It is sometimes said that such 'sense-data statements' as 'Red here now' are basic propositions, propositions with the peculiarity that the person who utters them cannot be wrong. He can lie, and he can be guilty of idiosyncrasies, and his tongue can slip; so he certainly can misinform others. But his statement can only go wrong in these three ways, so he cannot himself be mistaken.

There are, in Austin's opinion, two sorts of aberration. In the first type of case I recognize something as a so-and-so, but I bring forth the wrong word for the correctly identified thing. In the second kind of case there is no slip of the tongue; although I know my language perfectly well and say the word I intend to say, my utterance goes wrong because I have misidentified the thing. My failure to recognize it correctly may be due either (*a*) to my poor memory, or (*b*) to my bad present discernment. (*a*) I think this is the taste of laurel but I don't know—not because my sense of taste is not sufficiently developed to make fine discriminations, but because I don't quite remember the taste of laurel. (*b*) 'I'm not sure it *is* the taste of pineapple: isn't there perhaps just *something* about it, a tang, a bite, a lack of bite, a cloying sensation, which isn't *quite* right for pineapple?' (1946.60f.) To answer that question I do not scan my memory of the taste of pineapple, for I know its taste perfectly. What I have to do is to sharpen my present discernment—I have to savour again, intensely.—Both (*a*) and (*b*) seem ridiculous when transferred to such well-known colours as red; but take a shade like magenta or mauve, and the two sorts of non-trivial aberrations are no longer impossible.

'It may be said that, even if I don't know exactly how to describe it, I nevertheless *know* that I *think* (and roughly how confidently I think) it is mauve. So I do know *something*. But this is irrelevant: I *don't* know it's mauve, that it definitely looks to me now mauve. Besides, there are cases where I really don't know what I think: I'm completely baffled by it.' (1946.61f.) Of course I may very well know at times that something looks mauve to me now; but there still remains the purely negative point that the mere fact that a speaker says something about his own 'sense-data' does not by itself guarantee that he is not mistaken.

We have now discussed aberrations of classificatory words.* What about aberrational misreferrings?

If the I-words are real proper names ('Robin', 'Jones', and—

---

*[It is important that these aberrations occur in statements about what I *see*. Austin thought that his argument is applicable also to statements about what I *feel*. This is to my mind a mistake, for reasons given in Ch. 7 of my unpublished *This Language-Game Is Played*.]

in S_0 and S_1—'1228') the same sort of remarks hold good. That I gave the man over there a wrong name may be due to a slip of my tongue or to the fact that I was too tired to bother to remember his name although I know it. But it may also be due either to (*a*) the fact that in my memory I mixed up two names or (*b*) to the fact that I was too short-sighted to see that it was Brown instead of Jones, although I certainly know the names of both these gentlemen.

Austin does not discuss whether the two non-trivial sorts of aberration are possible when an 'egocentric particular' occupies the place of the I-word: in 'How to talk' he is not concerned with those kinds of demonstrative devices. If we put the question to ourselves, our answer will, I believe, be tied up with what we think about referring. If we take the Aristotelian view that we cannot refer to something without singling it out as a so-and-so, the two non-trivial sorts of aberration clearly may occur. If on the other hand we join Locke in holding that it is not necessary that the referent is singled out as anything at all, they are ruled out.

Aberration and language (1946.64f). Why have philosophers failed to see that there are other aberrations than slips of tongue or pen? Austin suggests that one reason may be that they have been taken in by the use of a direct object after the verb 'know'. They have seen that we can say 'I know my own mind' and 'I know my own feeling on the matter'; and they have also noticed that we can say, and say correctly, 'I know what I am feeling (seeing, tasting, etc.)'. If I really know what I am seeing, it seems the merest common sense that I know that which I am seeing; I am acquainted with it. And this gives rise to the idea that 'I can literally *say* what (that which) I *see*: it pipes up, or I read it off. It is as if sensa were *literally* to "announce themselves" or to "identify themselves", in the way we indicate when we say "It presently identified itself as a particularly fine white rhinoceros".' And if we are acquainted with that which we see, hear, etc., it seems difficult to be mistaken about it—if we stray here, where can we hope *not* to stray?

In Austin's opinion, this is a welter of mistakes. In the first place, the idioms 'I know my own mind' and 'I know my own feelings on the matter' are rather special expressions, which do not justify any general usage. 'Feelings' here has the sense it has in 'very strong feelings' in favour of or against something: perhaps it means 'views' or 'opinions' ('very decided opinions'). . . . To extend the usage uncritically is somewhat as though, on the strength of the legitimate phrase 'knowing somebody's tastes', we were to proceed to talk of 'knowing someone's sounds' or 'knowing someone's taste of pineapple'. If, for example, it is a case of *physical* feelings such as fatigue, we do not use the expression 'I know your feelings'.

In the second place, the transition from 'knowing what I am feeling (seeing, tasting, etc.)' to 'knowing that which I am feeling (seeing, tasting, etc.)' is

a grammatical mistake: 'what' *can* of course be a relative, but in 'know what you feel' . . . it is an interrogative (Latin *quid*, not *quod*). In this respect, 'I can smell what he is smelling' differs from 'I can know what he is smelling'. 'I know what he is feeling' is not 'There is an *x* which both I know and he is feeling', but 'I know the answer to the question "What is he feeling?"' And similarly with 'I know what I am feeling': this does *not* mean that there is something which I am *both knowing and feeling*.

In fact, a man does not even 'know his pain', although pain seems to be the sort of sensation for which the acquaintance theory is most plausible: 'he feels (not knows) what he recognizes as, or what he knows to be, anger (not his anger), and he knows that he is feeling angry. Always assuming that he does recognize the feeling, which in fact, though feeling it acutely, he may not'. There is no construction with a direct object after 'know' which 'lends support to the metaphysical "He knows his pain" (in a way we can't)'.

Thus the argument from language to acquaintance with the 'objects of perception' is a failure. There is no form of statement that is not even *liable* to failures of identification.

B. 'EXTERNAL SEMANTICS'

In the previous subsection we were concerned with how a speaker who knows the vocabulary and syntax of a language and does not want to deceive his audience may nevertheless err by idiosyncrasies and aberrations. In this subsection we shall assume that even these ills are cured. An utterance which is unexceptional in all these respects may be used in different ways, and our present task is to study what Austin has to say about them. An examination of the functions of an utterance as a whole may be called a study of its 'external semantics'. We shall be concerned only with the functions of a statement of the form S in the speech-situation S_0.*

A certain type of utterance has a limited number of *standard* functions. But a speaker may use it in new and unexpected situations for new ends, as e.g. in satire. So when we study the 'external semantics' of an utterance, we may either be interested in what standard speech acts are performed by a certain sort of utterance, or we may want to make clear what unusual speech act is performed by an individual utterance on a certain occasion. Literary critics are often engaged in the latter sort of task; but Austin is concerned with the former.

9. Fitting and matching

In the 1953 paper Austin tells us that in S_0 an utterance of S may be given four standard interpretations. The context determines which of them is in question on a particular occasion—which speech act is performed by the uttering of S. The speech acts I may perform in S_0 by uttering the words '1227 is a square' are

identifying 1227 as a square (c-identifying);
identifying a square as 1227 (b-identifying);
stating that 1227 is a square (stating);
giving 1227 as an instance of a square (instancing).

The trouble with these acts is that Austin's description of them is almost hopelessly mixed up with his explanation of how they have come about. If one is not sure that one has understood what they are, his remarks are not very helpful.

A preliminary survey. Let us, however, start from the two speech acts he explicitly illustrates, c-identifying and b-identifying:

We use the useful word 'identify', understandably enough, in two opposite ways: we may speak of 'identifying it (as a daphnia)' when

*[For an account of the functions of a statement of the form S in speech-situation S_1, see Chisholm's 'J. L. Austin's Philosophical Papers', (*Symp* 102–104).]

G

you hand it to me and ask me if I can identify it, and I say that it is a daphnia: but we also speak of 'identifying a daphnia' (or 'identifying the daphnia') when you hand me a slide and ask me if I can identify a daphnia (or the daphnia) in it. In the first case we are finding a cap to fit a given object: hence the name 'cap-fitting' or 'c-identifying'. We are trying to 'place' it. But in the second case we are trying to find an object to fill a given bill: hence the name 'b-identifying' or 'bill-filling'. We 'cast' this thing as the daphnia.

(1953.189f.) When an act of b-identification has gone wrong, I have failed to keep clear for myself the sense of the classificatory word; when an act of c-identification has gone wrong, I am guilty of misperception. (Austin is anxious to stress that a failure of c-identification is to be distinguished from misclassification: in the latter case the linguistic rule assumed to be governing the vocable does not exist; in the former case the rule exists and I know it, although I err by not attending to the item carefully enough.)

The distinction between the two sorts of identification will then be this: In c-identification I produce a thing and suit it to a given classificatory word. In b-identification I produce a classificatory word and suit it to a given thing. The difference is, in Austin's jargon, a difference in *direction of fit*: fitting a word to a thing differs from fitting a thing to a word as 'fitting a nut with a bolt differs from fitting a bolt with a nut'. (1953.188.)

Let us now turn to stating and instancing. No examples are given of them, since the 'terms "stating" and "instancing" should need no explanation: to instance is to cite I as an instance of T' (1953.190). He only tells us that the two acts have opposite directions of fit: stating—like c-identifying—is fitting a classificatory word to a given item; instancing—like b-identifying—is fitting an item to a given classificatory word. What does then distinguish c-identifying from stating and b-identifying from instancing?

To answer this, Austin introduces the notion of *onus of match*: 'We fit the name [= the *classificatory* word] to the item or the item to the name on the ground that the *type* of the item and the *sense* of the name *match*. But in matching X and Y, there is a distinction between matching X *to* Y and matching Y *to* X, which may be called a distinction in point of *onus of match*.' (1953.188.) C-identifying differs from stating by the fact that in the former, the type of the item is taken for granted and what is questioned is whether the sense of the classificatory word really matches it; whereas in stating, the sense of the classificatory word is taken for granted and what is questioned is whether the type of the item really matches it. Instancing is kept apart from b-identification in the same way: in the latter, the sense of the classificatory word is taken for granted but it is questioned whether the type matches it; in instancing, the type is taken for granted and what is questioned is whether the sense of the classificatory word matches it.

Cox's objection. The jargon of 'matching the type of an item to the sense of the classificatory word' (or vice versa) is a confusing one. Although Austin does not explain what he means by 'the type of an item', it is clear that in S_0 two items are of the same type if there is no dissimilarity between them except their spatio-temporal locations. To say that the type of the item and the sense of the classificatory word match seems then to be a way of saying that there holds, between the vocable and any item of a certain type, a vertical convention which makes the vocable a classificatory word. A speaker matches the sense of a word to a type, if he questions whether the word really is tied by such a convention to the type; he matches a type to the sense of a word, if he questions whether the type really is tied by such a convention to the classificatory word. What is then the difference between matching and fitting? How does matching differ from fitting a word to a thing or vice versa?

This is the difficulty raised by J. W. Roxbee Cox.[7] He argues that 'in both fitting and matching we are taking one of the two terms of the relation as given or held fast' (p. 8). Take two acts with the same direction of fit, e.g. instancing and b-identifying. Then we are in the former case asked to perform an impossible feat, viz. to hold fast the classificatory word and at the same time to hold fast the type and seek among the senses for one that matches it. 'Name [=classificatory word] and sense on the one hand, and item and type of the other, are connected by such a relationship that the effect of taking as given or holding fast one from each pair at the same time is to produce immobility.'—The operations demanded for b-identifying are not impossible; rather they are 'a single operation, twice described': we take the classifi-

[7] Cox, 'Fitting and matching'. *Analysis* 16 (1955/56).

catory word for given and hold fast the sense of it. Cox concludes that if the two acts are to be distinguished, it must be done 'by something less vacuous than a difference in respect of meaningless rigmaroles artificially attached to them' (p. 10).

I don't think his criticism will do. Let us return to Austin's words. He always says that in the operation of fitting, something (either a classificatory word or an item) is *given*; he always says that in matching, something (the type of an item or the sense of a word) is *taken for granted*; but he never says—as Cox implies he does—that in fitting, something is taken for granted, or that in matching, something is given. So he seems to hold that there is a difference between being given something and taking something for granted. Moreover, he insists that when speech acts go wrong, those with the same onus of match go wrong in the same way: by misconception if the onus of match is on the classificatory word, and by misperception if the onus of match is on the type of item. There is, however, no failure in common to speech acts with the same direction of fit. (1953.190-2.) Therefore matching seems to have the upper hand in the speech acts. This is confirmed by Austin's words that fitting is performed 'on the g r o u n d that the *type* of the item and the *sense* of the name *match*' (1953.188; my spacing). Matching clearly concerns (but is not identical with) the vertical convention relating items of a certain type to a certain vocable which in this way is made a word; so matching is in some way or other tied up with a convention in *language*. But it seems to me that Austin does not assign fitting to language at all but to speech. And speech does of course rely on linguistic conventions—although language is, in the last analysis, a construction from past speech-episodes.

This clears the ground for a new account of the two distinctions.

A new account. Let us first consider fitting. If a conversation is not about all sorts of things, it has a theme. It is, I think, the theme—usually supplied by the context—that determines the direction of fit. If the theme is a classificatory word, the issuing of an utterance of the form S is a b-identifying or an instancing act. (A wonders what a daphnia is; B makes a gesture towards something and says 'That's a daphnia'.)—If the theme is the item, an utterance of the same form is a c-identifying or a stating act. (A asks what that is; B answers 'That's a daphnia'.) This agrees with Austin's assertion that in b-identifying and instancing the classificatory word is 'given', whereas the item is 'given' in c-identifying and stating. So I suggest that 'so-and-so is "given"' ought to be read 'so-and-so is the subject about which we speak, is our theme'. That suggestion makes sense of Austin's examples, even those in 1953.190n: A asks 'What part of speech is the word "downhill" in "He was going downhill"?'; B answers, 'An adverb', thus c-identifying the *item* (the part of speech). A asks, 'Which is the adverb in "He was going downhill"?'; B answers '"Downhill"', thus b-identifying the word.

Now over to matching. A conversation centres about a word, and someone issues an utterance of the form S containing it. Then it has the *word* as its theme, and a word is in S_0 a vocable tied by a certain convention to items of a certain type. As we have seen in the case of aberrations two sorts of failure are possible when a linguistic convention links a vocable and items to each other: although I know perfectly well what characteristic an item must possess in order to be correctly labelled by a certain word, I may err, because I have failed to scrutinize this particular item closely enough; and although I have scrutinized this particular item closely enough I may label it wrongly, because I do not quite remember the convention.

I now say that whether an utterance of the form S is to be labelled as an act of b-identification or an act of instancing depends on whether it *is assumed* that the speaker has perceived the item correctly or it *is assumed* that he has got the convention right. In the former case, he is instancing: since his keenness of perception is not questioned, his speech act can go wrong only if he has misconceived the sense of the classificatory word. (Misinstancing is of course different from misreferring. As Austin puts it in 1953.192, in misreferring 'the reference is "wrong" even *though* the sense *does* match the type, whereas here [in misinstancing] the reference is "wrong" *because* the sense does *not* match the type'.) But if it is taken for granted that the speaker knows the sense of the word, his utterance can go wrong only by *misperception* of the item; and if this is the only failure envisaged, his utterance must be a b-identification.

In an analogous way, an utterance brought forward with the items as its theme is an act of c-identification if the situation is such that it *is assumed* that the speaker has perceived the item correctly; it is an act of stating if the situation is such that it *is assumed* that the speaker has got the grasp of the convention governing the classificatory word. A failure of c-identification is due to misconception; misstating is due to misperception.

A criticism of the new account. I think that this account is what Austin's talk about the four speech acts amounts to; and it is not open to Cox's objections. But since it is based on the failure of the acts—the ways in which they can go wrong—, it may be doubted whether two speech acts with the same direction of fit can be kept apart if they work smoothly. I say, with the item as my theme and without any hitches, '1227 is a square'. Has it then to be the case that it is assumed that either the item is correctly perceived or the convention is correctly grasped? If both of them is taken for granted, what act am I performing? A fifth kind of act? Above all, can something more be said about what determines what is taken for granted in a certain situation? (The speaker's intentions? His audience's expectations? Some other factor in the situation?)

Moreover, are the Austinian acts models of what we normally call identifying, stating, and instancing? Suppose I say, 'So you don't know what a square is? Well, look here: *that*'s a square.' No doubt I have then given you an instance of a square. But am I in the Austinian sense instancing? The theme is the word 'square'; but if I go wrong, if I misinstance, do I necessarily have to admit that I am a victim of a misconception? Can't I say, without giving up my claim to have produced an instance (though a faulty one) and without being taken to be giving up that claim, 'Sorry, I did not *notice* that my specimen actually has a fifth side, though a very small one'?—I don't think that objection carries weight as long as Austin is just concerned with bringing out different ways in which the very same sentence can be used, and labelling them with stipulatively defined terms. But he sometimes speaks as if his model is a very simplified model of what actually happens regularly when we give an instance of something; and that claim does not seem true.

I shall not harp on this; nor shall I dwell on his account of four new ways in which a sentence of type S works in S_1 (1953. 193–7). But we may note his remarks (pp. 198–200) on the speech acts that can be performed by sentences of type SN—i.e. sentences of the type 'I is not a T'. He claims that with these sentences, the number of possible speech acts dwindles: the two forms of identifying disappear. For the point of identification in these primitive speech acts is to match the meaning of a classificatory word and a type. 'Identifying something as *not* a so-and-so' is a nonsense phrase. But in instancing and stating, something useful is done even when one produces a type and points out that the sense of the word does not match it, or when one produces a sense of a word and points out that the type does not match it. If this is right—and the observation seems uncontroversial—then an unobjectionable pheme may, when uttered with a certain sense and a certain reference, turn into a rheme which is not obscure or void or vague but nonsensical; and then Austin certainly has to qualify his assertion in *Words*.98 that the pheme is a unit of language, its typical fault being to be meaningless, whereas the rheme is a unit of speech, its typical faults being to be vague, void, obscure, etc.: the border between units of language and units of speech will at least have to be made rather indefinite.

Are fitting and matching philosophically important? Let us now turn around and ask, 'Even if all that Austin has to say about fitting and matching were true, would it be important?'

His main points seem to have been two. (1) Language is not used in a haphazard manner. The different expressions we use— e.g. 'identify', 'state', 'instance'—are used for different types of situation. (1953.197.)—This tenet (which we have found to be doubtfully true) may be taken as a plea for 'linguistic phenomenology': that approach really leads us to see the world more clearly and in more detail. This points forward to the 1956a paper with its careful studies of how different adverbs are tied to different situations. But since Austin's account of matching involves that two situations may differ by the very fact that something is 'taken for granted' in the one but not in the other, he has to elucidate what 'taking for granted' is. How do we know what is 'taken for granted' in a given situation? *Words* may perhaps be seen as an attempt to clear the ground of a part of this area. (2) Constructions of models of speech-situations can help us to clarify the varieties of possible speech acts (1953.197f).

Is the investigation of the 'external' semantics of these primitive speech acts philosophically important, irrespective of these vague hints of future developments? Do they clear up any philosophical muddles? Austin does not tell us whether he had any specific confusions in mind. In Ch. 4 I shall suggest that there is a puzzle about truth which his distinctions may help us to solve; but I am not sure he was thinking of that problem. Perhaps he only held that there *may be* troubles which we can avoid by paying attention to his results. Then he would be offering us a kind of preventive therapy.[8] It is perhaps more likely that he did not think of any philosophical benefits but was just pursuing something which might prove relevant to the projected new 'science of language'. He often shows an intense interest in speech acts for their own sake, and sometimes he does so in the middle of otherwise traditionally philosophical inquiries. That has earned him the distrust of those who want everyone to keep within the historically given boundaries of his chosen trade.

[8] In *English Philosophy since 1900*, p. 148, G. J. Warnock asks us to see at least part of Austin's philosophy in that light.

CHAPTER 3

The Illocutionary Act

I. TWO PRINCIPLES OF SERIOUS SPEECH

At the very end of 'Other minds' Austin insists (1946.83) that believing in other persons, in authority and testimony, is an essential part of the act of communicating, an act which we all constantly perform. It is as much an irreducible part of our experience as, say, giving promises, or playing competitive games, or even sensing coloured patches. We can state certain advantages of such performances, and we can elaborate rules of a kind for their 'rational' conduct (as the Law Courts and historians and psychologists work out the rules for accepting testimony). But there is no 'justification' for our doing them as such.

The passage is perplexing. Is the 'irreducible part of our experience'

(i) 'the act of communicating'

or

(ii) a certain part of that act, viz. our belief in other persons, etc.?

Austin can hardly have wished to argue that there is no justification of the habit of communicating between beings who have human capacities and human needs and who live on our planet. What he hinted at was, I think, that there is no justification for (ii). But earlier in the same paper he has, in fact, adumbrated two important kinds of 'justification' for our habits of believing what other people say:

(*a*) 'It is fundamental in talking (as in other matters) that we are entitled to trust others, except in so far as there is some concrete reason to distrust them. Believing persons, accepting testimony, is the, or one main, point of talking. We don't play (competitive) games except in the faith that our opponent is trying to win: if he isn't, it isn't a game, but something different. So we don't talk with people (descriptively) except in the faith that they are trying to convey information.' (1946.50f.)

(b) 'Reliance on the authority of others is fundamental . . . for the correctness of our own use of words, which we learn from others.' (1946.51n.)

The remarks are hardly clear as they stand. They require supplementation and even explication. But what I am going to say about them is, I think, borne out above all by Austin's treatment in *Words* of performatives and illocutionary expressions. His observations in 'Other minds' might even be regarded as gropings after the illocutionary dimension of a speech act. What he stresses in them is that in normal speech situations it is tacitly taken for granted that the speaker is *trustworthy*.

1. *The principle of the speaker's trustworthiness*

It is a truism that language is a means of communication. It is also a truism that in most cases we use it to further our interests. A consequence of these two platitudes is that there is a tacit convention that we are not to say something seriously unless we believe we can back it up. This is not a moral rule as much as a rule without which talking would be pointless. Why should we bother to listen to a person's statements, advice, or promises, unless we assumed that he had evidence for his assertions, reasons for holding that the course advised was practicable, and was in a position to see to it that his promises were carried out?

Well, we could listen to him for fun. But then he is 'stating', 'advising', and 'promising' only by courtesy, in a way reminiscent of or even identical with that in which a story-teller 'states', 'advises', and 'promises' when he, in spinning out his yarn, goes through the motions of stating, advising and promising. Fiction presupposes the normal non-fictional activities of reporting events, giving advice and promising, and not the other way round. A person who does not know what it is to assert something is *a fortiori* ignorant of what it is to pretend to assert something, to assert something as a joke, and so on. There could not be a world in which all speakers always pretended to assert, promise, and advise but never did any of these things in earnest. It would be a world in which the mock-uses would have nothing to mock. It would be a world in which a speaker went through the motions of asserting, advising, and promising without giving his hearers to understand that they were entitled to trust him—that they could be confident he had good evidence for his assertions, that he thought his advice practicable, and that he intended to stand by his promises. His speech acts would not entitle his audience to do such things; and then his utterances would be neither true nor false statements, neither good nor bad pieces of advice, neither true nor false promises. They would not be any such speech act. For in stating, advising, and promising we do give our hearers rights to a certain kind of inference: *A serious utterance does in our world entitle the audience to infer that the speaker thinks that he, when asked to, can back it up in a way appropriate to it.*

That a serious utterance entitles the audience to infer that the speaker thinks he can back it up does not, of course, entail that he in fact believes he can do so, still less that he can do so. If A does not believe there are any good reasons for what he says but nevertheless utters it with all signs of sincerity, he has given his hearers to understand that he believes he can back it up—otherwise he could not hope to deceive them with his utterance. (Cf. 1940. 31–2). So the inference 'A seriously says that S is P (or that S ought to be P, or that he promises to make S P, etc.); hence he believes he can back it up' is valid, whether or not A in fact believes what he says. If he does not, the conclusion is false; but that does not affect the validity of the inference. (Oddities arising when the speaker asserts that the premiss holds but that the conclusion is false—i.e., utterances of the form 'S is P, but I don't believe it'—will be thrashed out in Ch. 5:8.)

It is reasonable to ask of every speaker's utterance 'Is it serious?' (i.e., 'Is there something in the situation, in his way of saying it, etc., that indicates that he does not want us to take it in its usual way?') But it is not reasonable to raise the general question 'Is anyone ever serious in what he says?', for this is to ask 'Do we always speak like story-tellers?'; and the answer to that query is obvious. It is obvious that we sometimes want to be taken as having committed ourselves, as intending to stand by our words, in a way a story-teller does not; and obvious that the latter's story presupposes the normal acts of stating, advising, etc. It is obvious that we *normally* intend our utterances to be committals; and that they *normally* are so taken—otherwise liars, welshers, and deceitful advisors would find their task more arduous. It is obvious that unless our speech normally is serious, we would not listen to others as much as we do; and that we otherwise would find it difficult to make others listen to us. All this is surely uncontroversial. But it explains why serious utterances entitle the audience to infer that the speaker thinks he can back them up. And it also gives us a perfectly good justification for our habit of believing what others say.

2. *Trustworthiness and the demands of a common language*

I have now explicated the first of two passages which I take to be justifications of our belief in the trustworthiness of others. The second quotation is more straightforward. It runs, 'Reliance on the authority of others is fundamental . . . for the correctness of our own use of words, which we learn from others' (1946.51n).

Suppose we are to learn a simple language like that of S_0. Call it 'L'. Imagine three different kinds of language-masters. All of them teach us correctly how to use the assertive link. Some of them are faultless also in the rest of their lectures: they always follow the rules of L. They are henceforward ignored.

Their more interesting colleagues go wrong in their instructions as to how to apply and withhold the application of I-words and T-words to items and types. (The items and types are, however, correctly perceived.)

Let there be two groups of these masters. Members of the first group follow the rules of L half the time and other rules the other half. They do so at random—i.e., there is no regularity in their shift from one set of rules to another set. Members of the second group *never* follow the rules of L, although they certainly follow rules.

Teachers of the first group are useless. They both teach and un-teach the very same rules, and the result is the same as if they had given no rules at all. If we are not taught any rules, explicitly or implicitly, we are not taught a language. If *all* speakers talked like these teachers, the sounds they emitted would not be governed by rules. No listener would know what sense he was to attach to the sounds heard. Consequently, there would be no common language. Hence, the supposition that everybody always uses words as these ineffective language-masters do is nonsensical. A common language requires common rules which have to be learnt by anyone who wants to become a member of the language-community.

How do we fare if our teachers are of the second group and *never* follow the rules of L although they follow rules? Well, in a very Pickwickian sense we do learn L; but we get it, as it were, upside down. We can communicate with those who follow the rules of L only if certain transformation rules are found by means of which our masters' utterance '1225 is a circle' can be turned into an utterance in L, e.g. '1227 is a square'. I.e., the teachers do follow the rules of *a* language, L', systematically correlated with but unfortunately not the same as the one they are paid to teach. If *all* speakers followed their practice, L would fall into oblivion. If everyone always tied the individuating expression '1225' to an item which in L was called '1227', '1225' would become its correct name; and the same holds *mutatis mutandis* for classificatory words.

The supposition that no speaker of a language *ever* follows its rules is nonsense. So is the idea that all language-users employ a word as often in discordance as in accordance with a rule. If linguistic communication is to be possible, vocables must be used according to conventions which the communicants have in common and observe more often than infringe. Since we do speak intelligibly to each other, we must have and follow such conventions. Hence lying, though frequent enough, must remain an exception. And this gives a new and independent justification for believing what others say.

3. *The principle of relevance to the addressee*

We seldom listen to a speaker unless we assume that he has something interesting to say. Someone who wants us to prick up our ears consequently tries to avoid saying things which do not tie up with our concerns. There is therefore a tacit convention that a speaker ought to say things relevant to the addressee.[1] This *principle of relevance* (to the addressee) may be formulated in the following way: 'Never say anything that cannot be expected to interest your addressee; and when you have started on a topic which interests him, don't omit parts that are important to him.'

[1] P. H. Nowell-Smith, *Ethics* (Pelican ed.), p. 82. He stresses that the convention is fundamental to moral discourse.

This principle is as little as the principle of trustworthiness a moral principle. It is a principle without which a speaker would not be listened to and hence without which talk would lose its point.

This is a principle we often tacitly appeal to in deciding how an utterance is to be taken. If I tell you that I feel like going to the cinema and you say that you enjoyed the film at the Scala, I normally take it for granted that you are not merely giving me a piece of autobiography but dropping me a hint. In this situation your words would be pointless unless they were intended as advice.

The fact that someone says something to somebody therefore entitles us to infer that the speaker thinks that the things said are relevant to the addressee.

4. *Pragmatic implications*

The words 'imply' and 'implication' are used in a variety of ways. Thus it is said that A's being a bachelor implies A's being unmarried; and here the vehicle of implication is the word 'bachelor'—i.e., the vocable together with its rules of language. These rules include that nobody is to be called a bachelor unless he is unmarried. It would, I think, be better to use the word 'entail' here.

Again, logicians have stipulatively used 'imply' or 'materially imply' in such a way that a proposition p implies a proposition q if the truth-value table of $p \supset q$ is satisfied. This is an entirely new use of 'imply', leading to the consequences that every false proposition implies any other proposition, true or false, and that any true proposition, implies every other true proposition. When these results are found perplexing ('paradoxes of material implication'), the reason is, in Moore's words, that 'if we use "implies" in any ordinary sense, they are quite certainly false'.[2] (But the logicians are not 'wrong'. Their use is explicitly stipulative, and they are not likely to confuse it with our everyday employment.)

Consider next another use of 'imply', illustrated in an example which the OED dates to 1581: 'he that forebydethe a thynge to be done in after tyme, doth he not covertly emplye that the same

---

[2] G. E. Moore, *Philosophical Studies*, p. 295.

was done before?"³ There is usually no point in saying something that the audience has not explicitly or implicitly questioned, been ignorant of, or been in danger of forgetting—no point in forbidding things nobody does, or commanding things everyone does without being ordered to, and so on. The fact that someone forbids x therefore entitles the audience to infer that he thinks there is a risk of x's being done.

This is the use of 'imply' I shall be concerned with: the use in which the performance of a certain deed (including a speech act) gives the audience a right to infer something about the performer's beliefs. The right is given not by the speaker but by the action and its occurrence in a certain type of situation. In a speech act the implications are, however, carried not only by the saying but also by the things said. The saying entitles the audience to infer that the speaker thinks he can substantiate the content of his utterance and (at least in most cases) that he also thinks that the addressees ought to be interested in that content; the things said entitle the audience to infer that the speaker's reasons for his beliefs are of a certain sort. The beliefs thus inferred may with Grant's term (*op. cit.*) be called *pragmatic implications* (of serious talk).

The inference from somebody's saying of something to his having beliefs of a certain sort is inductive; but it is not based merely on there being an empirically testable correlation between saying and believing. Its peculiarity lies in the fact that unless we assumed that speakers in general held these beliefs, we would cease to listen to their words and to react in the way they desired. A speaker who wants to affect us with what he says has therefore every reason to pose as having these beliefs. It would be fatal to his purpose if his untrustworthiness or the irrelevancy of what he says became apparent; and it would be fatal to *all* talk (and to the very existence of language) if speakers in general did not hold the appropriate beliefs. In order to affect his audience in the way intended, the speaker must at least take on responsibility for what he says: he must be prepared to bear blame if he cannot substantiate the content of his utterance or show its relevance to the addressee.

³ Quoted from C. K. Grant, 'Pragmatic implication'. *Ph.* 33 (1958), p. 319f.

5. Violations of the two principles

Non-serious talk. Assume that an utterance is in perfect order. On at least two sorts of occasion we should deny that it is issued seriously.

First, there is the (fairly heterogeneous) sort of occasion on which the speaker obviously talks playfully or without binding himself—where only an extremely stupid individual would have the slightest inclination to believe that the speaker intended to present his utterance as something for which questions of evidence, good faith, or relevance to the addressee, are at all in the offing. The principle of trustworthiness does not normally guide the words to test a microphone or train one's vocal chords. The principle of relevance does not enter when I address a cow in my rehearsal of a phillipic of which I mean every word.

Secondly, there is the sort of talk appropriate to story-telling and play-acting. Nowell-Smith wants to keep them apart from utterances of the first sort, 'since the question "Does an actor make a statement?" is one to which we want to answer "Yes and no", as we do not in the other cases. - - - In a play, statements are made, questions asked, order given, as in real life; the rules hold within the play, but not across the boundary between the play and real life.'[4]

The distinction Nowell-Smith is driving at might perhaps be put in a more general way. In non-serious talk of the first sort, questions of consistency are not always relevant. If I want just to test a microphone or train my voice or construct tongue-twisters, it does not matter whether my utterance is consistent. In normal cases, self-contradiction and inconsistency defeat the purpose of linguistic communication: if I say something and then take it back, the result is the same as if I had remained silent. But if I do not intend to tell anybody anything but am going through the motions of speech for some reason of the sort outlined, it does not matter if I say something and then in the same breath cancel it. In story-telling or play-writing, on the other hand, the author usually wants to tell us something. Hence an inconsistency would be serious for him. Moreover, the characters he creates are normally, though not always, intended to resemble us in the

---

[4] P. H. Nowell-Smith, 'Contextual implication and ethical theory', *PASS* 36 (1962), p. 7f.

respect that they want to communicate in speaking. Hence it would be fatal to their purpose if they were guilty of inconsistency (though the author may make them contradict themselves, since that may contribute to the characterization of their personalities). They would be guilty of something like inconsistency (in the respect that their talk would be self-frustrating) if they revealed that they did not themselves believe what they said and that they were not prepared to back it up: for then another fictional person, created in the likeness of us, would not react in the desired ways. An actor who on the stage says something logically inconsistent is, in his role, a fictional person; so the illogicality does not reflect unfavourably on the actor's, as distinct from the character's, power of thinking and communicating.

In the first type of non-serious talk, then, inconsistency does not always matter. It does matter in the second type. But it does so only *within* the boundaries of that piece of talk and not *across* them. Swift's statement in *Gulliver's Travels* that there is a species of man less than a feet high does not conflict with a statement of his, outside his study, to the effect that no species of man is less than a foot high.

Serious talk. What we say is sometimes serious in one respect but not in another. It cannot be classed *in toto* as serious or *in toto* as non-serious. A person who jokes does not normally want to be taken at his word; but a joke may cover a deadly serious intention. Hamlet sees his mother die from a drink in which a precious stone, a union, is allegedly dissolved. He forces the King to drink from the same goblet and exclaims 'Drink off this potion;—is thy union here?' This is a pun upon 'union'; but one part of his question is 'Will this cause your union with my dead mother? Will this drink kill you?' And that is no joke. But the example hardly shows us an etiolation of serious talk; it is an utterance in which some ingredients are serious and others jocular, however grimly.

Talking in order to deceive seems to be an etiolation, a free-wheeler on the standard implications of serious talk. Such a use of language would be ineffective if speakers tried to hoodwink us. But according to Grant it involves no violation of the principle of trustworthiness. For when I assert something seriously, I may also be correctly described 'as saying what I believe or know, *or else as saying what I pretend to believe or know*' (*op. cit.*, p. 314). Hence, he claims, I do *not* imply that I believe what I say.

This will not do. If a speaker gives his hearers to understand that he only pretends to believe what he says, his utterance will not be effective. If you know that I only pretend to believe that you ought to take the vows, you do not regard my utterance 'I advise you to take the vows' as bearing on the question of what you ought to do. If Grant rejoins that the addressee must not know whether I believe or just pretend to believe, it suffices to point out that in saying seriously that S is P, I have taken on the responsibilities of a person who does believe in his words. If you find that I didn't believe that S is P, I cannot defend myself by saying that I neither said nor implied that I believed so. The excuse is no good: I stand committed by my in all appearance sincere words 'S is P'.

That A may say that S is P without believing that S is P does not show that his apparently sincere utterance that S is P does not entitle his hearers to infer that he believes that S is P. An apparently sincere speech act does give the hearers that right. But since the vehicle of implication is the performance in a normal situation, the inference is not warranted when the words are uttered in very abnormal circumstances or are followed by explicit disclaimers, such as that of the recovering drunkard who says as a piece of autobiography, 'I still see pink rats on the window-sill, but I don't believe they are really there any longer' —an utterance which will be discussed in Ch. 5.

II. PRAGMATIC IMPLICATION AND DISCOURSE IMPLICATION

6. *Discourse implication*

The pragmatic implications now discussed hold for all sorts of serious communication—statement, advice, prayer, promise, command, expression of wishes, grading, ranking, value judgment, etc. If these are issued seriously, the audience is entitled to infer that the speaker thinks both that he can back them up and that they are relevant to the addressee.

But different types of utterance are backed up in different ways. If I seriously say 'He is angry', I give it to be understood that my backing is of a type showing e.g. that some criterion of anger is satisfied or that a reliable person has reported that he is angry. If I seriously state 'I always do so in that type of situation', I give it to be understood that roughly the same kind of evidence is available. But if I mean my speech act as a piece of advice, I entitle my audience to infer that also other factors enter —e.g. that I can show that the course advised is within the addressee's ability. And if I seriously say 'I wish I had a silent flat', my implied backing is again of a partly different type—e.g. that I should move to a silent flat if I could and if other things were equal. So the backing seems to be drawn from partly different categories in wishes, advice, and statements of fact. The three forms of speech act entitle to partly different inferences about the speaker's beliefs. But a thing common to all promises seems to be that the speaker gives it to be understood that his audience can trust him to do (or to abstain from) a certain kind of act in the future; all advice seems to give it to be understood that the speaker thinks the addressee able to follow the course advised, and so on.

All serious speech presupposes that the speaker thinks not only that he has backing for what he says, but also that his message gears in with the addressee's interests. The gears are not of the same make in every discourse. In advising, promising, and ordering, a course of action is sketched; but it is variously related to the addressee's interests. In a piece of advice or in a promise, the action is presumed to be to his advantage, though in a piece of advice the action is up to him and in a promise up to the speaker. But in an order, the action—to be done by the addressee—is not necessarily presumed to be particularly favourable to him; what *is* assumed is that its omission will bring down a punishment upon him.

Let us say that when a speaker states, or promises, or advises (etc.) something and does so seriously, then those among the types of things given to be understood that are common and peculiar to all serious speech acts of stating are *discourse implications* of stating; the things given to be understood that are common and peculiar to all serious speech acts of promising are *discourse implications* of promising; etc.

Not all utterances fall squarely into one and only one discourse. It may be unclear what speech act I am performing. Is 'I shall come tomorrow' a promise, a forecast, or what? Even if it is clear that I am, say, advising, my speech act may at the same time be an assertion, as when I tell a driver 'That road is the shortest one'. Further, the discourse implications may be criteria-delimited. Thus, the speaker's intentions are certainly important in helping us to determine what speech act he performs, but they are neither necessary nor sufficient for determining it. 'In that situation nobody could take it as anything but a promise, so whether you intended to or not you have committed yourself, you have promised.' (I suspect we can learn from the law here.)

As in serious talk in general, the question whether a speaker in uttering something has given it to be understood that a certain discourse implication holds is logically independent of the question whether he in fact has the appropriate beliefs. The inference 'A seriously uttered U as a piece of discourse D; hence addressees are entitled (in a sense that is *not* paraphrasable with "are in fact right") to infer that he believed that the discourse implications of D held' is valid, whether or not he held the beliefs. For nobody would care to listen to that sort of discourse unless he assumed that the speaker held the appropriate beliefs. If I did not assume that advisors were trying to tell me how to act to my own good, I should disregard what they say. Unless I assumed that assertors think they have evidence for their view, I should not bother to take it into account. And so on. This truism seems to give an excellent justification for our inclination to believe that a man who states something also believes that what he says both has a backing and is relevant to the addressees.

Summing up:

(i) The vehicle of a discourse implication is not certain word-types or expression types but the *serious issuing*, the serious utter*ing*, of an utterance as belonging to a certain discourse.

(ii) In a paradigmatic case, an utterance is issued as belonging to discourse D if the following criteria are satisfied:
    (a) the speaker intends his utterance to be a piece of D;
    (b) the audience takes him to be issuing a piece of D; and
    (c) the circumstances in which it is issued are such that to take it as a piece of D is the only reasonable interpretation.

(iii) What is discourse implied is

(a) those substantiations of the utterance that are common and peculiar to all clear speech acts of that discourse, and

(b) the relevance of what is said, in respects common and peculiar to all clear cases of speech acts belonging to that discourse.

(iv) The point of the discourse would be lost if the appropriate inference was not made. Unless it were assumed that speakers of that discourse held the appropriate beliefs, the addressee would not take their words as having a bearing upon his own beliefs and actions.

Being specifications of the general implications of all serious speech, discourse implications are pragmatic: carried by the performance of a certain speech act rather than by certain words of that act, and holding because their abolishment would have as a consequence that this kind of speech act would lose its point, cease to influence the addressee's beliefs and actions in the way it was designed to do.

An important philosophical task is to sift our discourse implications, making explicit what we all take for granted when using or hearing a certain kind of discourse and what we take advantage of when we abuse it by lying, giving deceitful advice, etc. Much moral philosophy after *Principia Ethica* may be seen as attempts to show that the discourse implications of moral talk are different from the discourse implications of stating and informing, and that 'moral discourse' is far from homogeneous and can be divided into very many kinds: hortative, advisory, contractual, and so on and so forth.

The word 'discourse' is obscure. It is as it were a sign marking a gap. But we know, roughly, what sorts of thing we can insert into the gap. We can roughly distinguish moral talk from, say, stating and commanding; and that is enough. The task of sifting out discourse implications is the task of laying bare the tacit conventions determining our intuitive awareness that the kinds of talk are different. Therefore we cannot *start* from definitions of what a given discourse is—we can, at best, hope to end up with them.

Discourse and requirements of a common language. Prerequisites for the possibility of linguistic communication in general are prerequisites for the special case of linguistic communication within a certain discourse. This is, I believe, a truism. Not all philosophers agree. Thus Grant suggests that we could account for Hamlet's words 'I'll make a ghost of him that lets me' by saying not that 'let' has changed its meaning, but that the sort of talk peculiar to allowing a person to do something has changed place with the sort of talk peculiar to prohibiting him to do something —we could say 'that nowadays when people want to be restrained they imply a desire not to be restrained' (*op. cit.*, p. 323).

This idea involves a violation of the prerequisites for the possibility of linguistic communication. There are words or sets of words which typically are at home in certain types of discourse, e.g. 'advice' and 'promise'. For the reasons given in the three teaching situations of §2, it would be nonsense to maintain that 'advice' could keep its present meaning and yet that *every* language-user employed it to give his addressees to understand that the course of action specified was to the contrary of their interest. 'Advice' would then mean what we at present mean with 'dissuasion', since part of the current meaning of 'advice' is that the course the word applies to is to the addressee's interest. It would be patent nonsense to maintain that the word could keep its present meaning and yet regularly and by all speakers be used for dissuasion as well as for advice. In the same way 'let' is a word peculiar to talk about permissions and inconsistent (except when negated) with talk about prohibitions. To say 'Let me do it, but don't allow me to' is to contradict oneself.

In an attempt to make his idea intelligible, Grant asks us to imagine a society in which people help each other as little as possible: 'in that case, in order to persuade another person to do something that I wished, I would use language implying that I desired the opposite, so that in his desire to displease me he would fall in with my wishes' (*loc. cit.*).

Generalize the point! *All* speakers regularly use words 'implying that they want the opposite of what they in fact wish'. Then these words would be the standard way of expressing their actual wishes. That is, the sense of the words expressing wishes would alter to the opposite of their present one. It is impossible that all language-users could regularly employ words peculiar to a certain type of discourse in those and only those situations where they want their audience to react in the way appropriate to the opposite type of discourse implications. For then the words now peculiar to advice would become words of dissuasion and the other way round. When serious utterances contain words peculiar to discourse D it is necessary, for the very sense of the words and not merely for the point of that sort of talk, that it remains exceptional that such an utterance is employed for purposes inconsistent with the normal discourse implications of D. The utterances would not have their present meaning if most people used them dishonestly and this was a well-known fact.

7. 'Practical' and 'theoretical' discourse

Consider a new type of speech situation, not discussed in Austin's writings. I propose to call it S_f. It is the same as S_0 except for the fact that we now speak about future states of affairs. Our utterances are therefore of the form

I will be a T.

In the speech situations sketched in 1953, Austin seems to have regarded the individuating convention as independent of the classificatory one. S_f makes his view questionable. I utter, '1227 will be a square'. Suppose that '1227' refers to a now existing item which is not at present a square. If my utterance is true, there must exist a convention relating '1227' not only to the item present but also to the one that, at a later time, *is* a square. This convention must enable us to trace the future item back to the present one. Such a feat seems impossible without the help of classificatory conventions. Or suppose that '1227' is used to indicate an item that does not yet exist. What do I then single out? Can I single out what is not there? Can you grasp what I am referring to? Is this form of singling out free from classificatory conventions?

The answers to these questions may point to an oversimplification in Austin's dichotomy between the individuating and the classificatory conventions. This would be important, since the dichotomy is essential to his theory of truth. But I did not invent S_f in order to spotlight weaknesses in his view of individuating conventions. I want to argue that in S_f two different kinds of speech act are possible. They indicate a watershed between 'theoretical' and 'practical' discourse and give us a clue to what is meant by Austin's term 'illocutionary act'.

I shall therefore set aside all puzzles about the individuating conventions and assume that the utterance '1227 will be a square' sometimes is in perfect order, at least when the subject expression refers to an item existing at the time of utterance. In using the words the speaker pragmatically implies that he has good reasons to think that his utterance and the world will conform. There is, however, a difference between

(a) having reasons to think that the utterance conforms to the world, and

(b) having reasons to think that the world conforms to the utterance. In (a) the speaker has reasons to think that 1227 will be a square without his or his addressee's meddling. In (b) he has reasons to think that

(i) there is a risk that the item will not be a square unless someone does something about it; and that

(ii) he or his addressee is able to take the necessary steps; and that

(iii) the ability will or ought to be so used.

Attempts at action would be otiose unless (i) held and in vain unless (ii) held. These clauses specify preconditions of any reasonable action; but (iii) takes the first step to initiate the action.

Let there be a discrepancy between '1227 will be a square' and the world. If the employment of the sentence pragmatically implies reasons of either type (a) or of the clauses (i) and (ii) in (b), the speaker has erred in judgment. But if the utterance pragmatically implies reasons of type (b) and if the clauses (i) and (ii) are in order, the discrepancy between his utterance and the world is due to a failure of performance.[5]

When an employment of '1227 will be a square' is backed up with reasons of type (a), I shall say that the speech act belongs to *theoretical* discourse. When the employment is backed up with reasons of type (b), I shall say that the speech act belongs to *practical* discourse. The (b)-clauses (i) and (ii) are, however, in the borderline between theoretical and practical discourse, for reasons which will emerge.

Let the phrase 'a mere observer in the broad sense' signify a person shorn of all ability of physical action. He can describe (state, forecast, etc.); but he cannot e.g. bring something about, and *a fortiori* he cannot reasonably praise or regret his action.

[5] Cf. G. E. M. Anscombe, *Intention*, pp. 56–7.

He knows what it is to praise and to regret, since he knows what it is to say something and to commend or to regret saying it. If he could not even talk, he would be a mere observer in a more narrow sense. 'Praising' and 'regretting' would then have as much sense to him as 'good' has to those philosophers who think that there is just an empirical correlation between saying that something is good and behaving preferentially towards it. He would see a correlation manifested among agents; but in his own passive world its foundations would remain a mystery.

Speech acts belonging to theoretical discourse can be performed and understood in a world of mere observers. Speech acts of practical discourse can only be performed and understood in a world of agents. Even if all of us always were totally unable to meddle with any course of events, we would still be able to forecast it and to bring our words into conformity with it; but we would not understand what it would be like to be able to interfere. Consequently we would not understand what it would be like to undertake to interfere. But if we know what it is like to meddle with things, we can as observers judge that a course of events can be changed and that someone, including ourselves, is able to change it. I.e., (i) and (ii) can be understood only by someone who knows what it is to act; but although they are prerequisites for any rational action, they are intelligible and acceptable to someone who, for the time being, prefers to remain an observer.

According to the principle of trustworthiness, the speaker always has to provide backing for his words, whenever he is asked to do so. He has to shoulder this obligation if he wants his addressees to listen to what he says. In S_f his utterance is in order only if the world and it conforms, in the sense illustrated. His responsibilities are of one kind when the conformity is one of words to world and of quite another kind if the conformity is one of world to words. The difference between these two kinds of responsibility indicates the difference between observers and agents, between recorders of actions and performers of actions. And normally the speaker has every reason to make these pragmatic implications known to the addressees. For if his hearers do not know whether he forecasts that 1227 will be a square or orders them to make it a square, his words will hardly affect them in the way he intended to.

8. Performatoriness and implications of trustworthiness

In S_f two kinds of practical discourse are discernible. They may be called performatory and non-performatory. Assume that I utter '1227 will be a square' with a 'practical' purport. My speech act then carries certain implications of trustworthiness, viz. at least (i) and (ii) in the (b)-type of §7. By means of the principle of relevance, my utterance pragmatically implies also that the man referred to in (ii) as the owner of certain abilities ought to use them.

Let you be the man referred to. Then my utterance is in order if certain implications of relevance are fulfilled; a piece of advice if others are fulfilled; and so on. I do not *forecast* any action of yours, I try to make you act. And I do not perform your action.

But let me be the man referred to. Then my utterance is hardly commanding or advisory. I do not usually coax myself, command myself, or even address myself: normally I address someone else and announce that I undertake to use my abilities. In this context, '1227 will be a square' is a promise. A promisory utterance is performatory. So in S_f there occur both performatory and non-performatory 'practical' utterances.

In S_f performatoriness is, I think, definable in terms of implications of trustworthiness:

DP 1 An utterance is performatory if, and only if, it carries the pragmatic implications that the speaker is able to bring the world into conformity with his words and that he, in uttering them, undertakes so to use his ability.

But the definition cannot be generalized to ordinary language as used in our everyday world. 'I swear to tell the truth' is a performatory utterance, but the man in the witness stand certainly does not undertake to make the world conform to his words. And if we try saying

DP 2 An utterance is performatory if, and only if, it carries the pragmatic implications that the speaker is able to bring his words and the world into conformity and that he, in uttering the words, undertakes so to use his ability

—well, then 'I know that p' almost qualifies as a performatory utterance. Since I think that this would be absurd, I doubt that performatoriness can be generally defined in terms of pragmatic implications of trustworthiness.

The implications of serious speech are not identical with the characteristic implications of performatives. (i) *All* serious speech is binding in the sense that when a speaker utters something in a serious tone of voice, in a normal kind of situation, and without any indications that he does not want to be taken at his word, that very speech act entitles his hearers to infer that he believes what he says and that he thinks he possesses an appropriate backing for it. We all agree that he is a right object to blame if he does not fulfil these expectations; and we all agree that he has then used language deceptively. But (ii) certain speech acts involve committals beyond those of *all* serious speech. Such acts are '*I swear* that this is so', '*I promise* I shall come', '*I give my word* that so-and-so is the case'. In these situations I have staked my reputation in a *new* way, taken up responsibility of a very peculiar sort. It is these committals that Austin baptizes performatives.[6] See Ch. 5:1.

III. THE ILLOCUTIONARY ACT

9. *Serious speech and the new 'science of language'*

The two principles of serious speech lay down necessary conditions of the possibility of *any* common language. Studies of these conditions have affinities to Kant's transcendental deductions and

---

[6] C. S. Peirce compares assertions to going before a notary and making an affidavit, executing a deed, and signing a note by which one voluntarily runs the risk of incurring penalties unless some proposition is true. In his book *The Pragmatism of C. S. Peirce*, Hjalmar Wennerberg comments, 'The act of asserting a proposition can be said to be "performatory", to use L. J. [*sic!*] Austin's term' (p. 129).

If Peirce really thought that to say 'S is P' is to take on as many and as definite responsibilities as those involved in saying in court 'I swear that S is P', he was obviously mistaken. But probably he was concerned with implications of type (i) and not of type (ii). In *Collected Papers*, Vol. V, p. 386 (quoted by Wennerberg in support of his interpretation), Peirce explains that his examples are 'very formal' assertions, 'the features of which have purposively been rendered very prominent'. I suggest that he makes a pedagogic exaggeration in order to bring out that every assertion is a committal. There is no need to think he was maintaining that the committal is of the sort typical to performatives. He may have made the point that serious talk involves the shouldering of responsibility.

lie close to traditionally philosophical pursuits. At the same time they are obviously relevant to linguistics. Are they constituents of Austin's 'new science of language'?

His phrase hints that the new discipline ought to be concerned with among other things the factors making all languages languages in spite of variances in vocabulary, syntax, and accidence. Perhaps there is no factor common and peculiar to them all. Wittgenstein may be right in holding that 'language' is a family term. But a science of language ought to investigate the truth of such suggestions; and then there is some plausibility in Austin's idea that philosophers, when linguistically trained, may be able to contribute to it.

I believe that *Words* is not merely an attempt at a general theory of what we in fact do when we say something. It is also an attempt at saying what conditions any speech act must conform to in order to be counted a speech act. If I am right, the illocutionary 'act'* is concerned with the pragmatic implications (mainly of trustworthiness) which, as we have seen, are necessary if speech is to be taken seriously.

10. Illocutionary and perlocutionary acts (*Words*. Chs. 8-10)

Austin has great difficulties in elucidating the illocutionary act. There is no term for it in English. It is, however, done *in* the performance of a locutionary act; hence the term of *il*locutionary act. It will not do to say that performing an illocutionary act is using language in a certain way—'use' is hopelessly ambiguous and refers indiscriminatingly to locutionary and illocutionary acts. Instead, he tries to make the issue clearer by distinguishing the illocutionary act from yet another type which he calls *perlocutionary*.

When something is said, it will often produce certain consequential effects upon the feelings, thoughts, or actions of the addressee; and the saying may be done in order to produce these effects. When these two conditions are fulfilled, the speaker has managed to accomplish an act the nomenclature of which only

---

*['Act' in the phrases 'locutionary act', 'illocutionary act', 'perlocutionary act' and 'speech act' is a dangerous term, as I shall argue in §12. I was not aware of the danger in the first edition of this book, and the text is sprinkled with the term. I can only ask the reader to be wary.]

obliquely or not at all refers to the performance of the locutionary or illocutionary act of his. If someone says 'Shoot her!' and I, in consequence of his words, do so, the situation can be stratified as follows:

    Locution   He said to me 'Shoot her!' (meaning by 'shoot' *shoot* and referring by 'her' to *her*).
    Illocution   He advised (ordered, etc.) me to shoot her.
    Perlocution   He persuaded (got) me to shoot her.

In an analogous way the locutionary act 'He said that . . .' can be distinguished from the illocutionary act 'He argued that . . .' and the perlocutionary act 'He convinced me that . . .'. (The name 'perlocution' alludes to the fact that the new type of act is often brought about not *in* but *by* (Latin *per*) a locutionary act.)

Austin tries to drive home the distinction between illocutionary acts and perlocutionary ones by the following points (*Words.* Chs. 8–9):

(i) There are linguistic devices for making clear that an illocutionary act is performed, but none for perlocutionary acts. We do not have such phrases as 'I convince you that . . .' or 'I alarm you that . . .', although we have phrases for telling what perlocutionary act we are *trying* to perform: 'I am trying to convince you', etc.

(ii) The question whether someone was performing an illocutionary act, e.g. arguing, may be answered without touching on the question whether he performed a perlocutionary act, e.g. convincing someone.

(iii) Consequences enter the two sorts of act in dissimilar ways. In performatory illocutionary acts, the so-called felicity conditions (see Ch. 5:1) delimit the stretch of consequences we may import into the act. To give two examples: The audience has to hear the performative and to take it in a certain way (take 'I warn' as a warning). Again, actions involving a breach of the commitment undertaken in the performative will be out of order. Certain illocutionary acts, such as asking and offering, involve by convention a response from the audience, but this response cannot be included under the initial stretch of action. In perlocutionary acts, on the other hand, there is no such limitation of the consequences. An undelimited stretch of them can be brought in under a perlocutionary act.

(iv) Although both illocutionary and perlocutionary acts can be brought about without words (I can warn someone by waving a red flag and alarm someone by wielding a stick), the perlocutionary but not the illocutionary act can be done without invoking conventions. The red flag is a *conventional* sign of danger. At this point (p. 117) Austin suggests that in the case of perlocutionary acts a distinction can be drawn between achieving an object and producing a sequel. It is not clear whether he meant something more than that a person can try to bring about one perlocutionary act (say, persuading somebody) but only succeed in doing another, perhaps an unintended one (say, alarming him), or that a person may successfully persuade somebody but simultaneously and perhaps inadvertently also alarm him.

(v) If the illocutionary and perlocutionary acts are brought about by means of words, the former are done *in* performing a certain locutionary act, and the latter *by* performing a locutionary act. Austin takes this linguistic test seriously and spends the better part of Ch. 10 on it. The upshot of his careful but not, I think, for his purposes very rewarding discussion is that the 'by saying'-formula can be used as a criterion of perlocutionary acts, provided that two conditions are fulfilled. First, 'by' must be used in an instrumental as distinct from a criterion sense. 'By' in 'By inserting a plate I was practising dentistry' or in 'By saying "I do" I was marrying her' gives a criterion of practising dentistry or of marrying. Secondly, 'saying' in the 'by saying'-formula must be used in the full sense of a locutionary act and not in a partial sense, e.g. the sense of phatic act. Further, it must not be used in a double-conventional way. 'Double-conventional' is explained by the example 'By saying I would take three tricks in clubs I informed him that I had no diamonds'. Here the speaker uses the illocutionary and strictly conventional act of saying 'I bid three clubs' as an indirect means of informing another person. And informing is also an illocutionary and conventional act.

(vi) Austin ends Lecture 10 by giving two tests which he regards as subsidiary and not water-tight. First, in the case of illocutionary verbs we can often say 'to say X was to do Y'. Secondly, the verbs we have classified as names of illocutionary acts are close to explicit performative verbs; and there is no analogue in the case of verbs naming perlocutionary acts. (The second of these tests seems to be a repetition of point (i) above.)

In spite of Austin's predilection for (v), I think that (i), (iii), (iv)

THE ILLOCUTIONARY ACT

and the first part of (vi) are equally or more elucidating. For they strongly suggest that whereas perlocutionary acts can *occasionally* be brought about by conventional means, illocutionary acts are *essentially* conventional. The most reliable test for distinguishing between perlocutionary and illocutionary acts seems to be '*Can I perform this act without any recourse to conventions (which need not be verbal)?*' If I can, the act is *not* illocutionary. If I cannot, the act may be illocutionary or locutionary.

11. *The locutionary and the illocutionary act*

When I say, '1227 will be a square', the locutionary dimension of my speech act is, according to *Words*.92–8, my issuing of certain noises (the phonetic act) belonging to and as belonging to a certain language and conforming to and as conforming to a certain grammar (the phatic act) and with a certain sense and reference (the rhetic act). Had I chosen to convey the same thing by pointing to 1227 and saying 'This will be a square', I should have performed quite another locutionary act, since one word would have been changed. '1227 will be a square' and 'This will be a square' are different as phones and hence different as locutionary acts; but since they have the same sense and reference, they are nevertheless rhetically equivalent.

Let the locutionary as well as the perlocutionary dimension of my speech act be perfectly clear. Questions about what I am doing in uttering words with this locutionary and that perlocutionary cash-value still remain unanswered. Am I forecasting? Or promising? Or warning? Investigations to answer this kind of questions are investigations of the illocutionary dimension of my speech act. (Cf. *Words*.Ch.8.)

As we saw in Austin's discussion of the differences between the illocutionary and the perlocutionary act, the former is conventional and up to the speaker. In these respects it resembles the locutionary one and differs from the perlocutionary act. I have not convinced you unless *you* react in a certain way. I have warned you if *I* do certain things, whether you react to them or not.

If I have understood Austin, a study of the illocutionary dimension of a speech act is a study of the discourse implications of an utterance issued in a given (type of) speech situation. These implications are indeed both (i) conventional and (ii) up to the speaker:

(i) There is a tacit rule, without which our talking would be in vain, that whenever we speak in such-and-such a manner in such-and-such a situation, our audience is entitled to infer that what we say has (we believe) such-and-such a type of backing and, in most types of discourse, such-and-such a type of relevance to the addressee. In any serious utterance we invoke such tacit conventions, since we want our words to be effective and know that they will pass unheeded unless our audience assumes that we shoulder certain responsibilities for what we say. The discourse implications of a speech act are *normally* those that the speaker wants to be implied; for if an utterance, when delivered in a certain manner and in a certain kind of situation, is always received in another way than the one intended, he would be a fool to continue his practice. Since the discourse implications are conventional, they are not brought into being by the current speaker's intentions. Suppose he uses '1227 will be a square' with the intention of merely forecasting that this will be so. If he says it in circumstances which make an inference to beliefs appropriate to a promisor a reasonable one but an inference to beliefs appropriate to an assertor far-fetched, then he will be judged to have promised, whatever his intentions.

(ii) The very conventionality of the discourse implications ensures, however, that the illocutionary act is up to the speaker. If I know the rules of language and utter '1227 will be a square' in a certain tone of voice and in a certain situation that, as all members of the language-community agree, are peculiar to acts of forecasting but not to acts of promising, then I have forecasted, whether *you*, my current addressee, grasp it or not.

I think, therefore, that the illocutionary dimension of a speech act is the dimension of discourse implications. We are concerned with questions pertaining to the illocutionary act when we ask (i) what the issuing of this type of words in this type of situation entitles the audience to infer about the speaker's beliefs about the backing and relevance of his utterance; or when we ask (ii) what responsibilities the speaker (= any speaker) shoulders in uttering the words in this type of situation. The two questions are not identical. The second is about what the speaker does, the first about what we are entitled to infer concerning his state of mind. Nevertheless they are intimately connected: if speakers did not in general have such-and-such reasonable beliefs, they would not take on such-and-such responsibilities; and we would not care what responsibilities they took on unless we thought that they had such-and-such reasonable beliefs. I think, however, that the second question is paradigmatically a question about the illocutionary dimension of the utterance.

12. Locutionary act/illocutionary act versus phrastic/neustic

Austin *says* that the study of the utterance of certain noises as words in a certain construction and with a certain sense and reference is 'the study of locutions, or of the full units of *speech*' (*Words*.94; my italics). This sounds as if he thought of a locution as a dimension of a speech *episode*—as something lasting for a certain time, etc. In the same vein he speaks as if an inquiry into the illocutionary dimension is an inquiry into certain aspects of a speech *episode*. But this is surely misleading. He thinks he can shed light on the nature of statements and promises. A statement or a promise is not a speech episode, although the act of stating or of promising is. A statement can be true or false; but what is true or false is not, in contradistinction to a speech episode, something clockable and datable. These things are true of the act of stating but not of the statement itself.

It is more plausible to maintain that the statement or the promise is a result of the act of stating or promising, and that inquiries into the locutionary and the illocutionary dimension are inquiries into aspects of the statement or the promise. Then they are certainly not inquiries into any act at all. The result of the act of stating, viz. the statement, is no more an act than is the result of the act of scribbling, viz. a scribble. And in practice Austin does not confuse the two. In Ch.4:1.1 I shall argue that he did *not* think of a statement as a speech episode.

It may be helpful to consider Austin's distinction in other terms than his own. Husserl's distinction between the content and the quality of a mental act has been revised in a more linguistic form by R. M. Hare.[7] What he calls the *phrastic* and

---

[7] Edmund Husserl, *Logische Untersuchungen* II, Pt. 1, Sect. V, Chs. 2–3. R. M. Hare, 'Imperative sentences', *Mind* 58 (1949); *The Language of Morals*, Pt. I; review of Everett W. Hall's *What is Value?*, *Mind* 63 (1954).

Husserl the *matter* (*Materie*) is the core common to, say, the order 'Donald, wear your wellingtons!' and the prediction 'Donald will wear his wellingtons', provided they are issued at approximately the same time and refer to the same Donald. The phrastic is a common core of meaning-cum-reference. It singles out a certain person and ascribes certain characteristics to him. It does not, however, indicate whether the speaker orders Donald to satisfy the description, or constates that he will, as a matter of fact, satisfy it, or just imagines he will satisfy it, or . . . Which, if any, of these things the speaker is doing depends on the *quality* (Husserl) or *neustic* (Hare) of his utterance. If we follow Erik Stenius[8] in using the expressions of the form 'that S is P' for the phrastic, the neustic may be made clear by the prefatory phrase 'I order (constate, etc.)'. If 'You go nowhere' is uttered as an order, it will be paraphrased 'I order/that you go nowhere'. If it is a statement, it will be paraphrased 'I constate/that you go nowhere'.

It seems to me that when 'locutionary act' is used not for a dimension of a speech episode but (breeding confusion) for the dimension of the semantic result of such an episode, this term and the term 'phrastic act' come close to being two names of the same phenomenon: the meaning-cum-reference which different kinds of speech acts, such as stating, ordering, and appealing, may have in common. But they are not identical. 'Phrastic' seems to be used in such a way that when '1227 will be a square' and 'That will be a square' are used at the same time and with the same reference, they have the same phrastic. But in spite of being rhetically equivalent they are, because of their different wording, not the same locutions.

A locution becomes a statement by the addition of a constative neustic and an order by the addition of a certain kind of imperative neustic, etc. The neustic entitles the audience to draw certain conclusions about how the locution is backed up, how what is said is intended to gear in with their interests, and so on. These rights are given by the speech episode but are not an aspect of it. The gift is not a part of the act of giving the gift. A neustic is, I

Hare's view has been discussed e.g. in R. B. Braithwaite's review of *The Language of Morals*, *Mind* 63 (1954), and by B. Mayo and B. Mitchell in 'The varieties of imperatives', *PASS* 31 (1957).

[8] Erik Stenius, *Wittgenstein's* 'Tractatus', Ch. 9.

think, what Austin meant most of the time by the phrase 'an illocutionary act'; but it is no part of any speech act.

Nobody would normally listen to a mere locution. Until the speaker has undertaken to supply a backing to it, he is just playing with words. Serious talk requires that a phrastic also has a neustic. What is said must not merely have sense and reference but also commit the speaker in certain ways. To use Austin's phrase, it must have *illocutionary force*.

The rest of this book will be concerned with different kinds of amalgams of locution and illocutionary force. The simplest kind of amalgam, the unguarded constative, will be considered in the next chapter. In Ch. 5 I shall look at various kinds of neustics and how they affect their locutions.

CHAPTER 4

Unguarded Constatives: Truth and Knowledge

The term 'constative' is a neologism, coined by Austin in his lectures on Words and Deeds and explained thus in *Words*.6n: 'to issue a constative utterance is to make a statement'.

But what is it to make a statement? I suggest the following analysis as a first shot:

When a sentence of the type

I is a T

is used with the pragmatic implication that the speaker believes that his locution conforms to the world, a typical act of constating is performed. The semantic result of this act is a constative. (In conformity with Austin's and Strawson's terminology in their discussion of truth, I shall in the following often use 'statement' in place of 'constative'.)

A constative always involves both some locution or other and a certain illocutionary force. What characterizes constatives is that they are typically true or false. They carry the pragmatic implications that the speaker is truthful and well-informed. An elucidation of truth and knowledge therefore sheds light on constative force.

Austin did not come to pay heed to the illocutionary force of constatives until fairly late. His discussions of truth and knowledge often takes it for granted. Nevertheless his views seem to have remained fundamentally the same even in his late writings; he only changed the emphasis.* He discussed truth in 1950, 1954, and in Chs. XI and XII of *Words*, esp. pp. 142–6. The startling suggestions in *Words* are, however, merely hinted at in 1950. Knowledge is treated in 1946. The ideas of that paper are taken up and developed in *S&S*. Ch. X.

*[I still think that this is correct, in spite of John R. Searle's misgivings in his review of *LIA* in *Ph.R.* 75, 1966.]

The constatives discussed in these writings are all unguarded. Problems arise when the constative force is qualified. They will be elucidated in Ch. 5 of this book.

I. TRUTH

Austin's discussions of truth aim at smartening up the Correspondence Theory but also at telling how stating, asserting, describing, etc., differ from other types of discourse. Sometimes he also talks as if he were concerned with a problem raised by P. F. Strawson, viz. 'How do we use the phrase "is true"?'

The three problems are connected, but it may be well to keep them as far apart as possible. Since the one Strawson worries about is the easiest one to detach, I shall begin there.

1. *The use of the phrase 'is true'*

Strawson describes the use of 'is true' in his paper 'Truth' which originally appeared in *Analysis* 9, 1949. My references will, however, be to the reprint in *Philosophy and Analysis* (ed. M. Macdonald). A note added to the reprint (p. 260) says that Strawson's contribution to a symposium of 'Truth' (*PASS* 24, 1950) is a later, 'extended and in some ways modified version' of his views. I shall call the papers 'Truth I' and 'Truth II'.

An account of 'Truth I'. Strawson sets out to destroy Tarski's Semantic Theory of Truth, in so far as it is not merely concerned with the construction of artificial languages but also wants, as Strawson puts it, 'to throw light on the actual use of the word "true"; or (which I take to be the same claim) on the philosophical problem of truth' (p. 260f). Philosophers have, he says, maintained that to say that an assertion is true

(1) is not to make any further assertion at all, but to make the same assertion;

(2) is to make a statement about a sentence of a given language in which the first statement is made.

These contentions go against each other. Strawson proves it thus: If 'It is true that moths fly by night' makes the same assertion as 'Moths fly by night', it is about moths and not about the English sentence 'Moths fly by night'. Hence at least one of the two tenets must be rejected, and then preferably the second. For it is clear that 'is true' is not used to talk about sentences. Such statements as 'The sentence ". . ." is badly formulated (ungrammatical, misspelt)' are about sentences. When they are translated, the sentence they are about will occur quoted and untranslated; otherwise the translation is faulty. But a correct translation of an 'is true'-utterance does not contain an untranslated and quoted sentence to which the phrase is applied. Hence (2) is false.

After an ingenious suggestion as to how meaning may be confused with truth, Strawson argues for the correctness of (1). The use of 'is true' (and 'is false') has, in his opinion, resemblances to that of 'Yes' or of 'Ditto'. The normal use of 'Yes' requires a 'linguistic occasion', viz. that of a question. In a way it is to state something, for if you employ it to answer 'Is Jones there?', I am entitled to report to a third party 'He says Jones is there'. And if you make an assertion and I say 'Ditto', I assert what you assert, though I do it in a way which requires that someone has spoken. The ordinary use of both 'Yes' and 'Ditto' (*a*) requires a linguistic occasion (that someone has asked a question or made an assertion), (*b*) does not constitute a meta-linguistic remark about the sentence used on that linguistic occasion but (*c*) is a speech act which, as far as it is an assertion, has the same content as that of the question or assertion which constitutes its 'linguistic occasion'. There is no temptation to say that 'Yes' and 'Ditto' are about the sentence employed on the occasion. Now an utterance containing 'is true' behaves in the same way: requires a linguistic occasion, has—in so far it is an assertion—the same content as the assertion uttered on that occasion, and does not say anything about it but is an act of agreeing with, endorsing, underwriting that content.

Strawson claims that his account helps us to avoid e.g. the paradoxes arising from the isolated utterance 'What I am saying now is false' or the text on an otherwise clean blackboard: 'Every statement on this blackboard is false'. Adherents of the Semantic Theory of Truth treat these examples as sentences, used to make second-order statements to the effect that (i) there is some statement of the first order made by me now or written on the blackboard, and (ii) that first-order statement is false. Then the examples can be dealt with in two ways. Either they are false, since there is no first-order statement; or we treat them as hypotheticals vacuously true since no first-order statement occurs—i.e., 'Every statement on the blackboard is true' is taken to mean the same as 'If there is a (first-order) statement on the blackboard, it is true': a hypothetical which is vacuously true, since the antecedent is false. Both solutions are formally successful but unnecessarily complicated. There is no need to assume that to say that a statement is true (or false) is to make a further statement, or to say that this second-order statement is about a sentence or sentences. Strawson's view is that the words 'true' and 'false' are not used unless someone has made, is making or is about to make a statement. They are employed to confirm that statement; but the indicative clause having 'is true' as its grammatical predicate 'does not in itself make any kind of statement at all . . . and *a fortiori* cannot make the statement, the making of which is required as the occasion for the significant use of the words 'true' or 'false'. . . . The phrase 'is true' *never* has a statement-making role.' (Pp. 270–1.) Hence the paradoxes do not arise.

There are, says Strawson, some indicative sentences with 'is true' or 'is false' as their grammatical predicate which make implicit claims that some statement has been made. Examples are 'What I am saying now is true', 'All statements made in English are false' and 'What the policeman said is true'. They imply 'I have just made (am about to make) a statement', 'Some statements are made in English', and 'The policeman made a statement'. These existential claims are 'part of the analysis' of the former sentences. (In a note in the reprint Strawson wants to change this—presumably in view of what he has said in 'On referring' and *Introduction to Logical Theory*, esp. p. 175. He now says that any statement made by using the former sentences would presuppose the truth of statements which might be made by using the latter sentences.) The heart of the matter is as follows (p. 272):

The sentence 'The policeman made a statement' clearly has not the same use as the sentence 'What the policeman said is true'. To utter the second is to do something more than to assert the first. What is this additional performance? . . . [The] sentence 'What the policeman said is true' has no use *except* to confirm the policeman's story; . . . the sentence does not say anything further *about* [it] or the sentences he used in telling it. It is a device for confirming the story without telling it again. So, in general, in using such expressions, we are confirming, underwriting, admitting, agreeing with, what somebody has said; but (except where we are implicitly making an existential meta-statement, in making which the phrase 'is true' plays no part), we are not making any assertion additional to theirs; and are *never* using 'is true' to talk *about* something which is *what they said*, or the sentences they used in saying it.

'What the policeman said is true' has to be analysed something like 'The policeman made a statement. I confirm it.' Since I, in uttering 'I confirm it', 'am not describing something I do, but *doing* something' (p. 272f), Strawson labels the phrase 'performatory', with Austin's word. He admits, however, that it is a misnomer, since a 'performatory word, in Austin's sense, . . . [is] a verb, the use of which, in the first person present indicative, seems to describe some activity of the speaker, but in fact *is* that activity'; whilst the use of 'is true' does not fulfil that condition. That it can be analysed in terms of the strictly performatory 'I confirm it' is the only point of using Austin's word. (P. 275.)

'True' has also other uses. It is employed to concede, to agree, to express the novelty of something, and so on. But according to Strawson none of the uses is descriptive.

An analytical summary of 'Truth I'. The contentions of 'Truth I' are, I take it, these:
 (i) The traditional philosophical problem of truth is that of elucidating the use of the phrase 'is true'.
 (ii) To say 'It is true that p' is not to make a statement about p.
 (iii) The use of 'is true' demands that the speaker envisages a serious utterance other than the actual utterance containing the phrase—otherwise its use is pointless, like 'Ditto' uttered when nobody has spoken.
 (iv) To use 'is true' is to agree with, endorse, underwrite the serious utterance envisaged.
 (v) The serious utterance envisaged in the correct use of 'is true' is a statement.
 (vi) The points (i)–(v), with suitable alterations, also hold good for the use of 'is false'.

I am convinced by Strawson's arguments for (iii) and (iv). But (1.1) I doubt the truth of (ii) and (v), which together embody the tenet that to say 'It is true that p' is not to make a statement about a statement. And (1.2) I am convinced that (i) is profoundly mistaken.

1.1. Is 'It is true that p' a statement about a statement?

At first sight, the contentions (ii)–(v) seem to involve two logical inconsistencies. First, if to say 'It is true that p' is to confirm, endorse, underwrite that p, then it seems odd that it is not about p. I cannot confirm something unless there is something to confirm; and when I confirm that p, that p is the case is what I confirm. Secondly, (iii), (iv) and (v) suggest that 'is true' is used for assessing assertions and denials. It is then plausible to suppose that what is assessed is whether what they say to be so really is so; and that in saying 'It is true that p' we are usually, among other things, *stating* that the assertion or denial corresponds to facts.

Let us begin to polish these crude objections by considering the notion of a statement.

Strawson's account of statements. Strawson contends that the phrase 'is true' is not used for talking about what someone has said, is saying, or will say. What sort of entity is it that they are about? In 'Truth I' he often says, following Tarski,[1] that it is a *sentence*, but at other places he seems to think of it as a *statement*. The difference between these accounts is brought out in his later essay 'On referring': Sentences are grammatically well-formed, meaningful or meaningless, but not true or false. Statements are not (assessed as) meaningful or meaningless but as true or false or —on Strawson's well-known theory of 'presuppositions'—true or false on the condition that the claim they 'presuppose' is true.[2]— This explanation resembles Austin's distinction between the phatic and the rhetic act. Sentences are units of language. Statements are meaningful units of language which are issued seriously and have acquired referents for their referring expressions—i.e., statements are units of speech. But a rhetic act is, in contradistinction to Strawsonian statements, neither true or false until a constative force is added.

Strawson seems right in holding that sentences lack a truth-

[1] A. Tarski, 'The semantic conception of truth' in *Semantics and the Philosophy of Language* (ed. L. Linsky).
[2] P. F. Strawson, 'On referring' in *ECA*.

value. A sentence is no utterance (serious or non-serious), and its referring expressions are not given any referents. A definition of truth is not materially adequate if it only implies an equivalence of the sort exemplified in 'The sentence "Snow is white" is true if and only if snow is white', where the left-side occurrence of the phrase about the whiteness of snow is a name of the sentence on the right hand. In 'Snow is white' the subject-expression is used to refer to something; in '"Snow is white"' it is not used at all and has no correct or incorrect referent. A definition of truth is not materially adequate in the case considered, until what the expression 'snow' refers to *when used* has the characteristic designated by the predicate expression. This is presumably what Aristotle meant by the saying Tarski quotes, 'To say of what is that it is not, or of what is not that it is, is false, while to say of what is that it is, or of what is not that it is not, is true'.

In 'Truth II' Strawson goes on to specify in what sense of the word 'statement' a statement is something that can be true or false: '"My statement" may be either what I say or my saying it. My saying something is . . . an episode. What I say is not. It is the latter, not the former, we declare to be true.' My saying something may be a whisper or a shout. What I say cannot be (p. 129f).

In the same paper he also tells us that different sentences may be used for making the same statement. Examples are not only 'different languages or synonymous expressions in the same language; but also . . . such occasions as that on which you say of Jones "He is ill", I say *to* Jones "You are ill" and Jones says "I am ill". Using, not only different sentences, but sentences with different meanings, we all make "the same statement".' (P. 131f.) —It is plausible that necessary conditions for making the same theme and the same statement are that the utterances have (1) the same sense and (2) the same reference; but in the passage quoted, Strawson claims that (1) is not necessary. It is, however, remarkable that in his only counter-instance the differences in sense are due to the differences in sense between '*egocentric*' expressions. No doubt 'I', 'you' and 'he', 'am', 'are' and 'is' are governed by different linguistic rules. Consequently they have different meanings; for two expressions are synonymous—have the same meaning—if and only if they are governed by the same linguistic rules. The whole point of having 'egocentric' expressions is, however, that of having a linguistic means for handy *references*—they are the very paradigms of referring expressions. So it is not surprising that two persons manage to make the same statement in spite of employing sentences with different meanings—if the only difference in sense is due to the referring expressions *which on this particular occasion have the same reference.*

1.11. Are 'is true-' utterances not about statements?

Strawson's points about sentences and statements make it abundantly clear that 'is true' and 'is false' are not used for assessing *sentences*. They are used for assessing sentences *when used*—they are used for assessing statements. (Whether statements are the only entities they are used to assess is another question.) If what we assess by the use of the two phrases is a sentence, it is hard to account for the fact that 'It is true that Jones was there' is used for endorsing not only some utterance of the sentence 'Jones was there' but also utterances of quite different sentences, such as 'Henry was there' or 'The chap with a squint was in the pub'. So Strawson is right in his criticism of the Semantic Theory of Truth provided that that theory is an attempt to elucidate what is meant by saying that e.g. 'Snow is white' is true if it corresponds to facts.

This does not, however, show that he is also right in holding that 'is true' and 'is false' are not used for saying something about a *statement*; and one of my objections to him is simply that the naïve common sense view is that we often *are* assessing statements, be they actual or—as often in the concessive use of 'is true'—merely imagined ones.

Strawson on statements and speech acts. My objection is identical with one Austin brought against Strawson (1950.101). Strawson's reply is bewildering. He takes Austin to task for having said in 1950.87f,

A statement is made and its making is an historic event, the utterance by a certain speaker or writer of certain words (a sentence) to an audience with reference to an historic situation, event or what not

and in 1950.90,

A statement is said to be true when the historic state of affairs to which it is correlated by the demonstrative conventions (the one to which it 'refers') is of a type with which the sentence used in making it is correlated by the descriptive conventions.

In Strawson's opinion, these quotations show that Austin has confused a statement with the making of it—that Austin takes the constative itself, and not the making of it, to be an historic event. In view of Austin's remarks in the same paper about using different utterances for making the same statement and for making different statements (1950.88), the charge is most unreasonable. However, Strawson uses his doctrine that the same statement can be made by the use of sentences with different meanings, to put Austin in a dilemma.

(a) The first horn of this dilemma is that if we say that people make the same statement when the words are used in such situations that their users must (logically) either all be making a true or all be making a false statement—then 'true' is used in the elucidation of 'same statement'; and this begs the question at issue. ('Truth II', p. 132.)

(b) In Strawson's opinion, Austin can avoid this horn only by impaling himself on the other. We can say that sentences with different meanings are used for making the same statement, when their use in the situation constitutes an application of the same description to the same person at a certain moment in his history: anyone applying that description to the person would be making that statement. But it will not do to analyse 'The statement that Jones was ill is true' as, e.g., 'If anyone had issued or were to issue words which in that situation describe Jones in the same way as I do when I now say "Jones was ill", then the resulting speech-episode was or would be true'. For the grammatical subjects of 'true' never designate speech-episodes. 'If I endorse Plato's view, wrongly attributing it to Lord Russell ("Russell's view that p is quite true"), and am corrected, I have not discovered that I was talking of an event separated by centuries from the one I imagined I was talking of. . . . My *implied* historical judgment is false; that is all.' (Pp. 132–3.)

I am not impressed by the argument. In the first place it is misdirected, since the passages Strawson attacks do not discuss the use of 'is true' at all. I shall try to establish this in the next section. In the second place Strawson's case rests on an assumption for which he has produced no evidence, viz. that Austin thought that a statement is a speech-episode. I have found no support for this accusation in Austin's writings. He held in 1950 and 1954 that in a speech-episode, we use words with a certain sense and give them a reference; and that what is true or false is the combination of the sense of the sentence with the reference given in the speech-episode. Although the *giving* of a reference certainly is datable, it does not follow that the combination of sense and reference indicates any speech-episode (or the absurdity that it *is* a speech-episode). We can therefore accept Strawson's view about the undatability of statements and about the unplausibility of the suggested analysis of 'It is true that p'. It does not force us to admit that 'It is true that p' is about a speech-episode.

Why does Strawson deny that 'is true'-utterances are about statements? The common sense view that 'It is true that p' often is about a statement is quite compatible with some of Strawson's tenets, e.g. that the correct use of the phrase 'is true' demands that an utterance is envisaged and that its point is to confirm, endorse, underwrite the content of that utterance.

But 'To use X is to do Y' is sometimes a way of saying that to do X is to do nothing except Y. It seems to me that Strawson sometimes accepts this interpretation of what it is to say 'It is true that p'. He argues that instead of saying 'What the policeman said is true' I may repeat his story, and that this shows that 'to confirm his story is not to say anything further, *about* his story, ... though it is to do something that cannot be done unless he has told his story' ('Truth I', p. 272). If to say 'It is true that p' is to do the same thing (though in a special setting) as to say that p, then the former utterance is not *about* the latter but makes the same statement as it.

Is it true that there is no difference except in setting between repeating the policeman's story on the one hand and saying 'What he said is true' on the other? I doubt it. To repeat his story in a serious way is to confirm it, in the sense of agreeing with or concurring in it. But to say 'What the policeman said is true' is to deliver a verdict on his story; it is confirming it in the sense of ruling in favour of it. The role of the witness is not identical with that of the judge. Here another of my previous arguments comes in: if I deliver a verdict upon or assess something, then there is something I deliver a verdict upon or assess; and nothing has shown that this something is not a statement. Strawson has not succeeded in proving that saying 'It is true that *p*' is not saying something about *p* and that *p* cannot be a statement. Since his case is not proven and for the reasons given contravenes common sense, I shall henceforward assume that 'is true'-utterances are about something, and that this something sometimes is a statement.

1.12. Are 'is true'-utterances always about statements?

Strawson's contention that 'is true'-utterances are used to confirm, endorse, underwrite the content of an envisaged *statement* is, I think, too rash and ought to be broken up into two points, as I did in my summary of his paper: (*a*) 'is true'-utterances are used to confirm, endorse, underwrite the content of an envisaged *serious utterance*, and (*b*) the serious utterance in question is always a *statement*.—The first point seems to be true and important, whilst (*b*) is false

If you say 'The battle of Hastings was fought in 1066' and I say 'That's true', I have confirmed a statement; but 'is true' is also at home in other contexts. Even 'value-nihilists' cheerfully say 'It's true that she ought to have stayed indoors (that he is a saintly man, that this is an excellent picture)'; and defenders of an 'atheoretical' view of religious utterances can be caught saying 'It's true that God has mercy upon us (that Christ died for our salvation, that there is sin against the Holy Ghost)'. Are they necessarily inconsistent? Must their utterance show that in their opinion 'She ought to have stayed indoors' or 'God has mercy upon us' is a statement, and that it corresponds to a certain state of affairs? Hardly. Quite often they are just confirming, endorsing, putting their authority behind an utterance, whatever its nature. Thus a moral philosopher of Stevensonian persuasion may say 'It is true that this is an excellent picture' and mean something like 'A said he likes this picture very much. I like it, too. Do so as well!' This would not be a new and unheard-of use of 'is true'—it is a plain fact about our everyday speech that the phrase is often employed to endorse something, without any demand that the thing endorsed be a statement.

1.13. Are 'is true'-utterances themselves statements?

Even if an 'is true'-utterance is about the content of statements, there still remains the question whether it, too, is a statement. Suppose that to say 'It is true that p' never is anything but the performance of an act of agreement as to the content of p. The utterance is then a performative, and the received view of performatives is that they can be neither true nor false. But, it may be said, it is essential to statements that they are either true or false or at least true or false on the condition that their 'presuppositions' are true. Hence, 'It is true that p' cannot be a statement.

The argument contains many questionable premisses which we shall take up in the last chapter. At present it suffices to point out that Strawson cannot employ it. Since he has stressed that 'is true'-utterances are not clear performatives, they need not fulfil the requirements of typical performatives. Waiving this difficulty, Strawson must prove that 'It is true that p' is *merely* performatory. The fact that it has a performatory side has, as Austin points out (1950.101), no more tendency to show that it is not true or false than the insulting character of 'You are a cuckold' frees *it* from truth or falsehood.

It sounds plausible that 'It is true that the cat is on the mat' asserts that the constative that the cat is on the mat corresponds to the facts. How is this to be reconciled with the suggestion that to say 'It is true that this is an excellent picture' is not to assert that the content of 'This is an excellent picture' corresponds to the facts—that it is not to assert anything at all but just to underwrite a commendation? Is there a good reason to think that 'It is true that the cat is on the mat' is and 'It is true that this is an excellent picture' is not an assertion?

I think so. Traditional philosophical inquiries into truth have been concerned with the peculiar kind of relations which, we hold, obtain between the world and the statements which 'fit the facts'. A statement with this relation to the world is true; and when we discuss whether (say) value-judgments can be true, we discuss whether they can have this relation. Strawson's elucidation of the use of the phrase 'is true' is, however, not concerned with this type of problem: as we have seen, 'It is true that p' is an underwriting, endorsement, etc., even if p is not an assertion at all. It is then perplexing that in several languages the very same words—in English 'true', in German 'wahr', in Swedish 'sann'—are used both for saying that statements (but not other kinds of utterance) 'fit the facts', and for putting one's authority behind an utterance (which need not be a statement). How are we to explain this?

If the two uses are connected, it is reasonable to assume that we put our authority behind an utterance *because* we think that it is well-established—satisfies certain adequacy-conditions, etc. The reporting usage is then primary to the confirmatory one. We may then guess that the basic use of 'true' reports correspondence with facts. Since to say that an utterance is in this sense true amounts to confirming it, 'is true' also acquired a 'performatory' aspect. After that, it came to be used even in contexts where the fact-stating side dropped out and only the other remained.[3] This explains why we react positively to the suggestion that 'It is true that the cat is on the mat' is an assertion, and negatively to the suggestion that the same applies to 'It is true that this is an excellent picture'. This is, however, a matter which a philosopher had better hand over to philologists.

A summary of 1.1. 'It is true that p' is about the content of an envisaged utterance. It is, among other things, used to endorse that content. The content in question need not, however, be that of a statement. Strawson gives no good arguments for his tenet that 'It is true that p' *never* is a statement; and we have seen reasons to believe that the fact that it is *not* a statement when p is (not a statement but) a value-judgment, etc., does not militate against our natural inclination to think that it *is* a statement when p is a statement.

On p. 120, 'Truth I' was summarized in six tenets. All except the first of them have now been considered. If my arguments are right, Strawson's points (ii), (v) and (vi) have broken down, whilst (iii) and (iv) seem true and important. Thus revised, Strawson's theory is no rival to the Correspondence Theory of Truth. They are not concerned with the same problem, and they are complementary to each other.

---

[3] The account seems to be borne out by etymological dictionaries, as far as 'sann' and 'wahr' are concerned. 'True' is, perhaps, a more dubious case, being tied up with 'good faith'.

1.2. *The traditional problems of truth and Strawson's problem*

There is a vast difference between Strawson's problem and those which most inquiries into truth have been concerned with. The speech acts of assertion and denial have to be distinguished from the speech acts of appraising an assertion or denial as true or false. The latter speech acts can be performed only when the former have been performed, but not the other way round. Traditionally, philosophers have tried to elucidate in what respects an assertion or a denial can fail 'to square with facts', not with how and in what respects an appraisal of such a speech act can go wrong. Ordinary language has no general labels for the excellences or shortcomings of a speech act's 'correspondence to facts'. The only labels there are for them are the words used in appraisals—i.e., 'is true' and 'is false'. Hence, too heavy a reliance on words may entice us to turn this classical problem of truth into the problem of describing the usage of 'is true'.

Strawson falls into the trap. To 'throw light on the actual use of the word "true" . . . [is to throw light] on the philosophical problem of truth' ('Truth I', p. 261); 'the problem of Truth . . . [is] the problem about our use of "true"' ('Truth II', p. 142). Thus he confuses the traditional philosophical problem of elucidating *the felicity-conditions of assertions and denials* (elucidating under what circumstances assertions and denials square with facts) with the problem of elucidating *the felicity-conditions of ASSESSMENTS of assertions and denials* (elucidating under what circumstances the assessments 'It is true that so-an-so' and 'It is false that so-and-so' are in order).

Of course Strawson sees that there are differences between what he is trying to do and what earlier philosophers have attempted. He sees that they have wanted to account for how certain statements are related to facts—a wish which he regards as fostered by an unreasonable mythology. He also sees that they have sometimes been concerned with an elucidation of the fact-stating type of discourse. But such an elucidation does not, he claims, solve the problem of truth; for that problem is about the use of 'true'. 'The surest route to the wrong answer is to confuse this problem with the question: What type of discourse is this?' ('Truth II', p. 143). So convinced is he that he has got hold of *the* problem of truth that when he in passing notices that there *is*

K

a distinction between studying the felicity-conditions of statements and the felicity-conditions of assessments of statements, he does so only in order to reproach Austin for being concerned with the former! (pp. 143–5.)

2. *The Correspondence Theory of Truth*

An excuse for Strawson's reproach is that in 1950 Austin sometimes writes as if he wanted to know how the word 'true' is used:
(1) 'What needs discussing . . . is the use, or certain uses, of the word "true"' (1950.85). On the same page he asks,
(2) 'What is it that we say is true or is false? Or, how does the phrase "is true" occur in English sentences?'
More serious than these wordings is (3) that the core of what he says about truth—his definition of what it is for a statement to be true—runs (1950.90):

A statement is said to be true when the historic state of affairs to which it is correlated by the demonstrative conventions (the one to which it 'refers') is of a type with which the sentence used in making it is correlated by the descriptive conventions.

Had the last-mentioned passage been intended as a description of the use of 'is true', Strawson would certainly be right in his objection ('Truth II', p. 143) that Austin was guilty of

the fundamental confusion . . . between:—
(*a*) the semantic conditions which must be satisfied for the statement that a certain statement is true to be itself true; and
(*b*) what is asserted when a certain statement is stated to be true.

A person who says 'It is true that *p*' is of course not stating that the semantic conditions Austin mentions are fulfilled; but Austin did not think he was. For I shall argue that Austin was not talking about the felicity-conditions of assessments of statements; *he was talking about the felicity-conditions of statements.*

What problems of truth was Austin concerned with? I shall now try to establish (i) that the quotations from Austin do not show that he was concerned with elucidations of the use of 'is true' in assessments, and (ii) that the bulk of what he has to say on truth is clearly concerned with relations between statements (not their assessments) and the world.

(i) Saying something true is very different from saying of something that it is true. We can do the former without doing the latter, and the other way round. Yet to say something true is to say something *true*; so there is a use of 'true' that is not tied to the *assessment* of statements. It may be this use which Austin in quotation (1) said needed discussion.

Even if this be so, is there a use of the phrase 'is true' (as distinct from the use of the word 'true' alone) which is not tied specifically to assessments? Austin thought there was. He held that although 'It is true that p' has a performatory aspect, it is at the same time a statement about a statement, reporting that the felicity-conditions of the statement that p are fulfilled (1950.101). He may have been wrong here, but it shows that the second quotation is not fatal to my thesis. If the felicity-conditions of 'It is true that p' do not differ in kind from the felicity-conditions of the statement that p, it is indifferent to investigations of truth whether we ask 'What is it to say something true?' or 'What is it to say of something that it is true?'

As to the third quotation, it must be noticed that Austin did not want to describe his own reactions only but also those of the majority of plain men. His task was to report under what conditions that majority would unanimously hold

(a) that the statement that p is true;
(b) that it would be correct to say of the statement that p that it is true.

In order to mark that it is about the customs of the majority and not merely about his own reactions, it would be natural for him to preface a report on (a) by 'It is agreed that the statement that p is true when and only when . . .' or, *as an alternative way of making the same point*, 'The statement that p is said to be true when and only when . . .'. The latter form of words is not a report on (b), which would rather be phrased 'The statement that p is true, is said (agreed upon) to be true when . . .'

(ii) I maintain, then, that the passages in Austin's text which seem to support Strawson's interpretation can be understood in another way. More important is, however, that the bulk of both the 1950 and the 1954 papers is concerned with the felicity-conditions of statements and not with the felicity-conditions of their assessments, whatever the most natural interpretation of the three quotations may be.

The question Austin poses in the central part of 'Truth', section 3, is 'When is a statement true?' and not 'When is a statement correctly said to be true?' The latter question may, but need not, be interpreted as the question what the felicity-conditions are of 'It is true that p'; the former question can hardly mean anything but 'What are the felicity-conditions of the statement that p?' One of Strawson's main objections to Austin's account of truth is that Austin asks '*When* do we use the word "true"? instead of the question: *How* do we use the word "true"?' ('Truth II', p. 145). Strawson takes this to show that Austin confuses the problem of truth with the problem of elucidating the fact-stating type of discourse. Surely it is more plausible that he *avoided* Strawson's confusion of elucidations of the felicity-conditions of statements with elucidations of the felicity-conditions of assessments of statements.

Having posed his question 'When is a statement true?' Austin lists some conditions which 'for present purposes' are important: that there are symbols; that there is something (the world) which they are used to communicate about; that the world exhibits similarities and dissimilarities which the communicating persons can observe; and that there are two kinds of conventions, descriptive ones and classificatory ones, which in different ways relate the symbols to the world. We shall soon have to consider them. Here I mention them just to point out that Austin does not make more than a very brief hint (1950.100 on 'is true' and 'is probable') at what he in *Words* was to call illocutionary devices, i.e. symbols used in order to warn the audience as to how an utterance is to be taken—as a confident statement, a tentative opinion, a guess, a warning, a confirmation, etc. Although the doctrine of illocutionary devices remained implicit until *Words*, it was adumbrated already in 1946. (Cf Ch. 5:9.) Performatory phrases are paradigms of illocutionary devices. In 1950 he mentions both that 'it is true' has a performatory aspect and that it is used to signal how an utterance is to be taken; but he says it in passing. That is remarkable—if he really intended to discuss the felicity-conditions of *assessments* of statements.

When Austin gives his version of the Correspondence Theory in section 3 of 'Truth', his only examples are of the sort 'The cat is on the mat' and 'I'm feeling sick', not 'It is true that the cat is on the mat' and 'It's true that I'm feeling sick'. When he discusses the felicity-conditions of assessments of statements (in sect. 4), he is concerned with the statement-making aspect only; and he tries to explain it by the model outlined for the felicity-conditions of statements. He declares that the performatory aspect is irrelevant to his purpose. This warrants us to hold that his main problem is the traditional one: What are the general felicity-conditions for statements? Further, his sections 5 and 6 seem trivial if they only discuss whether we say of certain utterances that they are true or false; but if they are concerned with the question whether there are any basic felicity-conditions that all statements have in common, the issue is no longer merely about the use of words. His language allows both interpretations, and then the latter and more exciting one is to be preferred. The choice is not arbitrary. As we shall see it gives a natural and easy transition to the doctrine of statements propounded in *Words*.

This point settled, I turn to his account of the felicity-conditions of statements.

2.0. *Austin's 1950 account of the felicity-conditions of statements*

The core of Austin's theory of truth is that a statement is true if, and only if, the sentence employed in the act of stating describes a state of affairs of the same type as that which the demonstratives used in the act refer to. That the unit of language describes a state of affairs of the same type as that to which the demonstratives refer means that the state of affairs referred to is sufficiently like the standard state of affairs described in the sentence. 'Thus, for a statement to be true one state of affairs must be *like* certain others, which is a natural relation, but also *sufficiently* like to merit the same "description", which is no longer a purely natural relation. . . . That things are *similar*, or even "exactly" similar, I may literally see, but that they are the *same* I cannot literally see—in calling them the same colour a convention is involved additional to the conventional choice of name to be given to the colour which they are said to be.' (1950.90n.)

He stresses that he is concerned with a *model*. Things are more complex in reality. Some 'sentences contain words or verbal devices to serve both descriptive and demonstrative purposes (not to mention other purposes), often both at once. . . . [Many] demonstrative conventions are non-verbal (pointing, &c.), and using these we can make a statement in a single word which is not a "sentence". Thus, "languages" like that of (traffic, &c.) *signs* use quite distinct media for their descriptive and demonstrative elements (the sign on the post, the site of the post).' (1950.90.)

In every Correspondence Theory of Truth there are three elements that deserve consideration: (*a*) the message that is true or false, (*b*) the relation between the message and the world, and (*c*) the world. Let us take these points in order.

Statements. Let us glance at what statements Austin was concerned with in his discussion of truth.

In his list of conditions for 'communication of the sort that we achieve by language', he says that there 'must . . . be something other than the words, which the words are to be used to communicate about: this may be called the "world"' (1950.89). Together with his demand that there must be demonstrative conventions correlating words and world, the quotation shows that he was thinking only of empirical statements of fact, not e.g. of analytic statements or of statements occurring in fiction. Although he thought of analytic statements as at least rhemes and not phemes as late as in *Words*.97, they are ruled out in his discussion of truth. We are commonly told that analytic statements are true in virtue of the meaning of the words they contain. Meaning is here, I suppose, contrasted with reference: such statements as 'This exists' or 'I exist' or 'I am here now', where the references are essential, are not normally said to be analytic, although it is often conceded that they are trivially true whenever they are seriously used. Since reference is not important for analytic statements, they are not among the statements Austin discussed. Nor did he include the statements of fiction, for they are not intended to be about anything in the world.

Further, he seems to think that his investigations can be stretched to a good many types of statements which do not resemble his standard example by exhibiting the time-hallowed subject/predicate form. Existential, general, and possibly also hypothetical statements, 'raise problems rather of meaning than of truth' (1950.91n).

Finally, the statements he is concerned with are, or are treated as, unguarded—they contain no illocutionary device; or if they do, its illocutionary force is disregarded. Hence, such statements as e.g., 'It is probable that *p*' are ruled out. (In view of his later findings in 'Ifs and cans', the same ought to hold good of the hypotheticals whose 'if'-clause indicates doubt.)

The relation of correspondence. Austin is afraid that his model may be taken to suggest that to every true statement there corresponds one and only one fact which it, if true, refers to. He is anxious to dissociate himself from the idea, since he holds that there is no need for a true statement to be couched in a sentence mirroring features in the world or reproducing the structure of reality—the correlations between the words and the world are purely conventional. 'We are absolutely free to appoint *any* symbol to describe *any* type of situation, so far as merely being true goes' (1950.92). A rudimentary language may have a single word for a highly complex type of situation; but although the speaker of a more developed language can make statements which are more precise, accurate, etc., they are not 'any more capable of being true or capable of being any more true' than the statements in the more primitive language. In all languages truth remains a matter of 'the words used being the ones *conventionally appointed* for situations of the type to which that referred to belongs'. (1950.93f.)

That truth is connected with conventions is seen by the fact that other things which are also about the world but in which conventions do not enter in the same degree are neither true nor false:

A picture, a copy, a replica, a photograph—these are *never* true in so far as they are reproductions, produced by natural or mechanical means: a reproduction can be accurate or lifelike (true *to* the original), as a gramophone recording or a transcription may be, but not true (*of*) as a record of proceedings can be. In the same way a (natural) sign *of* something can be infallible or unreliable but only an (artificial) sign *for* something can be right or wrong. [1950.94.]

Austin claims that a study of the many intermediate cases between a true account and a faithful picture brings home that truth depends on conventions and perhaps also on what conventions it depends. That is my interpretation of the passage in 1950.94 where he claims that maps

may be called pictures, yet they are highly conventionalized pictures.

If a map can be clear or accurate or misleading, like a statement, why can it not be true or exaggerated? How do the 'symbols' used in map-making differ from those used in statement-making? On the other hand, if an air-mosaic is not a map, why is it not? And when does a map become a diagram?

The non-linguistic correlate. When a statement is true, it corresponds to something in the world which, by turns, Austin calls facts, situations, and states of affairs. They make a statement true or false and are *toto mundo* distinct from it. What exactly they are remains vague in the paper; but 'Unfair to facts' makes it clear that he thinks of them as *states* or *events*. What makes it true that the cat is on the mat is a certain spatio-temporal volume involving cat and mat; and what fits the statement that Charles I was executed is the execution of Charles I.

In 1950 Austin is anxious to stress that facts do not occur ready-labelled—it is we who single them out from among the heterogeneous configurations of things in the world. If we believe that every true statement corresponds to one and only one fact, we are led to 'populate the world with linguistic *Doppelgänger* (and grossly over-populate it—every nugget of "positive" fact overlaid by a massive concentration of "negative" facts, every tiny detailed fact larded with generous general facts, and so on)' (1950.91). He thought that his theory about the purely conventional character of the correspondence relation would help him to avoid the overpopulation; and it is fairly easy to see, on the lines suggested in 1953.196, how he would deal with a detailed fact including general facts. But how would he treat 'negative' facts? Is there anything that the true statement 'The cat is not on the mat' corresponds to? And if so, what is it?

His account of truth caters also for falsehood. A false statement does not correspond but *miscorrespond* to a fact, the demonstrative conventions pinning down the fact in question (1950.97n). But as Austin himself stresses, this is another question than 'What does a true negative statement correspond to?' It is only too common, he complains, that negative statements are explained as second-order affirmations to the effect that a certain first-order affirmation is false, and then to account for assertions that a statement is false by saying that they assert its negation. He rejects (p. 96f) attempts to explain negation by means of falsity:

Affirmation and negation are exactly on a level, in this sense, that no language can exist which does not contain conventions for both and that both refer to the world equally directly, not to statements about the world: whereas a language can quite well exist without any device to do the work of 'true' and 'false'.

Unfortunately he leaves the matter there. It remains unclear what a 'negative' fact is. Is it what corresponds to a true statement containing such words, prefixes and suffixes as 'not', 'un-', and '-less'? Perhaps he thought so. 'Negative' is certainly tied up with 'negation'; and in 1953.198 he claims that negation is something 'on the *language* side rather than on the side of the world'. His remark has to be taken with a grain of salt, since there may be important differences between 'not' in ordinary language and as occurring in the skeleton-language of 'How to talk'. It is also possible he held that a fact (state of affairs, situation) is something that cannot sensibly be classified as 'negative' or 'positive' *tout court*. The very same fact that guarantees the truth of '1227 is a square' also guarantees the truth of '1227 is not a circle'—the very same fact corresponds to both these utterances. Our interests dictate whether the fact is to be dressed up in a positive or in a negative wording. Such a view would cater for Ayer's[4] and Strawson's[5] doctrines of negation; and it also seems commonsensical.

That a fact is neither positive nor negative *tout court* does not entail that there is no sense in speaking of facts as positive or negative in certain respects. It seems to me that Austin's tenet of adapter-words demands that there are *semantically* negative facts which are stated in positive words; we don't know what 'This is real whisky' (if true) corresponds to, until we know exactly what shortcomings of the drink the speaker has excluded. And Ivar Segelberg holds that there are what we may call *epistemologically* negative facts which can be stated in positive words. The fact that a is exactly like b is an example, since we ascertain it by searching for dissimilarities and failing to find them.

Austin's criticism of Strawson's account of truth. The theory that for a statement to be true, there must be something in the world

---

[4] A. J. Ayer, 'Negation'. *Philosophical Essays.*
[5] P. F. Strawson, *Introduction to Logical Theory*, pp. 5–9.

that it, by convention, corresponds to enables Austin to give a different account from Strawson's of two problems.

First, Strawson's solution of the semantical paradoxes of truth is unnecessary. They can be solved thus: 'It takes two to make a truth. Hence (obviously) there can be no criterion of truth in the sense of some feature detectable in the statement itself which will reveal whether it is true or false. Hence, too, a statement cannot without absurdity refer to itself.' (1950.92n.)

Secondly, Strawson's account of the problem of truth as the use of 'is true' misses the point that the assessment 'It is true that p' is itself a statement which is not in order unless its demonstrative conventions tie it to a state of affairs with which the sentence used in making it is correlated by its descriptive conventions (1950.95). Exactly how Austin saw the relation is not clear to me; but as I read 1950.95, he suggests that 'It is true that p' is in order only if p is in order. This relation holds although 'It is true that p' does not *include* the statement that p in the sense in which 'The statement that q includes the statement that r' is taken to mean that someone who states that q, by that very fact states that r.

Now it may be said (i) that even if 'It is true that p' is in order only when the statement that p is in order, the converse also holds; and (ii) that if this is so, the two statements amount to the same. Austin seems to accept (i), though with certain reservations; but he objects to (ii). He is not sure whether it is in general a sound view that two statements must mean the same if they always have the same truth-value; 'but even if it is, why should it not break down in the case of so obviously "peculiar" a phrase as "is true"? Mistakes in philosophy notoriously arise through thinking that what holds of "ordinary" words like "red" or "growls" must also hold of extraordinary words like "real" or "exists". But that "true" is just such another extraordinary word is obvious.' (1950.95f.)

I think, however, that also (i) can profitably be challenged. For even if 'It is true that p' is in order only when the statement that p is in order (a view which I have called into question in 1.12), does the converse really hold? Of course it does in a language where we assess statements and do so in words; but as Austin himself remarked (1950.97), we may have had a language in which only assertions and denials were made and no assessments of them. So the felicity of the statement that p, is always a prerequisite for the felicity of the statement that it is true that p; but the converse holds only if there is an institution of linguistic assessments of statements. This is an important qualification of the view that the statement that p and the statement that it is true that p are *always* true together and false together.

These points show that Strawson's account of the felicity-conditions of 'It is true that p' *may* be incomplete. It is *possible* that correspondence to reality is important even for assessments. But Austin has not proved that it *is* important. He has not even shown that 'It is true that p' is a statement; he has simply assumed it is. Yet his version of the Correspondence Theory of Truth and the objections against Strawson which he draws from it are commonsensical; and the burden of proof is on the man who deviates from common sense.

2.1. Strawson's objections

In 'Truth II' Strawson takes up the burden. His contention is that the Correspondence Theory 'requires, not purification, but elimination' (p. 129). If it can be eliminated, then those of Austin's objections that are based on it will of course fail.

Strawson concedes that Austin's semantic conditions have to be satisfied if a statement can correctly be said to be true; but he thinks they are misleadingly put. When rendered in a more satisfactory form, they lend no support to the Correspondence Theory. On the contrary, they show that it is profoundly wrong. It assimilates stating to referring. Since what we refer to is typically things, persons and events, this involves treating facts, states of affairs and situations as kinds of quasi-things. They alone are plausible non-linguistic correlates of a true statement. But (*a*) they are not kinds of things at all; (*b*) nor are they anything in the world; (*c*) they are analytical accusatives to the notion of a true statement. Hence the demand that there is something in the world which makes a statement true 'is logically absurd: a logically fundamental type-mistake' (p. 134).

2.11. Facts as quasi-objects

Strawson's argument against facts as a kind of thing seems to go like this:

If statements are to be about something in the world, they have to involve referring. What we refer to is paradigmatically things and persons. They are what statements are about. If we say that statements are about or involve picking out facts, we seem to imply that facts are a kind of (perhaps complex) thing. It is, however, obvious that our recognition of the fact that the cat has mange does not involve that we accept the existence of two types of entities, the cat and its mangy condition. We have recognized a single entity, the cat, with a certain characteristic, viz. manginess. A fact

> is not an object; not even . . . a complex object consisting of one or more particular elements (constituents, parts) and a universal element (constituent, part). I can (perhaps) hand you, or draw a circle round, or time with a stop-watch the things or incidents that are referred to when a statement is made. Statements are about such objects; but they state facts.

So facts are not a kind of thing, and stating a fact is not referring to an entity.

He is nevertheless convinced that Austin treats facts as things; on p. 139 he insists that the

> whole charm of talking of situations, states of affairs or facts as included in, or parts of, the world, consists in thinking of them as things, or groups of things . . . Mr. Austin does not withstand it.

It cannot be doubted that in Austin's opinion a statement is not, as Strawson maintains, about things and persons. Things and persons are what the referring conventions of the sentence usually single out; but what the statement is about is some happening to, state of, or event involving things and persons. This complex event or state is the non-linguistic relatum of the statement.

This is how Austin thinks of the non-linguistic relatum, but he sometimes speaks as if 'fact', 'state of affairs' and 'situation' do not apply to any entity at all. It is, in his opinion, impossible to step from 'The statement that S is about (involves picking out) a fact' to 'The statement that S is about (involves picking out) the fact that F'; he maintains that although the premiss makes sense, the conclusion does not. We cannot speak of the fact that F; and when we say

'The fact ⎫
'The situation ⎬ is that the cat has mange',
'The state of affairs ⎭

the prefatory phrases do not name an entity of any kind, since they are not referring (nor classificatory) devices.

My interpretation is founded on what he says about the expression 'the fact that S'. The context makes it plausible that he thinks that 'the situation that S' and 'the state of affairs that S' do the same duty. He remarks (1954.107) that 'fact' resembles 'person' in the respect that it is not used unless we think that what is thus characterized actually exists or has existed ('there is oxymoron in . . . imaginary "facts" or "imaginary persons"—we prefer imaginary characters'). Then he suggests (pp. 113–14) that 'the fact that' functions like the apposition usage. Asking whether 'the fact that S' is a name or a description is like asking whether 'the person Cicero' is a name or a person. Both 'the fact that S' and 'the person Cicero' are designed for speaking compendiously about words and world together. To ask whether 'the person Cicero' is a name is absurd, since the phrase means 'a certain person, viz. the one designated by the word "Cicero"'; to ask whether 'the fact that S' is a name or a description is absurd, since 'the expression "The fact that S" *means* "a certain fact [or actual occurrence, &c.], viz. that correctly described [or reported, &c.] by saying now 'S' [or at other times 'S' with a change of tense]"' (Austin's square brackets.) Saying 'The mangy condition of the cat is the fact that the cat has mange' is like saying 'Cicero is the person Cicero'. These expressions 'are not designed for combination in this manner', Austin says.

He immediately adds 'But why?', without vouchsafing an answer. His whole discussion of the point is so rugged and disconnected that I suspect he had no intention to print his jottings. ('Unfair to facts' was published posthumously.) The context suggests, however, that he felt tempted to answer his own question by saying something like this: The expressions 'Cicero' and 'the mangy condition of the cat' require for their correct use a certain correlation between the words and the world, but they do not say that the requirement is fulfilled. The phrases 'the person Cicero' and 'the fact that the cat has mange' are, however, designed to declare that the requirement is fulfilled.

If he held that 'the fact that S' has this function, he presumably thought that 'The fact is that S' is employed to report that the statement that S is related to the world in a way satisfying certain adequacy-conditions. (This is of course compatible with the point that 'the fact is . . .' sometimes also indicates that what follows is an unpleasant truth.) The same holds for the phrases containing 'situation' and 'state of affairs'. If these three phrases are used to convey that statement and world are related in a certain manner, it seems the merest common sense that they do not themselves signify any item in the world.

All this may be conceded. We have, however, seen that to say that the relevant adequacy-conditions of a statement are fulfilled is to say that 'the historic state of affairs to which it is correlated by the demonstrative conventions . . . is of a type with which the sentence used in making it is correlated by the descriptive conventions' (1950.90). 'Historic state of affairs' is here to mean the same as 'fact', and in 'Unfair to facts' Austin is very anxious to establish that facts are actual events or states of affairs. It is difficult to avoid the conclusion that a fact, a state of affairs and a situation in his opinion are events or states, involving persons and things; and thus that a fact, etc., is a complex entity.

2.12. *The status of facts*

According to Strawson (p. 135), we cannot reconcile the Correspondence Theory with the view that the only referents of a statement are the things, persons or events picked out by its demonstrative conventions:

> What 'makes the statement' that the cat has mange 'true', is not the cat, but the *condition* of the cat, i.e., the fact that the cat has mange. The only plausible candidate for the position of what (in the world) makes the statement true is the fact it states; but the fact it states is not something in the world.

To Austin, this is a strange argument. The true statement 'The cat has mange' states a fact. What it corresponds to is not the cat but the mangy condition of the cat. Nevertheless that condition is 'something in the world'. Hence, a fact is 'something in the world'. (1954.104.)

Etymology and facts. Austin quotes etymology in support of his contention that facts are 'something in the world' (1954.112):

> For the first 200 years of its use (sixteenth and seventeenth centuries) it [sc. the word 'fact'] meant (cf. 'feat') a deed or action, either the thing done or the doing of the thing, and more especially a criminal action; during the eighteenth century this use gradually died out in favour of a more extended meaning which began to appear already in the seventeenth century: a fact is now *something that has really occurred* (even classical Latin extended *factum* to mean 'event' or 'occurrence') or something that is actually the case (a further extension to the meaning of '*factum*' found in scholastic Latin). *Hence* and thereafter it came to mean something *known* to have really occurred, and *hence* (according to the Dictionary) a particular *truth* known by observation or authentic testimony, by contrast with what is merely inferred or a conjecture or a fiction.
>
> From this brief history, I take it as obvious that: (i) 'Fact' was in origin a name for 'something in the world', if we may take it that a past action or past actual event or occurrence is 'something in the world', and there is no reason whatever to doubt that it often still is so. (ii) Any connexion between 'fact' and 'knowledge', and still more between 'fact' and 'truth' (in particular the use of 'a fact' as equivalent to 'a truth'), is a derivative and comparatively late connexion.

I think, however, that the pieces of etymology he has quoted are not sufficient to warrant his conclusions, for two reasons:

(*a*) Even if 'fact' historically was used in the way Austin reports, its current use may be different. The dictionary even indicates that this is so, when it says that 'fact' now can mean 'a particular *truth* known by observation or authentic testimony'. Is it in this new sense 'something in the world'? A truth is hardly 'in the world' in the way a deed or action is. Austin dismisses the new employment as a derivative; but it can at least be argued that it is an indication that the older uses themselves are in a state of change.[6]

(*b*) It cannot, however, be doubted that 'fact' is still used for past actual events. A description of a skidding car up to the time it struck the tree may end with the words, 'And then the accident was a fact'. But this use is *not the one relevant to the Correspondence Theory*. The fact which is to do duty as the non-linguistic correlate has to be roughly the same as a situation or

---

[6] J. M. Shorter, 'Facts, Logical Atomism and Reducibility'. *AJP* 40 (1962), pp. 284–6.

state of affairs (cf e.g. the definition of truth in 1950:90, and 1954.102f); but it will not do to say 'The accident was a state of affairs' or 'The accident was a situation'. This is, perhaps, what worries White when he objects to Austin that 'though we might call the collapse of the Germans a (terrible, lucky, disastrous, fateful) event, I doubt that we would call it a fact (though it is a fact that they did collapse) and therefore that an event can be a fact'.[7] He is wrong in calling in question that we say, e.g., 'In May, 1945, the collapse of the Third Reich was a fact'; but he has the sound feeling that there is a difference between events and the facts required by the Correspondence Theory.

A digression: the relatum of the Correspondence Theory. In *Studier över medvetandet och jagidén*, Ivar Segelberg tries to distinguish a fact from an event. A rectangle consisting of two squares in a certain relation R to each other is, he says (pp. 14–15), something different from the fact or state of affairs (*sakförhållande*) that R holds between the squares. The fact or state of affairs is no rectangle. In an analogous way, the execution of Charles I is different from the fact or state of affairs that Charles I was executed: the former is a spatio-temporal volume; the latter is not. A fact (e.g. the fact that Charles I was executed) is, according to Segelberg, something constituted by certain relations obtaining between certain components of the spatio-temporal volume (executioner, axe, delinquent).

It seems clear that the fact that Charles I was executed cannot be identified with the execution of Charles I; the fact is not the event. Many different facts are connected with the same event. That the executioner made a certain movement is a fact other than that Charles I died, but both of them are linked to the execution of Charles I. But is not the execution constituted by, among other things, certain characteristic interrelations between the executioner and the king? And do not these relations obtain for some time? I.e., can facts be distinguished from events by Segelberg's criteria that the former but not the latter are constituted by certain relations obtaining between certain components of a complex, whereas the latter but not the former are spatio-temporal volumes?

[7] Alan R. White, Review of *Philosophical Papers*. *Philosophical Books* 3 (1962), p.l.

To specify the difference between an event and Segelberg's fact is a difficult task which cannot be undertaken here. It is, however, plain that there *is* a difference; and further that it is the fact, not the event, that conforms to our common sense notion of the non-linguistic correlate of true statements. What makes it true that the rectangle consists of two squares is, according to common sense, not the two squares but that they are interrelated in a certain way; and what corresponds to the true statement that Charles I was executed is not the execution of Charles I but the fact that Charles I was executed. Austin identified the fact that Charles I was executed with the execution of Charles I. If Segelberg's distinction is sound, this cannot be correct.*

Nevertheless the connexion between the execution of Charles I and the fact that the king was executed is very intimate: it is a fact that he was executed if, and only if, the execution took place. It is uncontroversial that a world in which the king was beheaded is different from a world in which he was let alone. What (perhaps) *is* controversial is whether the relevant sense of the word 'fact' can be analysed in a way which makes a fact a spatio-temporal volume (a volume which, however, must be different from that of an event). If we can (which seems unlikely), a fact is 'something in the world' in roughly the same way as whispers, headaches, chairs and persons are 'something in the world'. If we cannot, there still remains a problem which, however, is not factual. It is this: Given that the fact that Charles I was executed is something other than his execution and given that it is a fact that he was executed if, and only if, his execution took place, *are we to say* that a fact, bearing this intimate relation to something which no doubt is 'something in the world', also qualifies as 'something in the world'? Studying the relations between facts and events, we see what tempts us to say a fact is 'something in the world' and what tempts us to say it is not; and then the problem dissolves. What remains is to make a *stipulation* as to how to talk about facts.

'*The statement that S corresponds to the fact that S.*' We normally say 'The statement that S corresponds to the facts' or 'fits the facts'; we do not say—as I did in the digression above—that the

---

*[The point I was trying to make has been made clear by Zeno Vendler in his paper 'Facts and Events', reprinted in his book *Linguistics in Philosophy* (Ithaca, New York, 1967).]

statement that S corresponds to the fact that S or fits the fact that S. According to Austin (1954.108), the latter phrases are both un-English and nonsensical:

> surely it is not sense either to ask whether the statement that S fits the fact that S or to state that it either does or does not. And I may add that it seems to me . . . equally nonsense to ask whether the statement that S fits or corresponds to the fact that F, where 'F' is *different* from 'S' not identical with it (though . . . it is *not* nonsense to ask something that sounds rather similar to this, viz. whether the statement that S *squares with* or '*does justice to*' the fact that F ('F' # 'S').

Austin does not explain why it is nonsense to ask whether the statement that S fits or corresponds to the fact that S; and the following suggestions are mere guesses on my part:

The assertion 'The statement that it is raining does not fit or correspond to the fact that it is raining' seems not false but nonsensical—unless we switch over from the un-English 'fact'-construction to the English one: 'The statement that it is raining does not fit or correspond to the facts (*i.e., is not true*)'. When a statement does not make sense, the same holds for its negation. Hence the assertion 'The statement that it is raining fits (corresponds to) the fact that it is raining' is also nonsense.

Is it really nonsense to say 'The statement that it is raining does not fit or correspond to the fact that it is raining'?—It is, I think, nonsensical and not merely false to say *in English* '"Red" does not in English signify the colour red' (though the statement would be merely false if uttered in other languages as a piece of information about English). The words 'the colour red' require for their intelligibility a rule of English, tying 'red' to a certain colour; but the utterance as a whole rejects that requirement. Hence it is impossible to say intelligibly *in English* '"Red" does not in English signify the colour red'. Attempts to express partly non-verbal rules of language in sentences which for their intelligibility presuppose these very rules must end in disaster—that is, I think, the not very mysterious cash-value of Wittgenstein's dictum that there are things we can show but not say.

'A gulf is fixed between this case and the one discussed by Strawson and Austin. An utterance is not tied to a fact in the way an ostensively defined word is tied to the characteristic it labels. Every occurrence of the word is tied to the property, but not every occurrence of an utterance is tied to the fact.'—Your objection confuses a statement with a sentence. A sentence is tied only to a *type* of facts and can in different occurrences be tied to different facts; but a statement is by its referring conventions tied to a certain fact which every occurrence of the same statement must be tied to. (This may be overlooked if we consider only utterances with a *formal* subject, such as 'It is raining'.) Then the un-English utterance 'The statement that the cat has mange fits or corresponds to the fact that the cat has mange' is rather like the attempt to express an inexpressible (because partly non-verbal) semantical rule such as '"Red" signifies in English the colour red', uttered in English. To say that the statement that the cat has mange does *not* fit or correspond to the fact that the cat has mange involves a rejection of the combination of referring and classificatory rules that alone make your utterance intelligible; just as saying (in English) that 'red' is not in English tied to the colour red involves rejecting a requirement for the intelligibility of the utterance. Then the negations of these negations—*i.e.*, the positive wordings we started from—are equally nonsensical.

It is possible that this argument demonstrates that it is nonsense either to ask whether the statement that S fits or corresponds to the fact that S or to state that it either does or does not. It is nonsense, since the so-called statement is an attempt to *say* the non-verbal parts or a semantical rule. Although the rule cannot be stated, it can be shown. The so-called statement is therefore nonsensical in another and less vicious way than e.g. 'Immortality died yesterday'—which cannot be made intelligible by even drastic reformulations. It seems to me that we know what we mean when we say 'The statement that S corresponds to the fact that S', even if our statement necessarily fails to say what can only be shown.

2.13. *Facts as true statements*

Strawson tries to establish that a fact is nothing but a true statement. There are in 'Truth II' two connected arguments to that effect: Facts are what statements, when true, state; and facts and statements are made for each other.

'Facts are what statements, when true, state' 'True statement' and 'fact' are, according to Strawson, related roughly like 'to eat' and 'food'. The dogma can be discerned in the following passage (p. 136):

'Fact', like 'true', 'states' and 'statement' is wedded to 'that'-clauses; and there is nothing unholy about this union. Facts are known, stated, learnt, forgotten, overlooked, commented on, communicated or noticed. (Each of these verbs may be followed by a 'that'-clause or a 'the fact that'-clause.) Facts are what statements (when true) state; they are not what statements are about. They are not, like things or happenings on the face of the globe, witnessed or heard or seen, broken or overturned, interrupted or prolonged, kicked, destroyed, mended or noisy.

(i) Consider first the part that 'fact' is wedded to 'that'-clauses. Austin gives three counter-arguments to the thesis:

(a) The first is that according to the dictionary, 'fact' meant 'deed' and 'action' and then came to signify something that has actually occurred. The phrase 'fact that' is a comparatively recent linguistic device, says Austin (1954.111), introduced because of the already existing meaning of 'fact'. Its job is to avoid 'gerundial constructions as the subjects of sentences or as the domains of prepositions: i.e. in order not to say "I was unaware of the kitchen's being draughty" or "the kitchen's being draughty annoyed him"'. There is no reason to believe that 'fact' is used differently now than in the eighteenth century: 'When we say "The mangy condition of the cat is a fact" we mean it is an actual state of affairs; when we say "What are the facts?" we mean "what is the actual state of affairs?", "what has actually occurred?" or the like. This is the meaning, too, in such common expressions as "an *accomplished* fact" or "He has no personal experience of the facts he reports".'

This argument is open to the two objections already mentioned. First, the usage of a word may change and in the case of 'fact' seems to be changing: the phrase 'a fact' can now sometimes mean 'a truth', which, in turn, is closely connected with 'a true statement'. Secondly, the event-sense of 'fact' Austin is concerned with is irrelevant to the Correspondence Theory.

(b) Austin's second criticism is that there is no grammatical evidence of the alleged wedding between 'fact' and 'that'-clauses. Consider a sentence containing one of the verbs which according to Strawson take 'fact' as their object—'know', 'state', 'learn', 'forget', 'comment on', 'communicate', 'notice'. Then Austin complains that Strawson does not make it clear whether we *always* or only *sometimes* can replace the object with a 'that'-clause or a 'the fact that'-clause; whether 'fact' is to occur in singular or plural, with the definite or the indefinite article or neither; and whether the substitution alters the meaning of the original sentence or not. He thinks that Strawson holds that for any of the verbs listed 'the following three forms of sentence are equally good English and somehow interchangeable.

(a) *Fact-form.*　　　　　He verbed a/the fact/facts.
(b) *That-form.*　　　　　He verbed that S.
(c) *The-fact-that-form.*　He verbed the fact that S.'

Austin now maintains that not all the verbs occur in all three forms, and that there are important differences among those that do. With 'forget', (a) entails (b) and conversely; but 'He stated that S' does not entail 'He stated a fact'. It is good sense to say 'What he stated was a fact' or 'In stating that S he stated a fact'. It is not good sense to say 'What he forgot or knew was a fact' or 'In forgetting that S he forgot a fact'—'know' and 'forget' but not 'state' are achievement-words. (1954.114–16.)

Austin's point is, I think, that 'What he knew was a fact' and 'In knowing that S he knew a fact' are pleonasms, whereas 'What he stated was a fact' and 'In stating that S he stated a fact' are not. This is a slip. It is true that 'He knew that p' entails that p is true, whilst 'He stated that p' does not. But 'forget' is not on a par with 'know' in this respect. Having been told by an ignorant person that the battle of Hastings was fought in 1077, I may forget it.* Hence, 'He forgot that p' does not entail that p is true, and hence 'What he forgot was a fact' and 'In forgetting that S he forgot a fact' are *not* pleonasms. Nor do I see that these statements fail to make good sense in any other way.—But the slip does not matter, since Austin only wants to show that not all Strawson's verbs behave uniformly.

(c) In order to support the thesis that 'fact' is connected with 'that'-clauses, Strawson mentions verbs which in his opinion are connected not with facts but with things in the world—'witness',

*[The slip may be mine. Do I forget that the battle of Hastings was fought in 1077 or that *I was told that* the battle of Hastings was fought in 1077?]

'hear', 'see', 'break', 'overturn'.—If they really are connected with things in the world, rejoins Austin (1954.116), facts are something in the world; for we can witness, observe and have personal acquaintance with facts.

This reply will not do. I can, of course, witness how a marriage becomes a fact; but this is again the event sense of 'fact'. It is at least not evident that someone could have witnessed or observed the fact that Charles I was executed, as distinct from the execution of Charles I.

(ii) So much for the first part of Strawson's objection—the part that 'fact' is connected with 'that'-clauses. I now turn to the kernel of his argument: 'Facts are what statements (when true) state'. Austin remarks that this may mean no more than 'True statements state facts' but that Strawson presumably intends it as a definition of 'fact', 'reducing "facts" to an accusative so deeply and hopelessly internal that their status as "entities" is hopelessly compromised' (1954.117).[8]

(*a*) It is, says Austin, inconsistent of Strawson to allow that '"being a map of" or "being a photograph of" *are* relations, of which the non-photographic, non-cartographical, relata are, say, personal or geographical *entities*' (pp. 139-40) and yet to deny that there is a correspondence between statements and facts. Austin finds it illogical, since 'it is quite possible to say of a map that it does not correspond with the facts (e.g. a situation-map) and of a statement that it does not correspond with the topography'. It will not do to say that topography is what maps map, not what they are about; and if 'corresponds' means a relation in the case of maps, why should it not do so even in the case of statements? (1954.107-8.)

(*b*) Austin compares 'Facts are what statements, when true, state' to other statements with the same grammatical form: 'Births are what birth-certificates, when accurate, certify', 'Persons are what surnames, when borne, are the surnames of', 'Women are what men, when they marry, marry', 'Wives are what men, when they marry, marry', 'Events are what narratives, when true, narrate'. 'Which, if any of these, is Strawson's sentence to be taken to resemble?', he asks (1954.118). If it is the

[8] In *Filosofiske essays*, J. Hartnack makes the definition thesis Strawson's main objection to the Correspondence Theory of Truth. Hartnack seems to regard the argument as quite convincing.

case exemplified by 'Events are what narratives, when true, narrate', it does not make sense to go on, 'They are not what narratives are about'. Generally,

whatever the analyticity or internal accusatives or what not involved in any of these pronouncements, none of them have the slightest tendency to convince us that births, persons, or events, women (or even wives) . . . are *not* 'things or happenings on the surface of the globe'.

Why then worry about 'facts'?

The question is not quite rhetorical, since he argues that 'What statements state' can be taken in several ways. In this respect 'state' represents a large group of words used in talking about communication, he says; and he illustrates its different uses by means of the analogous verb 'to signal' (pp. 119–22):

Let us take a simple model situation in which all we are concerned to do is to signal targets as they bob up in an aperture. The targets are of various different recognizable types and there is an appointed signal (say a flag of a special colour) for each different type of target. Very well then—the targets keep on bobbing up, and we keep on wagging flags—the convention of reference being the simple one . . . that each signal refers to the contemporary occupant of the aperture.

'What we signal' can then be used in five ways.

The two first of them are typically couched in the form 'what we (=anyone) signals is always':

(1) What we signal is always a target.
    (What we state is always a fact.)
(2) What we signal is always a signal.
    (What we state is always a statement.)

There is no conflict between these pronouncements; nor is it either necessary or legitimate, in order to 'reconcile' them, to conclude that 'targets are signals': they are *not*, nor are facts statements, by the same token!

When 'always' and 'we' are not pedagogic generalizations, the 'what . . . signal (state)'-phrase is used differently:

(3) What we signal is sometimes, but not always, a target.
    'What we state is sometimes, but not always, a fact.)
(4) What we signal is sometimes, but not always (a) correct (signal).
    (What we state is sometimes, but not always, (a) true (statement).

The uses of 'what we signal' in (3) and (4) are of course *connected*, but they are *not* identical. If they were *identical* we should get the absurd conclusion that
  A target is (a) correct (signal)
and the conclusion, equally absurd I think, that
  A fact is a true statement (a truth).
The actual connexion between (3) and (4) is not so simple, though simple enough: If, and only if, and because what we signal (3) is a target, then what we signal (4) is correct; and derivatively, if, and only if, but not because what we signal (4) is correct, then what we signal (3) is a target.

In (1) and (3) we signal *targets*, in (2) and (4) *signals*.

And just as, in the signalling case, there is not the slightest temptation to say
  'Targets are not things in the world'
  'Targets are (correct) signals'
so there should be no temptation to say
  'Facts are not things-in-the-world'
  'Facts are true statements'.

In yet another use, illustrated by
(5) What we signal is now red, now green, now purple
   (What we state is now that S, now that T, now that U),
' "what we signal" is neither *always* x, as in (1) and (2), nor always either *x* or not *x*, as in (3) and (4).'

'Facts are what true statements state' is then, according to Austin, like 'Targets are what correct signals signal', and does not prove that facts are not 'something in the world'. If 'fact' and 'true statement' are definable in terms of each other, it is the former that is basic. Although the truth of (1) 'He stated a fact' and (2) 'He stated that S' allows us to infer 'What he stated was a fact' and 'What he stated was that S', (1) and (2) do not licence an inference to 'A fact is that S or that T'—for 'What he stated' does not mean the same in the two premisses.

In this criticism, Austin's point of departure resembles the views expounded in 1950.89–90 and in the 1953 paper. The communication situation involves a speaker; sentences; and something which they, when employed in speech-situations, are correlated with by their referring conventions. The audience is not considered; the situation is seen merely from the speaker's point of view. The only purpose is to impart information. Questions of accuracy, preciseness, etc., are not raised. The significance of these omissions will be seen later.

'What we state' can be either the vehicle of communication or what it conveys; hence uses (2) and (1). Although the vehicle usually conveys what we intend it to convey, it does not always do so. The failure may be due either to the sender's misperception of the fact or to his misconception of the sentence; hence the necessity of uses (3) and (4). Use (5) enters awkwardly; Austin's intention is, I presume, to pinpoint that referring expressions fix a statement to a *particular* state of affairs.

In spite of its definitional appearance, 'Facts are what statements, when true, state' may thus be read as an analogue to 'Targets are what signals, when true, signal'. Since Austin does not distinguish a fact from the event or thing whose constituents enter a fact, he takes the new interpretation to express a certain relation between the statement and the world. We have, however, seen that even if it is correct to take the statement as expressing a relation of correspondence, the non-linguistic correlate is hardly anything as unquestionably spatio-temporally located as an event.

'*Statements and facts are made for each other.*' Strawson asks ('Truth II', p. 137),

what could fit more perfectly the fact that it is raining than the statement that it is raining? Of course, statements and facts fit. They were made for each other. If you prise the statements off the world you prise the facts off it too; but the world would be none the poorer. (You don't also prise off the world what the statements are about—for this you would need a different kind of lever.)

To this Austin answers (*a*) that Strawson has quietly substituted the un-English phrases 'The statement that S corresponds to (fits) the fact that S' for the English phrases 'The statement that S corresponds to (fits) the facts', and that the substitutions do not make sense. We have considered that argument.

(*b*) Strawson cannot account for the locution 'statements correspond to facts'. In common language it is nonsense to ask—as we must, if Strawson is right—whether a statement corresponds to or first another statement—*p* can *fit in with q* but not fit it; clash with or be compatible with but not correspond to *q*. (1954.108.)

(c) For the sake of the argument we may, says Austin, allow Strawson to effect his substitutions and in some way give them sense. That does not force us to concede that statements and facts are made for each other. For, first, 'obviously, some statements *do not* fit the facts' (1954.108). There is a use of 'know' such that if someone knows that p, it follows that it is a fact; there is no use of 'state' such that if someone states that p, it follows that it is a fact that p. It would therefore be more adequate to say that knowledge and facts are made for each other than to say that statements and facts are made for each other—'though even then one would be inclined to protest that there may very well be facts that nobody knows or ever will know, and that to say the facts are made for knowledge is curious' (1954.116). Secondly, even if Strawson meant no more than that facts and *true* statements are made for each other, there is no more sense and no more malice in saying it than there is in saying, on the ground that well-aimed shots hit their marks, that marks and (well-aimed) shots are made for each other (1954.108f).

A summary of 2.1. Let us pause here to sum up the discussion of 2.1 and its sub-headings. Austin's replies (a)–(c) above seem sufficient to show that Strawson has not made good his bold claim that '[i]f you prise the statements off the world you prise the facts off it too'. The thesis that 'facts' and 'true statements' are analytically interrelated has then not been established. Both 'Facts are what statements, when true, state' and 'The fact that it is raining fits (corresponds to) the statement that it is raining' are capable of other interpretations than the definitional ones. In fact, Strawson's thesis goes counter to what we all take as an unquestionable truth most of the time—viz. that there are facts which nobody knows or will know and which therefore never will be stated.

So far, Austin's opposition is successful. He has, however, not managed to show that facts, in the sense demanded by the Correspondence Theory, are 'something in the world'. That they are 'something in the world' seems to mean that they are events or states. We have seen that this identification will not do. That a particular cat killed a particular mouse is a fact if, and only if, a certain event occurred (viz. the killing of the mouse by the cat); but the event is not the fact. Hence Austin's positive tenet is mistaken. Remaining problems as to the status of facts were indicated in the digression concerning the non-linguistic relatum of the Correspondence Theory.*

2.2. A digression: Austin's model of truth and Strawson's 'presuppositions'.†

Again I want to stress that Austin was concerned with a *model* of truth. In his eyes, 'truth is a bare minimum or an illusory ideal' (1950.98). A model is a simplification, not intended to fit reality exactly. It is a bad model if it does not help us to explain reality by ordering the phenomena in certain perspicious ways. Austin uses his model to bring out the differences between the utterances falling within the fact-stating type of discourse, and to elucidate the connexions which nevertheless make us place them all within that discourse. In the next section we shall scrutinize his attempt, and also a third attack by Strawson on the Correspondence Theory. In the remainder of this section I shall discuss how Austin's model tallies with Strawson's famous doctrine of 'presuppositions'.

Suppose that an empirical subject/predicate statement lacks a referent for the subject expression. According to Strawson, the question of the truth or falsehood of the statement does not then arise.[9] On his view of truth, this ought to be tantamount to saying that the question of *assessing* it by means of the labels 'true' and 'false' does not arise. B. Russell[10] and A. C. Danto[11] have, however, answered that it would be assessed as false if something important is at stake. An agent who tells a prospective customer, 'The house on the north-east corner is one of Wright's early masterpieces' cannot escape the charge of lying by the expedient of pleading that there is no house on the spot indicated; and lying is saying something false.

---

*[In 'Truth: a reconsideration . . .' Strawson has taken the controversy to partially fresh fields.]

†[Cf. P. F. Strawson: 'Identifying reference and truth-value'. *Theoria* 30 (1964).]

[9] See, e.g., 'On referring'; *Introduction to Logical Theory*, esp.ch. 6; 'A reply to Mr Sellars', *Ph.R.* 63 (1954); *Individuals*, esp.ch. 6; and 'Singular terms and predication', *J.Ph.* 57 (1961).

[10] 'Mr Strawson on referring' in *My Philosophical Development*, ch.18:III.

[11] 'A note on expressions of the referring sort', *Mind* 67 (1958).

I am not convinced by the objection. Of course the agent tried to deceive his customer; but it does not follow that what he said can be assessed as false. A simulation hoax can be performed without issuing any utterance or only such utterances as nobody would call true or false—orders, interjections, prayers, and blessings. Yet it would not be out of place to say that the deceiver lied—'lying' is sometimes tied up with 'deceiving', not with 'stating falsely'.

At least sometimes we are inclined to agree with Strawson that a subject/predicate statement is not assessed as true or false when its subject expression lacks a referent. It is easy to see why this is so. If a sentence, when issued in normal circumstances, (*a*) refers to something with its subject expression and (*b*) rightly or wrongly ascribes a certain property to that thing with its predicate expression, then something is seriously amiss if on a particular occasion the subject expression has no referent. For then there is trouble not only with the subject expression but also with the predicate expression, since the latter has nothing to ascribe a property to. It seems, then, as if the assessment as true or false is not an assessment of the success or failure of the referring part of the statement; it is an assessment of the success or failure of the predicate part. It is taken for granted that the referring part has done its duty, and what is assessed is merely whether the property signified by the predicate expression is a property of the referent.

Suppose that you and I walk together across the meadows. I indicate something far away and say 'That stone is very white'. You answer, 'It's not a stone, it's a horse'. I return, 'All the same, it's very white'.—Something is wrong with the referring part of my original utterance. It did not mislead you, since you grasped what I intended to refer to. But my tongue did not slip, nor was I ignorant of the rules governing the use of the English word 'stone'. I used the word faultlessly, in as far as I really intended to *signify* a stone—the referring part of my statement contains a classifying element, though its duty as a whole is to secure that you grasp what I refer to. So I am guilty of a misidentification and not merely of a trivial slip of the tongue. Nevertheless it would probably be conceded that if the object referred to really was white, I have said something true. But if I intend to refer to that stone and say 'That stone is black', my utterance can be allowed to be true only if my tongue has slipped or I am ignorant of the English vocabulary. If I know the rules governing the vocable 'black' and follow them without failure, my statement must be false and not true in the circumstances envisaged. This strengthens the point that what is assessed true or false is the predication. That the right referent has been singled out is taken for granted in such assessments; that issue is not *sub judice*.

Thus the question whether one of the pair of labels 'true' and 'false' is applicable in the assessment of a statement depends on the peculiarities of the statement. It is plain that a statement which cannot be so assessed is not related to the world in the way a statement is which can. In the former there is no referent for the referring part; and this causes trouble even for the predicate part.

Austin's account of truth is given only for statements which can be assessed as true or false, although he, in contradistinction to Strawson, takes no great interest in the assessment. So he is committed to the view that statements without referents are not true or false in the traditional sense—are not fit subjects for the Correspondence Theory. That he in fact accepts this consequence is shown by e.g. 1940.36 and more clearly in *Words*, especially lecture 4.

It must, however, be admitted that statements lacking referents for their referring part are *sometimes* assessed as true or false. The defendant who says 'A man in a bowler hat gave me the stolen crates of beer' may not only lie but also say something false. Our conviction that the giver is fictitious may be our ground for assessing his utterance as false. If this is granted, why is an assertion, whose subject term fails to refer, sometimes assessed as false and sometimes as neither true nor false?

Austin's distinction between fitting and matching may be helpful here. In normal statements the referent of the subject term is the theme of discussion; but this is not so in the defendant's statement. There the crates of beer are the theme. The assertion is therefore judged as if it were of the form, 'The stolen crates of beer were a gift of a man in a bowler hat'. In that utterance, the subject term certainly has referents, and something is predicated of them. Hence the utterance can be assessed as true or false; and if 'the crates' is made the logical subject of the defendant's utterance, the same sort of assessment is due to it also. But then the utterance seems to be a fit object not only for assessments in terms of truth and falsehood but also for the Correspondence Theory of Truth.

If this is right, there seems to be a connexion between the traditional philosophical problem of truth and Strawson's problem of assessments of statements in terms of truth and falsehood: a statement can be correctly assessed as true only if it fulfils the requirements of the Correspondence Theory; and it is correctly assessed as false only if its *referring* part fulfils the conditions it has to fulfil according to that theory. I hope I have shown that it does not follow that an investigation of the felicity-conditions of assessments of assertions as true or false, is the same thing as an investigation of the felicity-conditions of these assertions themselves.

3. *The constative discourse*

Austin's account of truth is a model, and its job is to exhibit a certain unity or lack of unity within the field of statements. In 'Truth II' (pp. 141–2), Strawson denies that a model of truth founded on the Correspondence Theory ever can fulfil that function. I quote his argument in full. It claims that

> the word 'fact' (and the 'set-of-facts' words like 'situation' 'state of affairs') have, like the words 'statement' and 'true' themselves, a certain type of word-world-relating discourse (the informative) *built in* to them. The occurrence in ordinary discourse of the words 'fact' 'statement' 'true' signalizes the occurrence of this type of discourse; just as the occurrence of the words 'order' 'obeyed' signalizes the occurrence of another kind of conventional communication (the imperative). . . . [I]t would be futile to attempt to [elucidate the first type of discourse] . . . in terms of the words 'fact', 'statement', 'true', for these words contain the problem, not its solution. It would, for the same reason, be equally futile to attempt to elucidate any one of these words . . . in terms of the others. And it is, indeed, very strange that people have so often proceeded by saying 'Well, we're pretty clear what a statement is, aren't we? Now let us settle *the further question, viz.*, what it is for a statement to be true.' This is like 'Well, we're clear about what a command is: now what is it for a command to be obeyed?' As if one could divorce statements and commands from the point of making or giving them!

Suppose we had in our language the word 'execution' meaning 'action which is the carrying out of a command'. And suppose someone asked the philosophical question: What is *obedience*? What is it for a command to be *obeyed*? A philosopher might produce the answer: 'Obedience is a conventional relation between a command and an execution. A command is obeyed when it corresponds to an execution.'

This is the Correspondence Theory of Obedience. It has, perhaps, a little less value as an attempt to elucidate the nature of one type of communication than the Correspondence Theory of Truth has as an attempt to elucidate that of another. In both cases, the words occurring in the solution incorporate the problem. And, of course, this intimate relation between 'statement' and 'fact' (which is understood when it is seen that they both incorporate this problem) explains why it is that when we seek to explain *truth* on the model of naming or classifying or any other kind of conventional or nonconventional relation between one thing and another, we always find ourselves landed with 'fact', 'situation', 'state of affairs' as the non-linguistic terms of the relation.

The passage seems to contain two arguments. The first of them is the old one, that 'fact', 'statement', 'true' (and 'false'?) are defined in terms of each other. There is then no point in elucidating one of the terms by means of the other terms of the set—what we are unclear about in the definiendum will remain unclear in the definiens.

The other argument is that an elucidation of what a statement is, must give an account of why statements are made. Strawson assumes the purpose is to convey a fact. Since on his view a fact is a true statement, there is small wonder that he finds this approach 'barren' (p. 142).*

Both arguments are wrong, and for the same reason: there is nothing to Strawson's definition thesis. 'Facts are what statements (when true) state' is not analytic. So the premiss of the first argument will not do, and I see no way to redeem it. And when the definition thesis is gone, the second argument does not show any circularity in saying that statements are made to convey facts.

Nevertheless Strawson is right in holding that the assertion that a statement is what is said in order to convey a fact, has no great candle-power. It is not even true until qualified. To make the nature of a statement clear we have to distinguish both different kinds of statements from each other, and the family of

*[This is too short a shrift. *Vide* Strawson, 'A reconsideration . . .'.]

statements from other kinds of utterances. In this section I shall begin to consider how Austin set about these tasks, but the theme will continue to be developed in the next chapter.

3.1. *The criteria of statements*

A trend in Wittgenstein's *Philosophical Investigations* is that there is nothing all statements have in common. They are only related to each other by a network of family resemblances. In §§ 134–6 he ridicules his idea in *Tractatus* that the statement (*Satz*) 'This is how things are' is the general form of statements. 'Statement' is a criteria-delimited term.

It seems to me that Austin rejects Wittgenstein's idea and holds that there are certain criteria that must be satisfied by every utterance qualifying as a statement. These necessary conditions are, however, functional and not grammatical.

Grammatical criteria of statements. When asked what makes an utterance a statement, we fairly often take our first shot at a grammatical criterion or set of criteria. The most plausible one is that of mood. Thus we may think that an utterance in the indicative mood is a statement. But it certainly is not, Austin objects, when 'it is a formula in a calculus: when it is a performatory utterance: when it is a value-judgment: when it is a definition' (1950.99). Here 'definition' has to be defined, since a dictionary definition, being a report on actual usages, *is* true or false, whereas e.g. a stipulative definition is not. Still, Austin's objection is acceptable to most philosophers, though perhaps not to some brands of Platonists, value-objectivists and adherents of the view (later to be discussed) that performatives (including stipulative definitions) cause their own truth.

Isn't the indicative mood of an utterance at least a necessary condition of its being a statement? Austin would presumably have denied it. Consider a one-word utterance, like 'Water'. Isn't it sometimes a statement?—'Quite so; but then it can be expanded into an indicative statement.'—But does it have to? Can't we, even in a primitive language allowing only of one-word sentences, distinguish between different uses of one and the same sentence? 'Water' may be a statement, a command, a wish, a prayer, depending on when it is uttered and in what tone of voice. Can't we then speak of statements, commands, wishes and prayers in that language?

This is not to deny that one way of making out whether an utterance is a statement is to consider its mood. Function and mood are intimately connected: moods are developed to show what function an utterance is to be taken to have. (Cf the next chapter.) But in some cases there is a friction between mood and function—the angry mother who yells to her child 'You'll do nothing of the sort!' is hardly *stating* anything. (Though we may feel that there is an element of stating in what she says: because she can see to it that her order is obeyed, she can squeeze command and statement about the addressee's future behaviour into one linguistic form. Before the events in the spring of 1962, it would have been pathetically absurd for President de Gaulle to address the leaders of the OAS in that way.) The mood of an utterance helps us to recognize it as a statement. But it is neither a necessary nor a sufficient condition.

Functional criteria of statements. What is the function of a statement? Austin clearly insists that a statement says how things are; utterances which do not do that are not statements. (See e.g. 1946.71, 1950.99, 1956c.222–4; *Words, passim.*)

To use a subject/predicate sentence to say how things are is, I think, to use it with the implications that I, the speaker, shoulder the obligation to conform my words to the world and that I am well-informed about the relevant part of the world. This is how the *forecast* '1227 will be a square' differs from the promise or the order made in the same form of words; and this is also how the *statement* 'I am sorry for my clumsiness' (which perhaps requires that the speaker actually *is* sorry) differs from the *performative* uttered in the same words (which does not require more than that I try to abstain from offending in the same way in the future).

Statements are certainly sometimes used for other purposes than merely saying how things are. 'There is sherry over there' may occasionally be an invitation. But the standard function of a statement is to conform words to the world. This can be done even by a mere observer, in the broad sense of Ch. 3:6.

M

3.2. The ideally true statement

Assume that we discern, however vaguely, the general sort of job all statements have. How are we to sort them? The clearest, most paradigmatical, statements will be those for which Austin's model of truth works without a hitch. '1227 is a square', issued in speech-situation S_0, gives us as good an example as we can hope to find. *Ex hypothesi*, all squares in S_0 are exactly alike; there is no item similar to them and liable to be confused with them; and the label 'square' is attached to them alone. '1227' is a purely referring word which has a referent, and the assertive link is in order. So if the referent really is a square, we have a paradigm of words fitting a fact exactly.

In the sequel I shall assume that the reference is secured, so that I can concentrate on the problem of how the predicate fits the referent. The ideally true statement is one which is precise and whose words fit the facts exactly. The less an utterance approaches the ideal, the more dubious is its truth or falsehood. In 1950.97–8 Austin says,

There are numerous other adjectives... in the same class as 'true' and 'false', which are concerned, that is, with the relations between the words (as uttered with reference to an historic situation) and the world.... We say, for example, that a certain statement is exaggerated or vague or bald, a description somewhat rough or misleading or not very good, an account rather general or too concise. In cases like these it is pointless to insist on deciding in simple terms whether the statement is 'true or false'. Is it true or false that Belfast is north of London? That the galaxy is the shape of a fried egg? That Beethoven was a drunkard? That Wellington won the battle of Waterloo? There are various *degrees and dimensions* of success in making statements: the statements fit the facts always more or less loosely, in different ways on different occasions for different intents and purposes. What may score full marks in a general knowledge test may in other circumstances get a gamma. And even the most adroit of languages may fail to 'work' in an abnormal situation or to cope, or cope reasonably simply, with novel discoveries: is it true or false that the dog goes round the cow? What, moreover, of the large class of cases where a statement is not so much false (or true) as out of place, *inept* ('All the signs of bread' said when the bread is before us)?

In S_0 the perfect fit is due to a combination of world and language. If the squares lose their perfect form while the meaning of 'square' remains the same, '1227 is a square' will not be a paradigmatically true or false statement. It also loses that status if the meaning changes but not the world. The adverbs and adjectives which Austin mentions and which are used in appraising statements are, according to 1954.109, all of them

connected with the notion of fitting and measuring in ordinary contexts, and it can scarcely be fortuitous that they, along with fitting and corresponding, have been taken over as a group to the sphere of statements and facts. Now to some extent the use of this galaxy of words in connexion with statements *may* be a transferred use; yet no one would surely deny that these constitute serious and important notions which can be, and should be elucidated. I should certainly go much farther and claim ... that these are the important terms to elucidate when we address ourselves to the problem of 'truth', just as, not 'freedom' but notions like duress and accident, are what require elucidation when we worry about 'freedom'.

S&S, Ch. X, contains a few remarks on some of these words. The phrases fall into two classes. Some of them have to do with *precision*, others with *fit*.

Preciseness. 'Precisely' is taken over from the field of measurement, where it is a matter of using a sufficiently finely graduated scale. In the case of statements, preciseness is found in language, not in speech. A word is precise when its application is fixed within narrow limits; 'duck-egg blue' is more precise than 'blue'. There is no such thing as an absolutely precise expression, since we can always make still finer divisions and discriminations when our purposes demand them. Consequently, a linguistic specification such as a description 'can no more be absolutely, finally, and ultimately *precise* than it can be absolutely *full* or *complete*'. A statement can be as precise as you like and still remain false—preciseness is concerned with language and not with its application to the world; it is not a matter of speech. (*S&S*.127–8.)

Fit. Other adjectives and adverbs are tied up with the notion of fit. Accuracy is a virtue of maps, but an accurate map is not 'a *kind* of map, as for instance is a large-scale, a detailed, or a clearly drawn map—its accuracy is a matter of the *fit* of the map *to* the terrain it is a map of'. In the matter of statements, fit is concerned with relating language and the world, i.e., it is a feature of speech. Hence 'neither a word nor a sentence can, as such, be accurate'; only particular instances of their application to the world can.—In *S&S* as well as in 1950 and 1954 Austin gives no examples of what a perfect fit would be like; but I suppose that the relation between a characteristic and its classificatory word in S_0 may be taken as a paradigm.

Austin seems to count 'exactly' as a member of the words concerned with fit: 'If I measure a banana with a ruler, I may find it to be precisely $5\frac{5}{8}$ inches long. If I measure my ruler with bananas, I may find it to be exactly six bananas long, though I couldn't claim any great precision for my method of measurement.' The exactness of a measurement is not a question of precision: it does not matter a whit whether my rod is or is not finely graduated, provided that it can be brought to coincide with the thing measured, after one application or more; and provided also that the coincidence is (or for the purposes at hand can be regarded as) containing no gaps or overlaps. Austin stresses that exactness is connected with speech and not with language also when he remarks, *à propos* of our application of words to the world, that 'there's a kind of exhilaration in finding the *exact word* (which may not be a precise word'). (*S&S*.128.)

A proof that 'exact' is not a term of preciseness may be extracted from these remarks. Although the sentence 'She wore a honey-coloured dress' is much more precise than the sentence 'She wore a yellow dress', a statement made by means of the former need not be more exact than one made by means of the latter. On the contrary, the former statement is *less* exact than the latter if her dress is (say) lemon-coloured. We shall presently see other reasons for thinking that 'exact' stands much closer to 'accurate' than to 'precise'.

Fit and truth. Austin believes that there is a connexion between fit and truth. He comments on 'accurate' (*S&S*.128f):

One is tempted to say that an accurate report, for instance, must be *true* whereas a very precise or detailed report may not be; and there is something right in this idea, though I feel rather uneasy about it. Certainly 'untrue but accurate' is pretty clearly wrong; but 'accurate and therefore true' doesn't seem quite right either. Is it only that 'true', after 'accurate', is redundant?

If accuracy really is akin to truth, can the kinship be due to its membership of the family of terms concerned with fit? The suggestion seems plausible, if other terms of fit exhibit the same sort of oddity as 'accurate' when filling up the gap of 'untrue but ...'.

Austin does not pause to consider how 'exact' fills the bill. In fact it seems to behave like 'accurate' in all requisite respects. It will not do to say 'His statement that her dress was honey-coloured was untrue but exact'; so exactness and truth seem connected. Nevertheless, it is also strange to say that the statement was true because it was exact.

Austin pounces upon another terms of fit, viz. 'exaggerated' (*S&S*.129):

It would be worth while to compare ... the relation of 'true' to, say, 'exaggerated'; if 'exaggerated and *therefore* untrue' seems not quite right, one might try 'untrue *in the sense that* it's exaggerated', 'untrue, *or rather*, exaggerated', or '*to the extent that* it's exaggerated, untrue'. Of course, just as no word or phrase is accurate as such, no word or phrase is as such an exaggeration.

Let me digress here to expound the difference between exaggerating and telling the truth. If I say 'I've 2000 books at home' when I have got only half the number, I am exaggerating. But suppose I had spoken a language where the only numeral after '100' is 'many'! Then I could not have exaggerated in this example, since I should not have had the linguistic means for doing so. The statement corresponding to 'I've 2000 books at home' would be 'I've many books at home', and it would be true: a person would have proved it up to the hilt if he said the series of cardinal numbers, picking out one book for each of them, and found that when he had reached '100' there were still books on the shelf. The understatement 'I've 500 books at home' would also be impossible to make, for the same reason. But there is nothing in the sense of the words '2000' or '500' which makes sentences containing them exaggerations or understatements; nor is there any feature in 'many' which makes sentences containing it impervious to these shortcomings. In other situations the former two sentences could be used to make irreproachable statements, and the latter to make an exaggeration or understatement. It is the use of words, not the words themselves, that causes statements to be exaggerated or understated.

Exaggerations do, however, shade into falsehoods. An exaggeration must at least point in the right direction, give the addressee some idea of the quantity (etc.) of the subject. If Smith says he has two thousand books, when he in fact owns only his battered school bible, a crime story and a novel by I. Slaughter, the difference between the number he mentions and the correct number is far too big. His utterance cannot be allowed to pass as an exaggeration; he has told us an obvious lie. We draw the line between lies and exaggerations differently for children and adults. If a small boy says that his cat is as big as a lion, we pass it off as an exaggeration—he does not know or remember how big a real lion is, he has not yet learnt the standards of acceptable looseness in comparison of size, and so forth. But if *I* say that the cat is as big as a lion, I am either joking or saying something which is much too exaggerated to be a mere exaggeration: it is on or has already crossed the border of falsehood.

Strawson's remark that exaggerated statements cannot be made in a language which does not have a sufficiently rich vocabulary ('Truth II', p. 151) does not prove that 'true' and 'exaggerated' differ in the respect which interests Austin. I think Austin meant that terms of fit, like 'accurate', 'exaggerated' and 'exact', delimit the concept of truth, in our language though not necessarily in richer or poorer languages. They fence it in by marking off different respects in which a statement can fail to be *quite* true, true without qualifications.

Roughness and generality. Two of Austin's pet examples of rough statements are 'France is a hexagonal' and 'Lord Raglan won the battle of Alma'. Their roughness is not due to any fault on the side of language. The sense of 'hexagonal' is quite clear, but it is indeed questionable whether *France* is a hexagonal. Nevertheless the statement is not *just* wrong. From a bird's eye view the borders of France form a figure with some semblance to a hexagon, so to say that the country looks like a hexagon is to say something which, although very sketchy and in several respects very unsatisfactory, gives a useful idea of what it looks like. And the sense of 'won the battle of Alma' is straightforward enough, though it is very dubious whether *Lord Raglan* won that battle: since his orders were not transmitted he can hardly be praised for the victory. Nonetheless the statement is not *just* wrong: after all he was in command of the triumphant troops.

Has roughness to do with fit? Austin gives no answer; but there is an important difference between accuracy, exactness, exaggeration and understatement on the one hand and roughness on the other. For if an ignoramus confused the outlines of France and Scandinavia and said 'The map of France is like a resting dog', we can hardly comment that what he said was untrue *in so far as* it was rough or that it was untrue *or rather* rough—phrases which imply that when its roughness is cured, its falsehood is also cured. Nothing hinders a statement from being both false and free from roughness, whilst it is odd to speak of accurate (exact, not exaggerated and not understated) but false statements.

But roughness is not or not merely a failure of preciseness (being couched in too general terms, etc.). The *sentence* 'She had a yellow dress' is more general than the *sentence* 'She had a honey-coloured dress', but a *sentence* is never rougher than another *sentence*. The *statement* 'She had a yellow dress' is more general than the *statement* 'She had a honey-coloured dress' since the word-type 'yellow' is less specified than the word-type 'honey-coloured'. The difference between a general word and a more precise one is a difference of *language* and is marked by the appearance of entailment-rules: 'She had a honey-coloured dress' entails 'She had a yellow dress' (cf. 1953.196). But it is nonsense to say that a sentence is rougher than another or to say that the former is entailed by the latter in virtue of the latter's being less rough. It is units of speech, not of language, that are rougher than other units, and entailment rules belong to language. That Lord Raglan was in command of the victorious troops at Alma notoriously does not entail that he won the battle, and that the borders of France roughly resemble a hexagon does not entail that France literally has no more than six sides. What makes us dissatisfied with a rough statement is not what makes us dissatisfied with a general one.

It may be suggested that rough statements are characterized by a lack of preciseness: if the verb in 'Lord Raglan won the battle of Alma' is replaced by 'was in command of the victorious troops', the roughness disappears.—A decisive objection to this is that in 'France is hexagonal', 'hexagonal' is very precise and yet the statement is rough.

The truth seems to be—as Ivar Segelberg has pointed out to me—that in rough statements a *schematization* has taken place. The man who says that France is hexagonal is in all likelihood aware that France has many more sides than six. Yet his utterance is not (treated as) an understatement: he does not try to count the sides of France. What he attempts to do is to give an idea of the dominant shape of the country, and to do this he has to simplify. 'France is hexagonal' is not incompatible with 'France has many thousand sides', if the former is taken as a schematization; whilst an understatement of the number of sides is incompatible with the statement giving the correct number. Hence roughness has to be kept distinct from exaggeration and understatement: the latter are on the same level as the utterance which gives the correct account, whilst a rough statement is on another level and expresses a simplification. But an utterance may of course be both exaggerated (or understated) and rough: 'Lord Raglan won the battle of Alma' is perhaps an example.

In a rough statement I simplify my apprehension of something. If I remove the simplification, there is no guarantee that my statement is true: my apprehension may be wrong. This explains why a statement can be free from roughness and yet false, but not free from deficiencies of fit (such as inaccurateness, inexactness, exaggeration) and yet false.

I conclude that roughness ought to be treated neither as a deficiency of preciseness nor as a deficiency of fit; it is a phenomenon of a third kind which has not yet been sufficiently investigated.

Preciseness and fit. We have considered two main kinds of deficiencies of statements: bad preciseness and bad fit. The line between them is of course not sharp: being general is largely a matter of language, but often when something is condemned as *too* general, it is due to the speaker's purpose, etc.—i.e. to factors of speech. Again, the comments on roughness indicate that there are probably more kinds of deficiencies than the two we have been concerned with. Even if we keep to these, investigations are required to decide whether the different words within one kind single out different sub-classes; whether still more sub-classes can be found; and what their relations to each other are. For these reasons, we are at the beginning, not at the end, of an inquiry.

Austin has pointed to a field of research but was not given time to do much spade-work himself.

Even if he has not produced much more than a programme, it is fairly exciting. From it a picture of the ideal statement and of ideal truth takes shape; and by means of these notions we can achieve a principle for sorting our actual statements. So let us examine carefully his outline of different respects in which an utterance can fail to be quite true.

Preciseness and fit are intimately connected: the greater the preciseness, the greater the risks of an imperfect fit. As our knowledge and interests increase, we need a more and more subtle vocabulary in order, among other things, to report phenomena we have come across. But the more precise our vocabulary, the greater the risk that the predicate expression is governed by rules of application that are too wide or too narrow to fit without failure the referent singled out by the subject expression.

A statement can be as precise as you please and still be false; but its neatness of fit is linked to its truth. This seems to carry the unplausible suggestion that a very unprecise language serves truth better than one which is more precise, since the risks of failures of fit are reduced in the former. The greater risk we run in stating something in a more precise language is, however, easily outweighed by the great amount of information conveyed by a statement which has successfully avoided deficiencies of preciseness and of fit. A very unprecise language buys its immunity against falsehood at the price of being very uninformative.

But even the vocabulary of a rich language does not suffice to deal with all the varieties of phenomena we come across or can imagine. Nor are we always able to find the right words on the spur of the moment. Hence little would be said in an informative, fact-stating way if we always demanded great preciseness together with a perfect fit. In practice an utterance is usually tolerated if the predicate expression approximately fits the referent. An inaccurate or inexact or exaggerated statement is neither false nor true *tout court*; it is false, but only to the extent to which it is inaccurate or inexact or exaggerated.

The wish for preciseness and for a perfect fit produces the notion of what I hereby dub an *ideal statement*. A constative utterance which has secured reference is an ideal statement if, and only if, its predicate expression

(i) is absolutely precise

and

(ii) is capable of fitting the referent perfectly—i.e., of fitting it as in S_0 a classificatory word fits an appropriate item.

These requirements prevent any utterance from being an ideal statement. There is no such thing as absolute preciseness: we can always ask for finer graduations and discriminations. Since these more and more precise terms also demand as good a fit as that provided in S_0, there is no end to the demand for a perfect fit either.

The ideally true statement. We have seen that according to Austin a statement is true when its referring conventions tie it to a fact of the type which its descriptive conventions describe. If I have 1000 books at home, my statement 'I have 1000 books at home' will then be just as true as someone's statement about me, 'He has many books at home', made in a language where the only numeral after 500 is 'many'. This agrees with our everyday tendency to treat truth as a polar concept. A statement is not truer than another except perhaps in the strained sense that it is more precise or less rough, or that it can be broken up into or implies a greater number of true statements. If there are atomic statements, it is as nonsensical to suggest that some of them are truer than others as it is to say that some objects are more real than others.

But suppose now that we toy with the idea of what we may call *ideal truth* or the *ideally true statement*. A statement is ideally true when it is an ideal statement and the fact to which its demonstrative conventions tie it is of a type with which the sentence used in making it is correlated by its descriptive conventions. In this definition no two facts are counted as belonging to the same type except when their only difference is numerical. An ideal statement can, of course, fail to be of the type its descriptive conventions require—i.e., it can be *ideally false*. But since there can be no ideal statements, there can be no ideally true or false statements.—This is why Austin declares that truth (and falsehood) must remain but an 'illusory ideal' (1950.98).

I think, however, that we had better take the idea of ideal truth as an attempt to elucidate neither the employment of 'true' nor the relation holding between (say) 'The cat is on the mat' and the cat on the mat but the function of statements in general. We bother to have statements because we want to have a means of informing one another of what the world is like. This purpose cannot be fulfilled unless we single out an item, predicate something fairly distinct about it, and use the predicate only when the characteristic it designates really belongs to the item. (As I have tried to show, only the third of these conditions is ordinarily discussed in traditional philosophical inquiries into truth.) There would be no point in having statements unless they have some—and a pretty high—degree of preciseness and fit. The better a statement fulfils its informative function, the more precise is its predicate and the better does it fit its subject. The ideally true statement is the statement with a maximum of preciseness and fit.

3.3. *The ideally true statement and actual statements*

The closer actual constative utterances come to the illusory ideal statement, the more unquestionable is their status as statements. As we have seen, they can fall short of the ideal in different respects: the subject term may lack a referent ('The king of France is wise') or misrefer although the context nevertheless makes it clear what the referent is ('The king of France always spells "général" with a small "g" except when referring to himself'); the degree of preciseness of the predicate may be unusually low ('This is something'); the fit may leave much to be desired ('A cow is rather like a horse'); and there are probably several fairly common types of misfortunes to be added to the list. It is a philosophical task to find them and to see how we try to mend the statements. Take e.g. adapter-words. How far do they help us to a better preciseness and fit? Is it true without qualifications that true humour is sad? If not, why? (Because 'sad' is intolerably vague? Because the adapter-word 'true' is 'emotive'?)

Perhaps Austin thought that 'all'-statements may be subject to a new type of misfortune. In *Words*.143 he points out that 'All snow geese migrate to Labrador' is not proved false if a maimed bird does not go that far. The usual explanations of this resistance to falsification are that the statement is a prescriptive definition or advice to adopt a rule. Austin finds them unsatisfactory and wants to explain the resistance by saying that the reference of the statement is limited to the known. Thus the discovery of black swans in Australia does not prove the falsehood of 'All swans are white': its author may answer that he was not referring to swans anywhere but just to the swans in the regions he knows of—he is not, for example, referring to possible swans on the canals of Mars. Austin's conclusion is that this rejoinder is admissible—reference depends on the knowledge at the time of utterance. Hence we cannot quite say, in his opinion, that the truth of statements depends on facts as distinct from knowledge of facts.

Suppose we recognize that an 'all'-statement has a wider span of reference than its author intended. Is this a new type of misfortune that can befall statements? I think not: it is just a special case of making a misleading reference which nevertheless is correctly grasped. It is often obvious that the speaker must be taken as referring to *fit* snow geese or to swans in the parts of the world he knows of; and if what he says is true of these referents, then the characteristics of snow geese or swans outside his span of reference do not bother us. The span varies for different speakers. A Swedish farmer may even nowadays get away with 'All swans are white'—we may say, 'He refers, of course, to wild swans in this part of the world'. A biologist will find it much harder. But nobody except the pedant would think that his statement 'All swans are white or black' is refuted if a Russian comes across a species of purple swans on Mars—for even a biologist's statements are (today) limited to phenomena on or close to the earth. If this is so, then it is misleading to say that the truth of a statement depends on knowledge of facts; what depends on knowledge of facts is the width of the span of reference. That settled, nothing Austin says has the disquieting consequence that the truth of the 'all'-statement depends not on facts but on knowledge of facts; and 'all'-statements' resistance to falsification in the case envisaged is not a new type of misfortune.*

Still other utterances may be allowed the title of statements because their words are designed to conform to the world and not the other way round. Their degree of preciseness or fit is, however, very low, so low that the utterances do not even aspire to be

*[I am now inclined to think that Austin distorted ordinary parlance. His examples would more naturally run, 'Snow geese migrate (or The snow goose migrates) to Labrador' and 'Swans are (or The swan is) white'. What is said about snow geese or the snow goose does not necessarily hold good of all snow geese.]

true or false. Thus we may say that 'The essence of love is affinity' is a statement although we hardly give it a truth-value. Its standard role is to be a heading or a summary of a lengthy discourse (say Goethe's *Wahlverwandtschaften*); and as a summary its virtue is not truth but e.g. conciseness. (I have developed this theme in my discussion note 'Mr Halldén on essence statements', *Theoria* 27, 1961). Aphorisms, figurative expressions and metaphors are still more dubious statements—Tegnér hardly *stated* that in relation to religion, theology is a scull, placed over a lily. Yet many of these utterances stand closer to statements than to orders, advice, interjections, etc. In this way, statements may after all come to form a sort of family. If there is anything correct in the vision emerging from Austin's remarks on the ideal of truth and the ideal statement, the ideal statement is the father of the family. We may then hope that a serious investigation of different ways of failing to come up to the ideal may give us the principles of a sensible classification of the members of the family.

II. KNOWLEDGE

It is a pity that Austin did not use S_0 and S_1 to shed light on his view of knowledge. These simple models seem admirably suited to making clear some of his remarks in 'Other minds' and *S&S*. I shall therefore start my discussion from the assumption that we are transported to one of these primitive situations. A speaker utters '1227 is a square'. He is not guilty of idiosyncrasy or aberration, and the item he singles out has the characteristic he attributes to it. Under what conditions does he then *know* that 1227 is a square?

The question must not be confused with two others. I am not wondering under what conditions he is entitled to say 'I know'. Nor am I trying to elucidate the standard function or functions of the phrase 'I know'. Austin certainly discusses these two problems also; and when his contribution to epistemology is assessed, the major part of attention is usually given to his treatment of the latter of them. They will, however, concern us in the next chapter, not here: the phrase 'I know' is ruled out already by the syntactical requirements of S_0 and S_1; and the question to which we shall now address ourselves is another one anyhow. It is, 'Given that the speaker utters "1227 is a square" as a constative and without idiosyncrasies or aberrations, under what circumstances does he know that 1227 is a square, whether or not he says he knows it?'

The time-honoured answer is that it must be true that 1227 is a square, that he must be convinced it is, and that he has a backing which guarantees its truth—a backing which makes any suggestion to the contrary ridiculous. Austin accepts the answer but wants to brush it up. We have just considered the first condition. The second will be dealt with in the next chapter. This section will be concerned with how he trims the third condition.

Austin's demand is that the backing fulfils two requirements: (i) it has to be sufficient, in the sense that all reasonable people agree that *if* it is sound it puts beyond doubt the truth of the statement it supports, and (ii) it also has to be *actually* sound. Its soundness is proved by eliminating the possible sources of unreliability, one after another.

This answer seems disappointingly brisk, but when spelt out it gives important insights. In my discussion of it, I shall say that (i) deals with the *sufficiency* and (ii) with the *reliability* of the backing.

4. Sufficiency of backing (1946.44–65)

The question how I know that 1227 is a square can be answered in different ways. I can stress that I have often enough seen squares, that I have scrutinized the present specimen in broad daylight, that I have been trained to distinguish squares from, say, triangles and pentagons, and that 1227 is a plane, closed figure bounded by four rectilineal sides. That is, I can answer by telling you that I have seen squares before, have been taught how to tell them from similar figures, have had an opportunity of mustering the present specimen under favourable conditions and have found that it satisfies all the criteria of a square. In this way I produce my backing, show you my credentials for the assertion. They are sufficient if they, when true, put the truth of my assertion beyond doubt. (Cf.1946.44–8.)

You may trust my credentials and yet claim that they are insufficient to show that I know my assertion to be true. But '[i]f you say "That's not enough", then you must have in mind some more or less definite lack' (1946.52): in my example perhaps that

I also have to remember what I have been taught about how to sort out squares from similar figures. 'If there is no definite lack, which you are at least prepared to specify on being pressed, then it's silly (outrageous) just to go on saying "That's not enough"' (*loc. cit.*). Suppose that in speech-situation S_0 my credentials are (*a*) that I have learnt and not forgotten how to tell squares from similar items (have learnt and not forgotten the characteristics of a square), (*b*) that I have learnt and not forgotten that the correct appellative for items of the first sort is 'square', (*c*) that I have scrutinized 1227 with necessary care and under favourable conditions, and (*d*) that the specimen has all the relevant characteristics of squares and no others. By (*a*)–(*d*) I have as it were proved my assertion; I have stated 'what are the features of the current case which are enough to constitute it one which is correctly describable in the way we have described it, and not in any other way relevantly variant' (1946.53f). Unless you query my credentials it would, I think, be outrageous to say 'That's not enough', for what is lacking? It cannot be that you demand a proof that 1227 satisfies the *geometrical* definition of a square—e.g. that it is bounded by four geometrically rectilineal sides. For in S_0 and S_1 item and type are 'apprehended by inspection merely' (1953.182). The only way to give sense to your protest is to take it as meaning that although the credentials *if true* do guarantee that I know, they are in my case unreliable. And unreliability is something different from insufficiency. (Cf. 1946.52-4.)

Sufficiency and criteria-delimitation. Criteria-delimited words give trouble in respect of sufficiency, for two kinds of reasons: (i) We cannot always describe the criteria in words, still less in detail, nor can we always describe them without apparently presupposing the notion we are giving criteria of.[12] (ii) The open texture of such words makes it impossible to specify their criteria even if these could be worded in detail, in non-committal ways, and by anyone.

Let us consider these reasons separately, starting with (i):

---

[12] A criterion of tar is a certain characteristic smell. Unfortunately, nobody except a chemist can describe that criterion except as 'a smell *of tar*'. This makes it sound as if this smell has to be recognized as a smell of tar before it is recognized at all; but in fact the smell is a criterion of tar and the recognition of it does not presuppose the notion of tar.

Nearly everybody can recognize a surly look or the smell of tar, but few can describe them non-committally, i.e. otherwise than as 'surly' or 'of tar': many can recognize, and 'with certainty', ports of different vintages, models by different fashion houses, shades of green, motor-car makes from behind, and so forth, without being able . . . to 'be more specific about it'—they can only say they can tell 'by the taste', 'from the cut', and so on. So, when I say I can tell the bird 'from its red head', or that I know a friend 'by his nose', I imply that there is something *peculiar* about the red head or the nose, . . . by which you can (always) tell them or him.—Often we know things quite well, while scarcely able at all to say 'from' what we know them.

When we answer the question 'How do you know that it is a so-and-so?' by a phrase prefaced with 'by' or 'from', we convey by these prefatory words that we are unable to state the criteria, whilst a phrase prefaced with 'because' conveys that the criterion it gives is sufficient to show that the specimen is a so-and-so.

When I say I know it's a goldfinch 'Because it has a red head', that implies that all I have noted, or needed to note, about it is that its head is red (nothing special or peculiar about the shade, shape, &c. of the patch): so that I imply that there is no small British bird that has any sort of red head except the goldfinch. [1946.53.]

So in Austin's opinion, 'from' and 'by' are at home when we want to convey that we cannot state the criteria of a word although we know it is applicable. I think they also often go together with criteria-delimited words whose main criteria we *can* state, although we do not bother to mention more than a sufficient number of them: 'How do you know it's a lemon?'—'From (By) the fact that it's yellowy-greenish, has a waxy skin, and tastes sour'. But since the question concerns sufficient conditions of application, we can also begin our answer 'Because . . .': I know it is a lemon because it is yellowy-greenish, etc.

The fact that a maker of 'by'- or 'from'-utterances is sometimes unable to detail his criteria or put them into words does not, of course, entail that they are uncheckable. If someone knows 'from its look' that the car OA 10989 is a Saab, he must at least be able to tell cars of that make from other cars. If he repeatedly fails to distinguish a Saab from a Volkswagen, he cannot *know* from its look that OA 10989 is a Saab, although he may by chance be right in his assertion. So although the speaker is unable to put his finger on the criterion or criteria he follows, we can unearth it or them by changing one after the other of the features of the item he has singled out and see whether he still would claim that the changed thing is a so-and-so; and we can test the sufficiency of the criteria by seeing whether they enable him to sort out the correct type of item from similar kinds.

(ii) Criteria-delimited words are often governed by an indefinite set of criteria; and it is logically impossible to enumerate all members of an indefinite set. This does not matter for our present point, since it is possible to specify not only one but many different sub-sets of a number of criteria *sufficient* to guarantee the correct application of the word. Since there are many different such subsets, the fact that mine does not include the same criteria as yours does not show that neither of them give a sufficient number of criteria.

Sufficiency and presumptions. An objector may, however, use open-textured terms to show that we never know whether a sufficient number of criteria have been given. He may argue, with P. Wilson,[13] that when a presumption underlying a term's rules of application is violated, we have to withhold the appellative from the thing violating it—a singing strawberry is no strawberry. Since it is always possible that something, which certainly has a sufficient number of relevant characteristics to qualify as a clear case of a so-and-so, will violate a presumption at some later time, we can *never* know that we have a sufficient number of criteria to guarantee the correct application of an open-textured term.

As we have seen in Ch. 2:5, there is no reason to take the decisive step of this objection. If a specimen violates a presumption, we are not logically forced to withhold the appellative from it. Language is not prepared for freaks; if they occur, we have to *decide* how to speak—our logic and our language do not enjoin that we are to deal with them in one way rather than another. Since presumptions are not necessary conditions for the correct application of an open-textured term, the objector's argument collapses.

This answer may be taken as an evasion. Austin has conceded that when a presumption is violated, we don't know what to say and have to decide how to speak; so he has conceded that under

[13] 'Austin on knowing', p. 51.

these conditions the ordinary term is not quite at home even if it is not forbidden. And then, the objector may say, Austin has conceded that we never know that an open-textured term is *quite* in place. We never know of any normal-seeming so-and-so (where the so-and-so is something designated by an open-textured term) that it really is an ordinary so-and-so, a so-and-so in the full sense of the term; for it may behave outrageously in the future.

To this there are two rejoinders. The first is that if the thing violates a presumption at some time in the future, there is no need to assume that it was a *lusus naturae* from the time it first came into existence. If I give you a sufficient amount of credentials for my claim that 1227 is a square and you test them and find them reliable, then we are in no way bound to say that since all of a sudden it changes into a circle it cannot, at the time of my assertion and your test, have been an ordinary square. We can maintain that it was an ordinary square right up to the time of its change. I take this to be the point of 1946.56f:

When I have made sure it's a real goldfinch (not stuffed, corroborated by the disinterested, &c.) then I am *not* 'predicting' in saying it's a real goldfinch, and in a very good sense I can't be proved wrong whatever happens. It seems a serious mistake to suppose that language (or most language, language about real things) is 'predictive' in such a way that the future can always prove it wrong. What the future *can* always do, is to make us *revise our ideas* about goldfinches or real goldfinches or anything else.

The second rejoinder—which I have not found in Austin's writing but which nevertheless lies fairly close at hand—is this. We are seldom aware of our presumptions and can, I suppose, never be sure we have found *all* the presumptions underlying a term's rules of application. If the objector maintains that presumptions enter the meaning of open-textured terms, he must accept the consequence that we can never be sure we know the full meaning of any open-textured word. Such words make up a very large part of our vocabulary, and they also give sense to a great many of our other, more exact terms—the more exact word may, for example, be introduced as the word whose range of application is to be the narrow range which several partially overlapping open-textured words have in common. Our objector is then forced to hold that we can never be sure that we know the full meaning of a very large part, perhaps the largest part, of our everyday vocabulary.

We may assess the consequence in two ways. Either we may take it to show that the sense of the phrase 'knowing the full meaning of the open-textured term "so-and-so"' has been tampered with, and then the objector is no longer dealing with what he presumably believes he is dealing with, viz. the ordinary meaning of an open-textured word. Or we may assume that 'knowing the full meaning of the open-textured word "so-and-so"' bears its ordinary sense, and then the tenet that we don't know the full meaning of a very large number of our everyday words is so obviously wrong that the 'proposition' from which it follows loses whatever remains of its not even initially great plausibility: the fact that we don't know all the presumptions for the use of open-textured words does not entail that we don't know their full meaning; and the fact that a thing which has stood up to all reasonable tests for being a so-and-so nevertheless may behave outrageously in the future has not the slightest tendency to show that our classificatory label *was* inept—even if it cannot be applied without qualms to the thing *after* the outrage.

Assume now that we are in a speech-situation slightly more complex than S_0 and S_1, since it admits open-textured terms as T-words. Someone says, without idiosyncrasy or aberration, '1224 is a lemon'. Then the facts that 'lemon' is criteria-delimited, that its set of criteria is indefinite, and that there in all likelihood exist, unknown to the speaker and his audience, certain presumptions for the normal application of the word, do not show that the audience can reasonably raise an unlimited or even an indefinite set of doubts as to the truth of the utterance. On the contrary. When the speaker has told us that he has learnt and not forgotten how to handle '1224' and 'lemon' and the assertive link, and that he has watched 1224 closely and under favourable conditions and found that it had a sufficient number of criteria of lemons, and that other people too have tested it and reached the same result, then we agree that if all these things are true and the testing has been thorough, then 1224 *is* a lemon, come what may. If there is a limited set of credentials sufficient to guarantee that even terms with open texture are correctly applicable to an item, then it is reasonable to infer that such a set exists also for less troublesome terms. In this light, Austin's attempt to 'prove' the truth of a statement by blocking up the sources of doubt is not obviously hopeless or even far-fetched. Perhaps some other words are less easy to bring to heel than those with an open texture. A good way of finding out is to put Austin's idea to work on a great many examples. This is yet another task which goes beyond the scope of this book.

Sufficiency and knowing on authority. In 1946.49–51 Austin discusses knowing on authority:

If asked 'How do you know the election is today?' I am apt to reply 'I read it in *The Times*', and if asked 'How do you know the Persians were defeated at Marathon?' I am apt to reply 'Herodotus expressly states that they were'.... [W]e know 'at second hand' when we can cite an authority who was in a position to know (possibly himself also only at second hand). The statement of an authority makes me aware of something, enables me to know something, which I shouldn't otherwise have known. It is a source of knowledge. In many cases, we contrast such reasons for knowing with other reasons for believing the very same thing: 'Even if we didn't know it, even if he hadn't confessed, the evidence against him would be enough to hang him.'

Wilson finds this extraordinary. 'It is now clear, for instance, that Gibbon was wrong to doubt that the martyrs of Tipasa in Mauretania continued to speak after their tongues were cut out by the Vandals; for he had the story not only from the philosopher Aeneas of Gaza, "a cool, a learned, an unexceptionable witness", who saw them himself, but also from Bishop Victor, who heard it from one of the victims.' (Wilson, *op. cit.*, p. 52.) In the very next paragraph of 'Other minds', Austin does, however, explicitly declare that the question 'How do you know that so-and-so?' cannot always be sufficiently answered by citing authorities. Human testimony may be unreliable because of 'bias, mistake, lying, exaggeration, &c.' But there has to be some special reason to doubt the testimony:

It is fundamental in talking (as in other matters) that we are entitled to trust others, except in so far as there is some concrete reason to distrust them. Believing persons, accepting testimony, is the, or one main, point of talking.... [W]e don't talk with people (descriptively) except in the faith that they are trying to convey information.

There are two stages in Austin's paragraph where Wilson sees only one. (i) Austin notes, as a piece of descriptive semantics, that when an authority says that S is P (P being a phenomenon within the field he is an authority on) and when there is no reason to think that he is, for example, biased or speaks about events for which he has no evidence, then (*a*) we do accept John's, Dick's and Harry's appeal to him as a sufficient *credential* for their assertion that S is P; and (*b*) we accept someone's knowledge that they can make this appeal as a sufficient credential for his assertion that they know at second hand that S is P. We think it reasonable to press John, Dick, and Harry for more reasons for their assertion only if there is some reason to hold that the authority is mistaken or dishonest, that they have misunderstood him, and so on. *Mutatis mutandis* the same point holds good of someone's assertion that they know at second hand that S is P. But to admit that we in fact usually hold that an appeal to authorities is in this way a sufficient *credential* for making an assertion is, as Austin indeed is at pains to stress in 1946.51 onwards, not enough to warrant us to accept the assertion as true. We are entitled to do that only if the sufficient backing also is reliable. So Wilson is in agreement with Austin and not—as he apparently thinks—scoring a point against him in holding that the fact that people correctly (= on sufficient credentials) speak of 'knowing at second hand' is not sufficient to establish the reliability of human testimony.

(ii) Austin, however, also adumbrates a reason for believing that human testimony is *in general* reliable. If there was no tacit convention that a speaker must be able to back up what he says, talking would lose its point. I discussed the issue in the last chapter. I hope that it will be obvious, without tiresome repetitions, that Wilson has got the passage all wrong when he insinuates that what Austin brings forth is the remarkably silly argument that since it is sometimes conceded that the speaker has produced sufficient credentials for his assertion that *p*, *p* must also be true!

Sufficiency and sense-data theories (S&S. Ch. X). Had Austin made that invalid inference, he would also have been guilty of inconsistency. For one of his objections against sense-data theories seems to be precisely that they are concerned merely with the sufficiency and not with the reliability of backings. He observes that the great charm of these doctrines lies in the combination of the two views (a) that if we know something, we cannot doubt its truth, and (b) that the truth of sense-data statements cannot intelligibly be doubted. Together they foster the idea that if we manage to give a complete analysis of a claim to knowledge of the external world (e.g. that there is a book on the table) into a claim about the speaker's sense-data, then the question whether he knows there is a book on the table is merely the question whether he has *enough* sense-data of the relevant kind. We don't have to ask whether his sense-data statement is true; for all sense-data statements are 'basic propositions'.

In Ch. 2, §8, we saw reasons for rejecting (b). Thus there is no guarantee of the truth of the statement 'There is a book on the table', even if it is completely analysed in terms of the claimant's sense-data and has a more than sufficient support. We also have to consider, say, whether there is no misperception; i.e. we have to consider also the reliability of the support. A doctrine of empirical knowledge which like sense-data theories considers only the *sufficiency* of backing for claims to knowledge is fundamentally misguided.

5. *Reliability of backing*

There is, claims Austin (*S&S*.124), no *general* answer to the question 'What is reliable backing for all empirical statements?', for (i) different kinds of empirical statements have different kinds of backing, and (ii) a statement which in one situation supports another might in a different situation be supported by it: what is counted as backing what depends on the total speech-situation.

Take the latter point first. It may seem tempting to suppose that singular statements must support general ones and not the other way round. Nevertheless it is a mistake: 'my belief that *this* animal will eat turnips may be based on the belief that most pigs eat turnips; though certainly, in different circumstances, I might have supported the claim that most pigs eat turnips by saying that this pig eats them at any rate'. Again, not all empirical evidence has to be based on how things appear, look, or seem: 'I may say . . . "That pillar is bulgy" on the ground that it looks bulgy; but equally I might say, in different circumstances, "That pillar looks bulgy"—on the ground that I've just built it, and I *built* it bulgy'. (*S&S*.116-17.)

The last example does not seem convincing. The fact that a philosopher has built a pillar with the intention of making it bulgy does not guarantee that he has been successful: to be sure that he has executed his design he has to look and see. Hence it is circular to quote the fact that he built it bulgy as a support for its looking bulgy. But the case is different when 'I' refers to an accomplished craftsman. A baker does not need to eat his cake in order to tell its flavour; he can give both sufficient and reliable support of his assertion about its gustatory qualities by speaking about what ingredients he put into it, how he baked it, and what the chemistry of baking is.

To this a sense-data theorist may reply that speaking about the ingredients of the cake is speaking about what they look like, taste like, and smell like; or rather, that it is speaking about constructs of visual, gustatory and olfactory qualities. The transition from 'The thing looks so-and-so' to 'There is a visual quality of so-and-so' is, of course, one of the main ideas Austin is combatting in *S&S*; but we cannot discuss it here. Let us admit, for the sake of the argument, that such a statement as 'I put cocoa in the cake' always requires evidence in terms of sense-data. Even so, it is clear that if I swallow a slice of the cake and say 'I think it tastes of cocoa', the baker gives me support by saying 'Of course it does; I put cocoa in it'. So even if the 'material object' statement 'I put cocoa in the cake' is in a given situation borne out by such sense-data statements about an ingredient as 'It tastes of cocoa', the former may in other situations support the latter; and that is enough to establish (ii).

But is (i) true? Is Austin right in asserting that 'there *could* be no *general* answer to the [question about empirical statements] what is evidence for that' (*S&S*.124) and that the reason is that different statements have different kinds of support? Must not everyone of them be backed up by empirical evidence? And is it not possible to say something about empirical evidence in general?

Of course Austin had no wish to deny that empirical statements must be supported by what we see, hear, taste, smell, and feel. This does not, however, entail that we can lay down in general how this backing has to be conditioned in order to be reliable. That is I think the point, elaborated none too clearly, in *S&S*.124: The reliability of a backing depends upon the individual circumstances of each case. 'If the Theory of Knowledge consists in finding grounds for such an answer [i.e., an answer to the general question, "What is reliable evidence for an (= any) empirical statement?"] there is no such thing.' We can only ascertain the reliability of particular backings in particular situations.

Reliability and scholarly research. How do we test the reliability of a sufficient backing of a claim? Well, that notoriously depends on the nature of the backing, and on what part of it you are questioning. If you query that I ever mastered the technique of telling squares from other objects, recordings and testimonies of my past performances become relevant; if you wonder whether I scanned the present specimen closely enough, you have to set other types of inquiries afoot (e.g. into the keenness of my eyesight). Scientists and scholars have often worked out strict rules for accepting and rejecting results of such inquiries. Ophthalmologists can, in many cases, ascertain the state of someone's eyesight under different conditions of illumination, time of exposure of the things seen, etc.; and historians, psychologists and jurists have rules for assessing the reliability of testimonies. (Cf. 1946.83.)

Although Austin does not say so, the trend of his thought is, pretty clearly, that the philosopher is not qualified to teach ophthalmologists and historians how to deal with questions of reliability within their fields of research. They are the acknowledged experts on these questions, and the philosopher can only learn from them, not teach them. He cannot hope to answer even the more specific question. 'What is reliable evidence of this historical (psychological, etc.) statement?' without turning to the expert.

Reliability of common sense statements. But Austin has no doubt whatsoever that we can very often verify our credentials completely. As far as common sense statements are concerned, such as that there is a telephone in the next room, there is no need to call in experts. I can go and look, test whether it is a *trompe l'oeil* painting, take it to pieces to see if it has a real mechanism, use it for ringing somebody up and get him to ring me up too. '[If] I do all these things, I *do* make sure; what more could possibly be required? This object has already stood up to amply enough tests to establish that it really is a telephone; and it isn't just that, for everyday or practical or ordinary purposes, enough is *as good as* a telephone; what meets all these tests just *is* a telephone, no doubt about it.' (*S&S*.119.) I have verified your claim up to the hilt although I have not, e.g., tried to eat the telephone and failed (*S&S*.123).

In Austin's opinion there are, however, a lot of statements about material things which have sufficient backing but cannot be said to be based on evidence: 'evidence' is too weak a word for the backing, since it implies that we only have signs or indications of the truth of our statement, when we in fact are far better off. Crumbs of bread or traces of a pig are evidence that there has been a loaf of bread or a pig there; but if the loaf of bread or the pig actually is on display, it is of course no *evidence* of the truth of 'There's a loaf of bread (a pig) here': it guarantees its truth, provided that no illusion, etc., is involved. There is no need for further verification, and it is indeed doubtful whether it makes sense to speak of 'further verification' in this context. (1946.74–5; *S&S*.115–16.)

6. *Our knowledge of other minds*

Let us now consider how Austin employs the previous observations in his famous study of our knowledge of other minds. Very many of our 'mental' concepts are dispositional. The analysis of dispositional concepts is a major problem in contemporary philosophy of science, since it involves, for example, an analysis of contrary-to-fact conditionals. Austin ignores these problems, possibly because he first wants to deal with simpler problems or because he thinks that the former do not pose problems peculiar to questions about other minds.

It may be convenient to start a discussion of his paper from two truisms which he clearly takes for granted: (*a*) We have a common language. (*b*) In that language we can say and understand such phrases as 'He is thinking', 'She is cheerful', 'I am depressed'. We have presumably learnt to understand them. But how is that possible if they signify strictly private events? Does not a common language demand that the phenomena it has words for are public?

In 1946 Austin argues that knowledge of other minds does not require power of introspecting them. His procedure is, roughly, to single out some 'mental' word which allegedly signifies strictly private phenomena, and then to show that in fact it does not stand for any such thing: your anger is sometimes quite public, and then your behaviour is not just a 'symptom' of your inner, unwitnessable wrath (1946.71–82). This goes some way to show that we do sometimes know something about other minds. Yet, when he comes to grips with what he feels is 'fundamental to the whole Predicament', his question is not the one which his procedure seems to lead up to, viz.

(1) Can there be any conventionally accepted rule joining vocables to entities ('mental events', feelings, etc.) that are necessarily wholly private?

Instead he poses the problem

(2) Have I any reason to believe that other people ever give true introspective reports about their states of mind?

He answers that 'believing in other persons ... is ... an irreducible part of our experience' for which, however, no justification can be given (1946.83).

This is a surprisingly bad answer. It hands away the valuable remarks he made in the very same paper about the point of serious talk; and it is irrelevant to the 'Predicament'. Anyone really worried at the problem of our knowledge of other minds is likely to retort, 'Certainly I do[14] believe that people can generally back up what they say; but in all cases except that of their introspective reports I can, at least in principle, check what they say. What worries me is whether their general reliability in matters which I can control entitles me to infer that they are generally reliable in matters which I cannot control. To answer that I as a matter of psychology do accept their autopsychical reports, at least usually, is to confuse what I in fact do with what I am entitled to do.'

[14] The change from Austin's 'we' to 'I' is essential. Had the objector said 'We believe' etc, he would already have assumed that he had that knowledge of other minds he in the very same breath questions. He would then be guilty of the (typically philosophical) inconsistency Moore castigated in 'A defence of common sense' (*Philosophical Papers*, pp. 42–5).

The necessity of public criteria. I have suggested that the bulk of the paper more naturally leads up to (1) than to (2). An answer to the former question really sheds light on the 'Predicament', and Austin does in fact give a very good reply. His 'Final Note' is, I suppose, designed to spotlight the guiding idea of the essay, and it fastens only on that answer. I propose therefore to drop (2), as a dead end. Instead I shall develop what he has to say on (1). In order to explicate it, I shall use Strawson's notions of private and public criteria.[15] At one point Austin seems dimly aware of the former, but later on he forgets them; and I shall argue that it is because of that neglect he begins to wonder whether there is any justification of our belief in other men's introspective reports.

One of the main causes of doubt as to our knowledge of other minds is the assumption that at least some mental phenomena *for which our language has words* are unwitnessable and necessarily private. And this cannot be true. We can teach someone what 'angry' or 'unhappy' means by pointing to people who look and behave typically angrily or unhappily. In doing so, we establish a vertical convention between the vocable 'angry' or 'unhappy' and the look and behaviour: the latter become criteria of anger— witnessable, *public* criteria. Yet a pupil who has learnt the meaning of a word in this way does not, in an important sense, know what anger is until he has himself been angry. But how does he know that this sensation which he has is of anger? Well, he may be told 'Now you are angry' when he is in the appropriate state of mind. The teacher can tell his state from his behaviour, looks, etc. (Cf. 1946.78.) So from being told he is angry, the pupil learns to link the vocable 'anger' not only to public criteria but also to something strictly private, something which he alone can experience. That sort of experience might then become a *private criterion* of anger for him. Later on he recognizes that when public criteria tell him that another is angry, that person can also say he is angry, *without relying on public criteria*. This is everyone's ground for assuming that others than himself have private criteria.

Austin may hint at private criteria when he says that someone's introspective report 'is not (is not treated primarily as) a sign or symptom, although it can, secondarily and artificially, be treated

[15] P. F. Strawson, *Individuals*, Ch. 3.

as such. A unique place is reserved for it in the summary of the facts of the case.' (1946.82) But although he (perhaps) admits their existence, his arguments are designed to show that the public criteria are the important ones. My (honest) statements about my states of mind are not incorrigible and undoubtedly true, are not 'basic propositions'. I can wonder not only whether what I feel really amounts to pain (1946.60–1); I can also genuinely believe that I hate her and be told, and convinced, that I love her (1946.78). Those who told me what my feelings were did not have telepathic powers; they just studied my looks and behaviour and found in them the (public) criteria of love, not of hate. In conflicts between my behaviour and what I say about my state of mind, the former has the upper hand—deception of course excepted—in the sense that not only others but I too admit, at least at a cool moment, that since I steadily behave in such-and-such a way, I must have misidentified my feelings. How is this concession possible if my state of mind is something entirely private?

Strawson has shown that the truth of all this does not force us to dismiss private criteria. We can tell whether we are angry or in love without watching our behaviour or consulting a mirror; but if the private criteria clash with the public ones, the former have to give way. For the terms we are concerned with have conventional meanings; conventional meanings presuppose general consent to follow certain rules within a language community; but how are we to consent or dissent to rules tying a vocable to something necessarily private? Private criteria are held in check by public ones. There cannot be any term in linguistic communication whose criteria are wholly or even essentially private—for then we could never know whether it had the same meaning for you as for me.

So whether or not we accept the existence of private criteria, we must agree that they are inessential to the correct employment of the term. A common language cannot contain words governed by private criteria, unless these in their turn are kept in check by public ones. The answer to question (1) is in the negative.

Some solvable questions about other minds. We may now distinguish two types of difficulties concerning our knowledge of other minds.

A. I may take it for granted that others are sometimes angry but call in question that they have private criteria of their anger or that their private criteria resemble mine.

B. I may be more profoundly sceptical and wonder whether others ever are really angry. And it seems to me that Austin thinks the main problems of other minds are

A_1: When others are in a certain state of mind, do they have private criteria of it?

B_1: When others to all appearance are in a certain state of mind, are they merely feigning it to deceive me?

B_2: Am I correct in taking their behaviour, looks, etc., to be criteria of this instead of that state of mind?

These are straightforward empirical questions. A_1 can be answered by investigating whether others can apply 'anger' and its cognates to themselves without falling back on observations of their own behaviour, facial expressions, etc.; B_1 by unearthing and applying tests of hypocricy and simulation; and B_2 by going through our stock of criteria-delimited 'mental' words in order to see whether the same criteria enter two of them. No difficulty in principle seems to hinder us from finding sufficient criteria for settling these three questions or prevent the existence of reliable criteria for settling them. We all believe, for example, that there is some crucial test for deciding whether he just pretends to love her—though we may know the test and yet be unable to employ it. It certainly seems as if in lots and lots and lots of cases we can answer the three questions, and answer them confidently: and then we *do* have knowledge of other minds.

B_1 may, however, be given a less empirical interpretation. I may wonder, not 'Is this man trying to deceive me as to what his state of mind is?' but 'Does everyone always try to deceive me as to his state of mind?' This is a conceptual question, and I am not sure that Austin deals with it. The laconic saying '"You cannot fool all the people all of the time" is "analytic"' (1946.81n) may be a contribution to a reply which, I think, has to run something like this:

I wonder whether *anyone* who exhibits the public criteria of (say) anger is angry. But how can that be a problem? I have been taught the meaning of 'angry' by means of public criteria. Since I know that some pieces of behaviour, etc., which are public criteria of anger also enter the public criteria of, say, jealousy, I may wonder whether I am mistaken in thinking that he is angry instead of jealous; since I know that some pieces of behaviour can be feigned, I may wonder whether the ones I have witnessed are genuine; and since I know that there are private criteria of anger, I may wonder whether he feels anything private or what his feeling is like. But if *no* piece of behaviour is in any circumstance allowed as a criterion that another is angry, 'anger' and its cognates must signify something strictly private.[16] Consequently, they have no meaning in a common language. All that can be said of them is that they signify some private entity or other. But that entity is not *anger* any longer. The terms in which the problem was posed have been emptied of their old sense without having acquired a new one. I can wonder whether this or that man tries to deceive me now, or most of the time, or always. But I cannot intelligibly wonder whether all men are always trying to deceive me—that would be to pose the problem within a conceptual scheme which I in the same breath reject without putting something else in its stead. 'You cannot fool all the people all of the time' is indeed analytic—at least if linguistic communication is to be possible.

Austin and private criteria. I have said that although Austin does not deny that there are private criteria, he neglects them. They do not matter for the points just made. I think, however, that if he had considered them, he would not have taken the question why we trust other people's introspective reports to be fundamental to discussions of other minds. I cannot check your 'auto-psychical' report except by studying your behaviour. If I still give it a unique place in reciting the circumstances of the case even when I have no public criteria to go on, how am I to justify the practice? Austin's way out is to declare that our belief in others is 'an irreducible part of our experience'.

We need not in this way fall back on animal faith if we assume that there are private criteria. Reports based on them are mostly borne out by public ones; when the relevant outward behaviour

---

[16] Austin says that 'there is no call to say that . . . "the feeling" . . . *is* the *anger*' (1946.77n.) That is an understatement. What we all commonly mean by 'anger' *cannot* be purely private—though it has, or can have, a private side.

and looks are absent, we know—at least very often—that there are crucial tests for deciding whether they are suppressed or the report is false; and when we cannot test the utterance but have no reason to doubt it, we trust it because speech would be pointless unless speakers are usually honest.

A digression: unsolvable questions of other minds. Are the problems Austin has singled out the main ones in the cluster surrounding our knowledge of other minds? Perhaps; but there are others which have puzzled philosophers. Suppose we take it for granted that someone is angry. Then we may still wonder

A_2: Are his private criteria the same as mine?

A_3: Do his private criteria even faintly resemble mine?

These questions are not empirically solvable. Our common language contains no words for private criteria, nor can we as a rule describe what they are like (for we have then to take recourse to words with public criteria). Therefore we cannot inform another about them, nor can we point to them nor make any other form of ostension of them. Hence A_2 and A_3 cannot be answered and cannot, even in principle, be confirmed or disconfirmed. Yet they seem perfectly meaningful. In fact, such questions as 'Do others feel the same when they are in love as I do when I am in love?' are, I think, among the clearest counter-examples there are to the thesis that literal meaning is tied up with methods of verification and falsification.[17]

[17] But it does not show that anything is wrong with the Principle of Verification—as e.g. A. J. Ayer conceives of it in *Language, Truth & Logic*. For the principle is applicable only to propositions, and a question to which no answer can be given can hardly be given a propositional character. To rephrase it by an indicative sentence, e.g. 'It will forever be doubtful whether' etc is no good, since this may very well be a pseudo-proposition. Finally, the principle is merely a *criterion* of sense.

CHAPTER 5

The Performative Thesis and the Force Thesis

Austin's general thesis of the illocutionary 'act' is far from clear. It was, I think, designed to cater for his best-known discovery, *the performatory utterance*. Such an utterance, also called a *performative* (*Words*.6), has the grammatical form of a statement, but to utter it is not to describe how things are. Already in the 1946 paper, two different positive views of performatives are discernible. The first is that to issue such an utterance in appropriate circumstances is to perform an action, not to say anything true or false. I dub this suggestion the (genuinely) *Performative Thesis*. The second idea is that the characteristic verb phrase of a performative serves to give the audience to understand how an utterance is to be taken—what its *illocutionary force* is. This hypothesis I name the *Force Thesis*.[1]

I believe Austin never saw that the theses need not concern the same type of phenomena. It is true that in 1946 he puts the Performative Thesis in the lime-light, whilst in *Words* the Force Thesis takes its place; but even in the latter work there are passages suggesting that he thought of the performatory and the illocutionary function as connected 'aspects' of (the semantic result of) the very same type of speech act, the illocutionary act. If he did, he was mistaken. An act which satisfies the Performative Thesis does not have to satisfy the Force Thesis, and *vice versa*. To class both of them as examples of illocutionary acts is too rash. This is the theme of my first section.

[1] Scandinavian discussions of performatives have exclusively pivoted upon the Performative Thesis. At the second Scandinavian congress of philosophy (held at Sigtuna in 1961) none of the three symposiasts on performatives— I. Hedenius, 'Performativer'; J. Hartnack, 'The performatory use of sentences'; and G. H. von Wright, 'On promises'—touched on the Force Thesis. In British philosophy, however, lines of thought parallel to or coincident with that thesis have been developed by S. Toulmin ('Probability', in *ECA* and also as part of Ch. 2 of Toulmin's *The Uses of Argument*) and J. O. Urmson ('Parenthetical verbs' in *ECA*).

The second section is more an appendix than an integral part of the book. In it I try to develop the Force Thesis in two directions: as a theory of discourse-showing devices and as a theory of degree-showing devices. In the course of that undertaking, a few problems about promising and about saying and disbelieving will be discussed. Finally I try to give a new turn to Austin's comparison between saying 'I know' and saying 'I promise'.

I. PERFORMATIVES AND THEIR FUNCTIONS

1. Performatives

Before the two theses can be stated, we have to make it clear what kind of utterance it is that is paradigmatically performative, and in what kinds of situation a performative is in order—what its *felicity-conditions* are. Both these points are discussed at length in the first chapters of *Words*. Let us start with what Austin says about what he calls *explicit* performatives.

Explicit performatives. Paradigms of explicit performatives are utterances of the form 'I promise to do so-and-so', 'I guarantee...', 'I swear...', 'I name this ship *Queen Elizabeth*', 'I give and bequeath my watch to my brother'.[2] None of these utterances contains such words as 'good', 'all', 'ought', 'can'—phrases which normally indicate that the utterance containing them is not, or not clearly, a constative; nor does it exhibit philosophically bewildering constructions like the hypothetical. Every explicit performative has the grammatical form of an indicative utterance. Nonetheless it
   (1) is not assessed as true or false;
   (2) is not a record or a description of an action;
   (3) is (a part of) the doing of an action that would not normally be described as (just) *saying* something in the sense of (just) performing a locutionary act.
Let us take these points from *Words*.Ch.1 in order.

(*i*) *Grammatical form.* The grammatical form is that of the first person present perfect indicative active. If any of our para-

[2] A sample of legal performatives is given in Hedenius' paper 'Performatives'. [Cf. also R. Samek: 'Performative utterances and the concept of contract' *AJP* 43 (1965).]

digms is put in another person, tense, or mood, the result is usually not a performative: 'He promises to do so-and-so', 'I guaranteed', 'I should swear if . . .', 'I am bequeathing my watch to my brother'[3] are *not* performatives. They are assessed as true or false, are records or descriptions of actions, and would not normally be described as pieces of promising, guaranteeing, swearing or bequeathing. (*Words*.63–4.)

We cannot, however, say that whenever somebody utters 'I promise to do so-and-so', he has issued a performative. One reason is that a performative can go wrong in a variety of ways which will be mentioned in the discussion of its felicity-conditions (A.1)–(Γ.2). Another reason is that the present perfect may be habitual: such an utterance as 'Every New Year's Eve I promise to stop smoking' fails to satisfy (1)–(3). (*Words*.56.)

Our explicit performatives can, however, be couched in other grammatical forms than the one mentioned. 'I name this ship the *Queen Elizabeth*' can be put in the passive voice as 'This ship is (hereby) named the *Queen Elizabeth*'. Instead of 'I promise you to come tomorrow' I may say, with an outlandish turn of phrase, 'You are (hereby) promised that I shall come tomorrow'. A cricket umpire may say 'You are (hereby out' instead of 'I give (pronounce) you out'.—From this there is no great step to such utterances as 'Notice is hereby given that trespassers will be prosecuted' or 'Passengers are (hereby) warned to cross the track by the bridge only'. They pass (1)–(3) with flying colours. They may also, though slightly awkwardly, be brought to conform to the requirement of the first person present perfect indicative active: 'Notice is hereby given that trespassers will be prosecuted' may be rendered as 'We, the railway authorities [or whatnot], hereby give notice that trespassers will be prosecuted'. (*Words*. Ch.5.)

(*ii*) *Assessments in terms of 'true' and 'false'*. Suppose we have an utterance of the appropriate grammatical form. Then it is

---

[3] The continuous present is *the* tense for *stating* that I promise. In his essay on performatives Hartnack says, 'If I make a promise to come by signing a document I can at the same time answer the question "What are you doing?" by saying "I promise to come".' Can anybody who masters English really answer that question in those words? Mustn't he say 'I am promising to come'? (In Swedish the answer must be put in our counterpart to the continuous tense: 'Jag håller på med (är i färd med) att lova'.)

easy to see whether we use the epithets 'true' or 'false' when assessing it. But we do speak of false promises, so an utterance can be assessed as false and yet be a performative. (What Austin maintains is of course *not* that a performative cannot be assessed by means of the labels 'true' and 'false' but that it cannot square with facts in the way constatives do. We shall discuss that tenet in a while. For purposes which will soon be evident I have changed Austin's bold claim to the weak one that performatives are not called true or false. That this criterion by itself is neither necessary nor sufficient need not worry us. We are by now used to the idea of criteria-delimited words.)

(*iii*) *Performatives do not describe or record actions.* Were performatives descriptions of actions done by the speaker, there would be candidates for the descriptions even if the speaker kept silent. But I cannot normally be quiet and yet manage to apologize, to bid you welcome, or to swear to tell the truth, the whole truth and nothing but the truth. Austin recognizes, however, that this is by no means always true: I can, e.g., marry in deeds, or bet by putting a coin in the totalisator. (*Words*.8.)

Further, it always makes sense to ask whether a description is correct. Hence we can always ask 'Does he really do the action designated by the verb of our description? We describe him as running, but does he really run?' Where a performative is concerned, the question does not arise. If someone says 'I promise' and the felicity-conditions are fulfilled, there is no room for the query 'Does he really promise?'—it is already answered. This enables us to distinguish 'I bid you welcome' (which is a performative) from 'I welcome you' (which is not). (*Words*.79.)

That a performative is no description of an action may also be seen in a way which Austin does not mention. W. H. F. Barnes notes that when another person's statements are reported in *oratio obliqua*, this is normally done by the formula 'he said that he . . .': 'I love her' becomes 'He said that he loved her'; 'I believe in God' becomes 'He said that he believed in God'; and so forth. But when the utterance reported is a performative, the 'he said that he' - formula is inept: 'I promise' does not become 'He said that he promised' but simply 'He promised'; 'I bid you welcome' not 'He said that he bade her welcome' but 'He bade her welcome', etc.

Barnes does not use the notion of performatives. He speaks of the practical use of certain verbs; and he does so for two reasons. The first is that he is under the misapprehension that Austin classifies certain verbs, and not certain employments of certain verbs in certain constructions, as performatory; and Barnes is rightly anxious to stress that 'promise', for example, is *not* performatory in any persons, tenses and moods other than the first person present perfect indicative (and of course in the reformulations of this grammatical form we have mentioned). The second is that he is worried about Austin's words (1946.69), 'The sense in which you "did promise" is that you did *say* you promised', which seem to admit of a gap between saying of somebody that he said he promised and saying of him that he promised.[4] It is true that Austin in that early paper held that there was such a gap: he held the obviously hopeless view that a false promise is no promise. But we shall see that he recants it in *Words*; and Barnes' remarks seem to fit in with the theory expounded in that book.

(iv) *Performatives are actions.* How are we to explain that no wedge can be inserted between my saying that I promise and my promising? Austin's answer is that my words are my promise. Performatives seem to describe actions but are in effect performances of them. In uttering the words 'I promise', I perform the act of promising; I do not describe or record it. I am an agent, not an observer.

That the act of promising is performed in uttering the words 'I promise' is indicated by the word 'hereby'. It can be slipped into genuine performatives and 'serves to indicate that the utterance . . . of the sentence is, as it is said, the instrument effecting the act' (*Words*.57). That act is, of course, done by a person. He is essentially involved in all performatives: as the 'I' of the first person cases; as the person or authority appending his signature to the third person passive voice cases and thereby setting them in effect; and as the person addressing you in the second person passive voice cases. (*Words*.60–1.)

That performatives are actions is further seen by the fact that they, like all other actions, can be done willingly or unwillingly. We can ask someone whether he is willing to apologize and also

[4] W. H. F. Barnes, 'Knowing'. *Ph.R.* 72 (1963), pp. 5–7.

whether he is willing *to say* he is sorry; but we cannot ask him whether he is willing to *be* sorry. To apologize consists in uttering the words 'I apologize' in circumstances satisfying their felicity-conditions; but to be sorry does not consist merely or even essentially in uttering the words 'I am sorry' as an apology. It consists in being in a state of mind; and that is not an action and hence nothing you can perform, willingly or unwillingly. (*Words*.80.)

Austin's example is not happy. To say 'I'm sorry' is sometimes to make an apology and nothing more: you can say it with a smiling face and without feeling of guilt, displeasure with yourself, etc. Hence there is no doubt that the utterance *occasionally* has the function of a performative; and Austin does not deny it. (Cf *Words*.Ch.6.) His point is presumably that its *standard* function is not, or not merely, or not essentially, performatory; it (also) serves to describe a state of mind. Whether this is true of 'I am sorry' may, however, be doubted. Cf §3.

Austin notes with satisfaction that 'in the American law of evidence, a report of what someone else said is admitted as evidence if what he said is an utterance of our performative kind: because this is regarded as a report not so much of something he *said*, as which it would be hear-say and not admissible as evidence, but rather as something he *did*, an action of his' (*Words*. 13). But he does not think that he really has to prove that performatives do not *describe* actions but *do* them—it is, he claims, obvious as soon as it is pointed out (*Words*.6).

Felicity-conditions of explicit performatives. Austin assumes that the points now elaborated are enough to enable us to single out a class of explicit performatives. In what situations is such an utterance in order? He lists six conditions, the violation of any of which makes the performative 'infelicitous'. They are (*Words*. 14–15):

(A.1) There must exist an accepted conventional procedure having a certain conventional effect, that procedure to include the uttering of certain words by certain persons in certain circumstances, and further,

(A.2) the particular persons and circumstances in a given case must be appropriate for the invocation of the particular procedure invoked.

(B.1) The procedure must be executed by all participants both correctly and
(B.2) completely.
(Γ.1) Where, as often, the procedure is designed for use by persons having certain thoughts or feelings, or for the inauguration of certain consequential conduct on the part of any participant, then a person participating in and so invoking the procedure must in fact have those thoughts or feelings, and the participants must intend so to conduct themselves, and further
(Γ.2) must actually so conduct themselves subsequently.

A performative violating one or more of the felicity-conditions (A.1)–(B.2) is a *misfire*. I have not then managed to perform the intended act. I cannot, in our present society, challenge someone to duel, since the institution of duelling is no longer accepted; I have not named the ship if I am not the person appointed to perform the ceremony; I have not bet you sixpence if you do not take me on.

If a performative of the kind specified in the preamble of (Γ.1) is issued in circumstances satisfying (A.1)–(B.2) but not one or both of the Γ-conditions, the act intended *is* brought off. A promise is a promise, even if given in bad faith;[5] and if I say 'I pardon you', I have pardoned you even if I say it without having the appropriate intentions and/or without abstaining from punishing you for the deed. A performative which fails merely in respect to the Γ-conditions is not a misfire but an *abuse*.

Austin's ingenious discussion in *Words*.Chs.2–4 of the borders between the different sorts of infelicities (and hence between the different fecility-conditions) is difficult to sum up. Since anyhow I have no general quarrels with it, I shall pass it over in silence. It shows that the conditions shade into each other: Austin holds that the infelicities are not mutually exclusive.

Are the violations of (A.1)–(Γ.2) the only ways there are in which a performative can be out of order? Of course not, answers Austin (*Words*.Ch.2). As *actions*, performatives are subject to

[5] Here Austin recants 1946.69, where he had included the Γ-conditions in (A.2) and therefore maintained that when a person says 'I promise to do it' without intending to perform the act promised, he has not promised: 'you *can't* then have promised to do it, so that you *didn't* promise'.

troubles which can affect *all* sorts of actions (e.g. they may be done under duress, or by accident, or otherwise unintentionally);[6] and as *utterances*, they are heirs to ills affecting *all* kinds of utterances (they may go wrong in various stages of the locutionary act, they may be etiolations, etc.). Since these sorts of unsatisfactoriness are not peculiar to performatives, he mentions them just to remark that he is not concerned with them.

Thus (A.1)–(Γ.2) are not sufficient conditions for the smooth functioning of a performative. Are all of them even necessary? Austin is not univocal. Sometimes he says they are. He introduces them by saying (*Words*.14; my italics):

Suppose we try first to state schematically . . . some at least of the things which are *necessary* for the smooth or 'happy' functioning of a performative. . . . I fear . . . that these *necessary* conditions to be satisfied will strike you as obvious.

Sometimes, however, he answers that one or other of the six conditions can be dispensed with in ordinary life. Examples of failures to conform to (B.1) are, he says on p. 36, more easily seen in the law than in ordinary life *where allowances are made*. Similarly, the performative 'I open this library' is misexecuted by violation of (B.2) if the key snaps in the lock; yet a certain lapse in such procedures is admitted—otherwise university business would never get done (p. 31).

These examples may be taken to show that he does not, after all, regard the conditions as necessary; but I am not sure. He probably means that they *are* necessary, although we often, in matters of minor importance, do not bother to repeat a performance if the first execution goes wrong. Their necessity may, e.g., show themselves in the fact that people who accept the relevant institution admit that the violation of one of these conditions constitutes a reasonable ground for maintaining that the performative is a misfire or an abuse. In fact, the six conditions ought perhaps to be regarded as necessary for the existence of the performatory institutions at issue—were they not in general satisfied, there would be no institutions of giving and accepting promises, entering marriages, promoting people, etc. This could, I think, be established with arguments parallel to those given in Ch. 3:2. But we shall soon see that the border between some

---

[6] Austin has taken up these problems in 1956a.

performatives and some non-performatives is far from clear. It is then small wonder that dubious cases arise.

2. *The Performative Thesis*

Let us shelve the question of implicit performatives for a while, and instead try and come to grips with the Performative Thesis.

When singling out the class of explicit performatives, I said that they were not *assessed* as true or false. Austin maintains that they also *are* neither true nor false. We have seen that truth and falsehood are connected with constatives; and that a constative is true when its locution specifies situations of a certain type—a type which is exemplified by the actual situation (the fact) to which the constative is tied down by its referring conventions. Austin can hardly doubt that such sentences as 'I promise to come tomorrow' or 'I name the ship the *Queen Elizabeth*' are intelligible specifications of certain types of situations, nor that they can be so used that their referring expressions pin them down to a certain historic situation (a fact). What he must maintain is that the difference between performatives and constatives is that their relations to their respective situations are totally unlike each other. The facts reported by constatives can exist whether or not the constative is issued; but *performatives constitute the fact they seem to report.* 'When I say, before the registrar or altar, &c., "I do", I am not reporting on a marriage: I am indulging in it.' (*Words*.6; cf 1956c.222.)

It is tempting to regard a promise as an inner unwitnessable act of which the words 'I promise' are at best a record. If they are, the performative cannot be the promise. But, in the first place, the idea of a promise as a *purely* inward, private act leaves it a mystery how we come to have such a word in our common language and how we can understand and ascertain that something is a promise. Secondly, the idea that performatives are *mere* reports on, and not performances of, actions contravenes common sense, as Austin shows (*Words*.9–10; 1956c.223). For if 'I promise' is just a description or record or of a report on something, a promise-breaker may excuse himself thus: 'I did indeed say "I promise to come" but I didn't promise; I didn't perform the inward spiritual act. I lied, but I didn't promise.' This is unacceptable. Our word is our bond.

PERFORMATIVES AND THEIR FUNCTIONS

Austin tries to bring out the contrast between constatives and performatives thus (*Words*.47):

in ordinary cases, for example running, it is the fact that he is running which makes the statement that he is running *true*; or again, . . . [the truth of the statement] 'he is running' depends on his being running. Whereas in our case it is the happiness of the performative 'I apologize' which makes it the fact that I am apologizing: and my success in apologizing depends on the happiness of the performative utterance 'I apologize'.*

No wedge can be inserted between a performative (when in order) and the promise, apology or whatnot performed by it; but a great gulf is fixed between the true constative 'I am sick' and being sick.

This difference between performatives and constatives is, I think, not controversial. There are, of course, cases where an act can be performed in other ways than by a performative. If I first confirm a deal with a handshake and then say 'I agree to your conditions', we may perhaps wonder whether my utterance is not just a verbal record of the act performed by shaking hands. That performatives often constitute the actions they seem to describe cannot, however, be reasonably doubted.

Two things can be and have been discussed: (2.1) Assuming that performatives are not true or false, what relations do they have to constatives? (2.2) May it not be the case that performatives always are either true or false, although they are performances of actions?

---

*[In a joint review of *Words* and *LIA* R. Brown remarks: 'Obviously the parallel is not correctly drawn. If there is to be a relevant parallel, the truth of "I am apologizing for John's running" must depend on the happiness (adequacy of utterance) of "John is running" and not on "I apologize". But then the dependency relation is quite different in the two cases. For if in neither case is John running, "I am stating that . . ." becomes false and "I am apologizing" remains true.' (*AJP* 41 (1963), p. 421.)

I admit that Austin's parallel is not correct. But if John is not running, my apology for his running is inept. Moreover, it is at least doubtful that I manage to apologize. The performance is perhaps not in order unless its supplementation is true. If this is so, it is not my success in apologizing that makes my performative 'I apologize for John's running' a happy one. The success of my apology depends on whether I issue the performative in the right circumstances.]

2.1. Connections between performatives and constatives

(i) Austin denies that performatives are true or false; but he insists that they nevertheless are linked up with truth or falsehood. A performative is not felicitous unless (A.1)–(Γ.2) are fulfilled; i.e., unless it is *true* that there is a certain conventional procedure of the sort described in (A.1), that the persons and circumstances are of the kind laid down in (A.2), and so on for the remaining conditions (*Words*.46–7).

For this reason it will not do to argue like Hedenius (*op. cit.*, §3) that since we can settle empirically whether the words 'I promise' constitute a promise on a particular occasion, the performative *must* be true or false. Hartnack's rejoinder to this allegation was that performatives are 'defeasible', i.e., that there is no set of conditions which together are *sufficient* to decide whether 'I promise' on this occasion is a promise. This may be right. It is, however, certain that when one of (A.1)–(B.2) is not fulfilled, the performative does not come off. They are necessary conditions; and since it is empirically checkable whether they are satisfied, we can tell at least misfires without considering whether the infelicitous performatives has any truth-value at all.

(ii) Granted that performatives constitute the action they seem to describe whilst constatives do not constitute the facts they report, we may wonder whether a performative cannot *simultaneously* have a performatory and reporting function. Is it not possible for me to say, with a defiant glance at my audience, 'I promise to help him; and now I've told you'? Does not 'I promise' then do duty *both* as a promise *and* as a piece of information? (Cf von Wright's paper.) I have already answered in the affirmative. See Ch.4:3.1.

Nonetheless the success of the reporting job is logically dependent on the performatory job, in the sense that one would be wrong to report that a promise, a marriage, etc., are performed unless they *are* performed; and their being performed is a matter of the performatory function of the expression. The agent has to do the act, before he can correctly report that it is done. Consequently, the performatory function of a performative expression is (*a*) not identical with its descriptive or reporting function; (*b*) it is, on the contrary, a pre-requisite for the success of the latter.

2.2. Are performatives true and false?

One can perhaps maintain, with Hedenius,[7] that there is no performative with a purely performatory function. A performatory act always involves uttering phemes with a certain sense and a certain reference; i.e., it always involves a locutionary act. This act characterizes the speaker as the performer of a certain action—viz. that which the performatory function of the utterance, if successful, brings about. The locution is happy only if there is a correspondence between it and the world. There is such a correspondence if, and only if, the performatory function of the utterance works smoothly. Isn't the correspondence enough to guarantee the truth of what is said?

A performatory utterance is an utterance with the social function of causing its own truth. Examples of false performatives (or better: examples of performatives which in their locutionary aspect are false) are, according to Hedenius, utterances of normally performatory sentences in situations which make them either crudely jocular or ironical, or which are such that the speaker does not have the appropriate authority.

Truth and non-serious constatives. There are two steps in Hedenius's argument. The first—which will be discussed later—conflates performatives with constatives. The second is that jocular constatives are true or false, i.e., that truth and falsehood adhere to utterances of a constative form even when they do not carry pragmatic implications of truthfulness. This is an odd assumption.

In a play, a child hands another a toy bank-note in exchange for a dish of sand and says, 'Here is a pound'. Compare him to a counterfeiter who hands one of his home-made products to a shopkeeper in exchange for some wares and says, 'Here is a pound'. Both the child and the counterfeiter know that they are not handling real bank-notes. Do both of them utter a falsehood?

As far as common sense is concerned, the answer is No. An utterance is given a truth-value only when it is intended and/or taken to be (*a*) *serious*—not a joke, a mock-utterance, etc.—, and (*b*) a *statement*—not an order, a value-judgment, an interjection,

---

[7] The reader is warned that what follows is an adaptation of Hedenius' arguments to the somewhat different concepts and distinctios of this book.

etc. The child's utterance is a mock-utterance, the counterfeiter's is a serious but false statement. A mock-utterance or a jocular statement is related to a serious statement in about the same way as a toy bank-note is related to a true bank-note; whilst a serious but false statement is related to a serious and true statement in about the same way as a counterfeited bank-note is related to a real bank-note. To say that a jocular statement is false is as correct—and as bewildering—as to say that the toy bank-note has no purchase-power. Since the jocular statement and the toy bank-note never set out to be the things they imitate, it is most unreasonable to judge them as if they did.

This is open to the objection that if I jocularly say of a man 'He's the Duke of Edinburgh' and you at the same time seriously say of the same man, 'By Jove, he's the Duke of Edinburgh!', our utterances have exactly the same relation to facts. Of course they differ in the respect that your utterance warrants the audience to infer that you think you can back it up, whilst mine does not entitle you to the corresponding inference about me. What is at issue in discussions of truth is, however, the relation of the utterance to facts, and not whether it warrants an inference about the speaker's beliefs. Hence jokes have truth-values.

It is, no doubt, convenient to use the notions of truth and falsehood in this way. Then they are, however, explications of our everyday notions. Explications involve reforms, and the elements discarded in the transformation may prove to be important. Our everyday notion of truth and falsehood is so entwined with notions of commitment and contradiction that a reform has far-reaching consequences. The tenor of Ch.3 was that there would be no point in having a language in which speakers were not obliged to commit themselves in their words (although the words might have been used for saying true or false things). In §8 we shall see that one and the same statement, e.g., 'The cat is on the mat', may be more and more weakened: 'The cat is on the mat', 'is probably on the mat', 'may be on the mat'. The closer we come to the 'may'-utterance, the less willing we are to assessment in terms of 'true' and 'false'; and the less does the clash between the utterance and its negation satisfy the standard conditions of a contradiction. 'The cat is and is not on the mat' is a clear contradiction; 'The cat presumably is and presumably isn't on the mat' is not so clear; and 'The cat may and may not be on the mat' is not a contradiction at all. The explanation, I shall argue, is to be found in the fact that 'The cat is on the mat' normally has a high degree of commitment, whilst the 'may'-utterance only commits the speaker to the view that it is not settled whether the cat is on the mat. ('May'- and 'probably'-utterances are 'problematic'— to use Kant's term—in the sense that they indicate a problem, not its solution.) If this hypothesis can be vindicated, truth and falsehood do not merely demand that certain relations obtain between statements and facts; they also demand that the statements carry a certain degree of commitment. Characteristic of the jocular 'I am king of Ruritania' is, however, that the speaker has not claimed to be king of Ruritania; he has not committed himself.

This does not, of course, show that a conceptual reform is impossible or that it is not needed. At most it indicates that, unless the related notions also are considered, there is a danger that the explication alienates truth and falsehood so far from their customary sense that it is merely bewildering to give the new concepts the old labels; and at the very least it indicates that the explication is not quite so free from difficulties as it appears to be.

Truth and performatives. As we have seen, Austin thought that constatives but not performatives are true or false. Both constatives and performatives are happy only if they and the world conform. It is, however, undeniable that they have different kinds of force. It is also undeniable that a command, for example, is unhappy when it and the world do not conform. If the likeness in respect of conformity is enough to make a performative true or false, the suggestion seems to be that the *locution*—or, less stringently, the *phrastic*—is true or false. And this is paradoxical. If a phrastic is what is true or false, then both the statement 'Donald will wear his galoshes' and the command 'Donald, wear your galoshes!' will be true or false—for they have the phrastic in common. Most philosophers fight shy of assigning truth-values to imperatives (Hedenius is no exception: cf. *op. cit.*, §3); and it is clear that an explication of truth and falsehood which has these consequences runs a risk to lose contact with our ordinary notions.

The only plausible alternative left is that what is true or false is the-locutionary-act-with-a-constative-force. It is, however, plain that a speaker seldom or never uses 'I apologize' to state that he apologizes: he wants to perform a certain action and not to convey a piece of information about his own behaviour. It is also uncontroversial that his hearers seldom or never take him to be informing them of anything or stating anything. Hence, 'I apologize' is neither designed to have a constative force nor normally taken to have it. If the thing that is true or false must have a constative force, it follows that 'I apologize' is *not* true or false. I conclude that performatives do not cause their own truth, in the sense required by Hedenius.

3. The Force Thesis

An utterance has a performatory function if, and only if, it seems to describe an action which the speaker in uttering it is performing. The statement 'The cat is on the mat' or the order 'Donald, wear your galoshes!' does not, however, seem to describe an action the speaker in uttering it is performing. Performatoriness and force must therefore be kept apart. Austin does not always realize this; for the force of an utterance may be brought out into the open by a phrase which resembles (and sometimes also is) an expression with a performatory function.

In order to make the Force Thesis clear, we have to consider the notions of *P-radical* and *illocutionary force*. The former of them is not to be found in Austin; it is an auxiliary construction made for this book.

P-radicals. In explicit performatives, it is always possible to isolate the operative clause, the part doing the performatory job. We get it thus: Put the performative in its classical explicit form, i.e., in the first person present indicative active. Pick out the grammatical subject and the grammatical predicate. They constitute the *P-radical*.

P-radicals always require supplementation. This is not the trite point that in such cases as 'I name this ship the *Queen Elizabeth*' the P-radical cannot be issued alone without violations to the syntactical rule that transitive verbs demand an object. It is the philosophically more relevant observation that for some reason it will not do to leave out the supplementation, even when the isolated P-radical is syntactically unobjectionable. 'I promise' is syntactically in order; yet I cannot use 'I promise' in a satisfactory way without indicating *what* I promise. 'I apologize' is grammatically faultless; yet I cannot say 'I apologize' without indicating what I apologize for. I do not always have to tell what the supplementation is: the context may make it obvious. The point is, however, that it always makes sense to ask for a supplementation, and that something is seriously amiss if I cannot give it—I am then either abusing the P-radical or ignorant of its conventional meaning.

The necessity of supplementation is stressed by the plain fact that in many cases it is not the P-radical but the supplementation which is the most essential part of the message. In these cases, I can get across what I want without using the P-radical, but not by using the latter without indicating its supplementation. Instead of saying 'I advise you to do so', I may say 'Do so' and still be engaged in advisory activity; but I cannot say 'I advise' without supplementation. It would be absurd to say 'I advise, but there's nothing I advise' or 'I promise, but there is nothing I promise': to advise nothing and promise nothing is not to advise or to promise.

Illocutionary force. Suppose I say 'I shall come tomorrow'. You may understand the words, their construction and their referents and still feel that my utterance is not clear. You may ask 'How am I to take it? Is it a promise or a warning or just a forecast?' My utterance is in a sense ambiguous; but not as 'He was sitting on a bank' is. It does not contain a vocable to which different rules of meaning are tied. 'He was sitting on a bank' can already on the rhetic level be given two interpretations: 'He was sitting on the rowing-bench (of a galley)' and 'He was sitting on the slope (of a river)'; but this is not possible with regard to 'I shall come tomorrow'. Nor has our ambiguity anything to do with reference. The *sentence* 'I shall come tomorrow' is of course 'systematically ambiguous' in the sense that when used, it necessarily changes referents for every new speaker and/or day. But in my example you know me and know that I issued the utterance, and you know what day I intended to refer to as 'tomorrow'; so you are not troubled about the referents of my utterance. My utterance is not ambiguous on its locutionary side. Its obscurity is due to the fact that I have not made it clear how I want you to take it, what its neustic is—whether I mean to promise or to warn or to forecast. I have not, in our example, managed to get across to what discourse my utterance belongs. In other cases the discourse may be clear. If I say that a certain series of figures will crop up in the development of π, I am usually constating. Still you may complain that you do not know whether I meant it as a piece of information or as a guess—i.e., that I have left it unclear how far I want to stand committed by my words. I shall say that utterances which show this indeterminateness concerning their discourse or to what degree they conform to the standard requirements of that discourse, are *force-ambiguous*. The fault of such an utterance is that its *illocutionary force* or neustic is not made clear.

We shall soon look at a number of different ways of avoiding force-ambiguities. At present only one of them will interest us, viz., the insertion of P-radicals. If I say 'I promise I shall come tomorrow', I have made it clear that I am not prognosticating; if I say 'I guess that such-and-such a series of figures will occur in the development of π', I have given you to understand that I am not conveying a piece of information. The P-radicals are, in these cases, linguistic devices whose standard function is to remove force-ambiguity; they are invented to tell the audience either to what discourse a certain utterance belongs on this occasion, or—if that is settled—how far the usual implications of that discourse hold. Certain P-radicals have to do both jobs at once.

These remarks do not make the notion of illocutionary force very clear. It has to be elucidated by a number of case-studies. But even in this rough form it may help us to state the Force Thesis.

The core of the Force Thesis. We have noticed that P-radicals need supplementation; that the supplementation sometimes is more important than the radical; and that at least in some cases the radical serves to eliminate force-ambiguities. We may attempt to string these features together by the theory that P-radicals are explicit linguistic devices for showing how the supplementation is to be taken: if our utterances never suffered from force-ambiguity, we should not need them.

The tenet that the main function of *all* P-radicals is to remove force-ambiguity may be called the *strong Force Thesis*. The *weak Force Thesis* is that *some* P-radicals have this main function. According to them both, a performative is an utterance where the main function of the P-radicals always (on the strong thesis) or sometimes (on the weak one) is to make it clear how their supplementation is to be taken.

Both versions allow that there are other expressions with the same aim. Instead of 'I promise to come' I may say 'On my honour I shall come'; instead of 'I state that Shakespeare died in 1616' I may say 'Shakespeare surely died in 1616'. When such substitutions are possible we cease, I think, to feel any inclination to speak of P-radicals as true or false. If there is any truth-value, it belongs to the supplementation. This is an additional explanation of why denials of the Performative Thesis seem so queer, as far as they are directed at performatives with a suppressed supplementation ('I promise', 'I apologize', 'I swear').

Both versions maintain that the speaker does not *state* the force of his utterance; he *signals* or *shows* it but he does not *say* what it is. Austin tries to illustrate this part of the doctrine. I may, he says (*Words*.69–70), bow deeply from the waist in order to ease my indigestion, or to tie my shoelaces, or to do obeisance to you. In order to make it clear that it is the latter I am performing, I may raise my hat or say 'Salaam' or 'I salute you'. Raising my hat is not stating or describing what I am doing; and since 'Salaam' performs the same duty, it is no statement or description either. By the same token, 'I salute you' shows but does not describe or state what my act is.

This is of course merely an illustration. That *a* and *b* have a function in common does not guarantee that they must be assessed in the same way—there may be a lot of relevant differences. Nor can we infer from the fact that *a* and *b* have a function in common and *b* and *c* also have a function in common that *a* and *c* have the same function in common. To save the illustration we have to assume (i) that whatever the function is, it is the only thing relevant to the assessment of the things having it; and (ii) that the function common to *a* and *b* is the same as the one common to *b* and *c*. In favour of (i) it could be said that a performative may—and, I think, in general does—occur without being a description of itself, having only a performatory function; and in favour of (ii) that the only *obvious* difference between raising my hat and saying 'I salute you' is that the latter has a verbal side and therefore may be afflicted with ills which the latter is not susceptible to, such as being muttered unintelligibly or said to a person who does not understand the language; and that this difference can be disregarded.

Force-showing and stating. It may be said that 'I salute you' has started its career as something which certainly was not just forceshowing. Consider, says Austin (*Words*.81), 'I slam the door thus' (he slams the door) or 'I spit me of you thus' (he spits). They hardly show the force of anything, and they are obviously *not* performatory: 'I slam the door thus' does not constitute a slamming of the door as 'I apologize' constitutes an apology. Nor are they clear cases of constatives. They are, rather, examples of suiting an action to the words. It seems likely that historically 'I salute you' was a case of that sort.

Austin leaves the matter there; but it can, I think, be maintained that very clear examples of performatives, conforming to both the Performatory Thesis and the Force Thesis, have the same origin. In his paper 'Om handslagets ursprungliga innebörd', Axel Hägerström claims that the Latin word 'promittere' acquired its sense of 'promise' from a suppressed 'dextram'—'to promise' meant, originally, 'to put forward the right hand [for a handshake]'.[8]—If this is right, 'Promitto' may in the past have had a fairly pronounced non-performatory side. Whether this side is to be labelled as *stating* or *describing* that I put forward my right hand is indeed questionable: probably it is nothing of the sort. Much linguistic information would be needed—could I, e.g., say 'Promitto' *before* I made the gesture or would that be like saying 'I slam the door thus' without slamming the door?

It may be said that these questions are of doubtful philosophical importance, since the origin of a formula is an unreliable guide to its present employment. But Austin cannot afford to treat them cavalierly, since he maintains that words seldom shake off their etymological meaning (1956a.149f). Yet they are hardly questions which philosophers are good at answering.

---

[8] A. Hägerström, *Socialfilosofiska uppsatser*, p. 176.—It would, I think, be rewarding to compare Hägerström's view of the magical use of language with Austin's doctrines of performatives (the Force Thesis as well as the Performative Thesis).

Implicit performatives. Austin says (*Words*.Ch.VI) that it is a plausible guess—which he, however, does not see how to test—that in primitive languages the force of an utterance would be unclear. It would be unclear because different forces were not yet distinguished. In a primitive one-word language, 'Bull' or 'Thunder' could be *both* a warning, *and* a piece of information, *and* a prediction, and so on and so forth. It would then be a *primary performative*. The explicit distinction of its force is a later, and considerable, achievement.

The force of an utterance may be brought out in a number of ways. Austin mentions tone of voice, cadence, emphasis; gestures and ceremonial non-verbal procedures; the circumstances of the utterance and the speaker's status; grammatical mood; adverbs, adverbial phrases and connecting particles such as 'still' and 'therefore'; and sub-headings such as 'A Novel' and 'A Manifesto'. The clearest device is, however, an explicit performative. He fights shy of saying that the primitive utterance is an *implicit* performative; for the distinction of forces is not just a discovery of something implicit, it is also a creative act. Whether he would call a force-ambiguous utterance an implicit performative is not clear; as we shall see, it would anyhow be a bad choice of words.

He illustrates the doctrine that the distinction of forces is partly a creative activity by saying that it is probable that 'I am sorry' originally was employed in situations where the speaker really *was* sorry. Later on it was transferred to contexts where it is agreed that people ought to be sorry, whether they are so or not. But there it makes sense to ask 'Are you really sorry?' To avoid that embarrassing question, new phrases were invented which took care of the normative aspect of the situation without being reports on inner states—'I apologize', 'I regret (that . . .)'.
—If I have understood him, he suggests that these phrases are *suggested* by a tendency in the transferred use of 'I'm sorry'; but that they do not just lay bare an aspect which is already there to be unearthed, they also carve it out—much as a sculptor may be inspired to create a certain sculpture by the form of a piece of scrap-iron and yet himself work much with it before the work of art has taken its final shape.

The explicit distinction of forces in an utterance goes hand in hand with sophistication and the development of social forms (*loc. cit.*). Austin does not develop this attractive idea. As long as a society is so small that a person can speak to everyone he wants to address, intonation, stress and gestures may perhaps suffice as force-showing devices; but when the community grows, they become insufficient. Not even such phrases from the deputy's lips as 'Thus speaketh the King, "- - -"' will do; for although the subjects understand that the words of the King are authoritative, there may still be doubts as to the force—do they constitute an order, or an advice, or a warning? Thus there will be need for such phrases as 'I, the King, hereby decree (advise, warn' . . .)'. The development of performatives in the law will perhaps afford examples of this process; and linguistic research might show that 'Promitto' asquired clear and dominating performatory and force-showing functions fairly recently.

4. 'Illocutions'

Austin seems to think that since both force-showing and the performance of a performatory act are done *in* the performance of a locutionary act, they must have a common genus, the illocutionary 'act'. He makes performatives the paradigms of illocutionary acts and concentrates on the performatives straddling the Force Thesis and the Performative Thesis. The words 'I promise I shall come' constitute a promise and at the same time remove a force-ambiguity from 'I shall come'. The speaker cannot do the latter without *eo ipso* being committed in the way typical of a promisor. Hence it is easy to take performatoriness and force-showing as two sides to the same act. Austin even says that in 'I promise' the commitments come into the illocutionary act (*Words*.102).

So far, it seems as if Austin has arrived at his illocutionary act by conflating a performatory and a force-showing one. This is, I think, why he is perplexed at the distinction between a performative and a merely polite phrase. Since 'I have pleasure in calling upon the next speaker', 'I am sorry to have to say . . .' and 'I am gratified to be in a position to announce . . .' unfortunately do not constitute having pleasure, being sorry or being gratified, they are not performatives. He confesses, however, that the exact nature of the distinction eludes him. (*Words*.80f.) I suggest that the polite phrases differ from the performative ones by lacking a performatory function and resemble them by having a force-showing function—the job of these phrases is to indicate how an utterance is to be taken.

The conflation fosters other difficulties. In an aside Austin wonders whether not *all* utterances are performatory, since they all have some force or other (*Words*.103n): as if the teacher's piece of information 'John F. Kennedy is President of the United States' constitutes John F. Kennedy's presidentship just as 'I promise to come' constitutes my promise to come! His way out seems to be to give up the Performative Thesis in favour of the Force Thesis.* I cannot help feeling that this is the trend of the last and (to me) very obscure chapters of *Words*. There he says, e.g., 'We said long ago that we needed a list of "explicit performative verbs"; but in the light of the more general theory we now see that what we need is a list of *illocutionary forces* of an utterance' (p. 148f). In the long list of such verbs 'doubt', 'know' and 'believe' occur, though accompanied by queries (p. 161). He cannot have thought of them as performatives—it would be absurd to hold that to say 'I know' is to know. As I shall argue in the next section, he must have held that they are force-showing devices, like a sub-heading such as 'Some Suggestions'.

Still more suggestive is the fact that he firmly attempts to make all constatives liable to the same infelicities as performatives if the (A.1)–(Γ.2) conditions are infringed. His argument seems to be (*Words*.Ch.11) that all utterances have a force, whether or not it is made explicit. It can be brought out in many other ways than by means of locutions, but P-radicals are also used for that purpose. If they are and if the utterances they enter are subjected to the (A.1)–(Γ.2) conditions, then utterances with the same implicit force also obey them. Here he seems to assume that all P-radicals are force-showing, and that there is no performatory edge to them. His backing is, however, not impressive. He alleges that 'The cat is on the mat' is infelicitous in the Γ-way, if the speaker later on says 'The cat was at that time under the mat'; just as 'I pardon you' is infelicitous if later on I punish you for your deed. But surely there are many relevant differences between breaking one's word and being logically inconsistent? And if insincere talk

*[This is an error, as J. W. Roxbee Cox, Tore Nordenstam and John R. Searle have argued (though with different, and sometimes incompatible, reasons) in their criticisms of *LIA*. But it has a point. My postscript is an attempt to bring out both the error and the important truth it points to.]

is treated as an infringement of a Γ-condition, all serious talk will threaten to become performatory, and then the difference between 'I promise' and 'The cat is on the mat' which the doctrine of performatives originally wanted to bring out is obscured.

The analogies between constatives and performatives with regard to the other conditions are a little more convincing, but not much. Is there, e.g., not a difference between saying 'The bat is on the mat' instead of 'The cat is on the mat' and producing a nut instead of a ring at the relevant point in the marriage ceremony? At least the ceremony can go wrong in the B-ways *both* by the production of a wrong word *and* by the production of a wrong thing, whilst the constative runs only one of these risks.

At the end of *Words*, then, the illocutionary act seems to become indistinguishable from the force-showing act, and the performatory aspect is dropped. Yet—how can Austin have dropped it, in view of the stress it receives in the beginning of the book?* He can make it a prerequisite of the force-showing function, as he seems to do in the case of 'I promise'; but how is he, for example, to treat 'I apologize'? Of course the lecture notes from which *Words* is composed were not designed for publication; but what he said on performatives in the almost identical series of lectures he gave at Oxford under the title of 'Words and Deeds' left the same doubt in my mind as to the nature of the illocutionary act—and I listened to the whole series twice (Hilary Term, 1957, and Summer Term, 1959).

Austin's notion of the illocutionary act is, then, far from clear. It would, I think, be convenient to restrict the term to the force-showing act; but I shall try to avoid it altogether—except, of course, in reports on Austin's words.

The rift between the two theses. Let us look closer at cases where the Performative Thesis and the Force Thesis part company.

(i) Austin's simile of the man who raises his hat in order to show that his bow is a salutation makes us wonder how the word 'supplementation' is to be taken. Hitherto we have assumed that it is something which is either verbal or can be made so. But if I

*[A poor argument. As Searle points out in his review of *LIA* I could just as well ask how Austin can have rejected sense-data in view of the amount of attention they receive in *S&S*.]

bow and say 'I salute you' instead of tipping my hat, the supplementation is the bow, not a verbal message.

Let us approach the problem by way of Austin's tentative classification of performatives (*Words*.Ch.12). 'I salute you' belongs, I think, to the group of *behabitives*. They are concerned with behaviour—especially reactions to other people's behaviour, including attitudes and expressions of attitudes to somebody's past or imminent conduct. Examples are 'I apologize', 'I thank', 'I deplore, commiserate, compliment, condole, congratulate, felicitate, sympathize', 'I resent, don't mind, pay tribute, grumble about, complain of, applaud, overlook, commend, deprecate', 'I welcome, bid farewell', 'I bless, curse, toast, drink to', 'I challenge, dare, defy, protest'.

Austin's other classes of performatives are: verdictives, exercitives, commissives, and expositives.

Verdictives are deliveries of an official or unofficial finding upon evidence or reason as to value or fact. A verdictive is a judicial act, whilst legislative or executive acts are exercitives. Examples of verdictives are 'I acquit, convict, interpret as, rule, reckon, estimate, date, place, make it, grade, assess, rank, value, describe, characterize, analyse'.

An *exercitive* is the giving of a decision against or in favour of a certain course of action. It is a decision that something is so, not a statement that it is so. Examples are 'I appoint, degrade, dismiss, name, order, sentence, fine, choose, vote for, claim, bequeath, pardon, resign, advise, plead, pray, urge, proclaim, announce, annul, reprieve, veto'.

The point of a *commissive* is to commit the speaker to a course of action: 'I promise, contract, undertake, bind myself, give my word, plan, guarantee, pledge myself, bet, consent, side with, favour, adopt'.

Expositives, finally, are used in acts of exposition involving the expounding of views, conduction of arguments, clarification of usages and of references. Many such performatory radicals may belong to other groups as well. 'I affirm, state, remark, inform, answer, ask, testify, report, accept, concede, recognize, correct, postulate, deduce, argue, interpret, distinguish, define, mean, refer, call, understand, regard as' are examples.

Austin found expositivies and behabitives troublesome. He thought that the former were not clear and perhaps could be broken up into verdictives, exercitives and commissives. Behabitives were unsatisfactory for partially the same reason; but although they seem to enter the other classes, they are nevertheless unique 'in a way', he confessed (*Words.*151), 'that I have not succeeded in making clear even to myself'.

I suggest that this uniqueness is at least partially due to the fact that it is fairly difficult to see behabitives as devices for freeing a linguistic expression from force-ambiguity. Sometimes they do this; but it is not their standard function, as is evident already from the facts that it is hard to find any adverbial expressions (except derivatives from behabitives) which do the same duty, and that such expressions as 'This is an apology' or 'This is a felicitation' are uncommon. Behabitives are usually not conjoined with any other utterance.

In this respect they differ from the other groups of performatives. These require linguistic supplementation. The Force Thesis is plausible for verdictives, exercitives, commissives and expositives but not for behabitives. The strong Force Thesis seems to be beyond help.*

(ii) In Austin's list of expositives we found 'I state'. What I state is often a statement, a constative. Yet 'I state' meets all the tests of the Performative Thesis. It seems as if such performatives have a truth-value.

The obvious dodge is to say that a performatory radical is neither true nor false. But Austin refuses to insert a wedge between 'He did not do it' and 'I state he did not do it': their truth-value is ascertained in identical ways, and the latter of them *makes the same statement* as the former. If I say 'I state that he did not do it', it will not do to retort 'That's a statement about you' (*Words.*134).

A minor objection to this that it is sometimes unsatisfactory to say that the two sentences can be used for making the same statement. In the first place, there is a performatory ingredient to 'I state that p'. To say it seriously is to state that p; to say 'p' seriously is not necessarily to *state* it—it can be to guess it, etc. Secondly, what matters in 'I state that p' is of course normally the truth-value of p, and then we treat 'I state that p' and 'p' on

---

*[This is true only if illocutionary devices *necessarily* remove ambiguities from the locution. Tore Nordenstam has pointed out that there may be only one standard way of taking some locutions.]

a par. But do we not sometimes pay heed merely to the force of the utterance? Do we not sometimes wonder not so much whether what he said is true as whether he meant it as an assertion and not as (say) a guess? Unless the force of 'p' is brought out by the circumstances of its utterance, it is vague in a way in which 'I state that p' is not. This is a reason for saying that to utter 'I state that p' is to make a more specified and to that extent a different statement than is made by saying simply 'p'. But the former is nevertheless either true or false. Consequently, the Performative Thesis no longer holds for the standard function of some P-radicals.

It would be neat if the word 'performative' was defined as in *DP 1* of Ch. 3:8. 'I state that p' and 'I swear that p' would not then qualify as performatives, although the act of uttering them is the act they seem to describe. If this definition of performative were to be accepted, 'I state' and 'I swear' could easily be classified as force-showing but not performatory devices.

(iii) It is, then, doubtful whether the Performative Thesis will hold in its general form; and the strong Force Thesis is probably false. The former is correct only in so far as behabitives are concerned, whilst the weak Force Thesis seems plausible for most performatives outside that group.

If we are to call the issuing of any performative an illocutionary act, such acts will span utterances which are true or false as constatives are, as well as utterances which are not. It is true that there will be a performatory edge to them all—for they are singled out as (parts of) actions. But (*a*) some are essentially actions ('I apologize'), others are taken in that vein only in odd situations ('I state'); (*b*) the latter are force-showing, the former are not; and (*c*) the force can be shown by words which are not performatory at all, such as 'on my honour' or 'perhaps'. To give such a heterogeneous collection of speech acts a unitary name, 'illocutionary act', is to imply the falsehoods that the overlap of functions is complete, not partial; and substantial, not accidental. If the notion of illocutionary acts has to be rejected, Austin's classification of such acts will of course also have to go.

5. *Constating, performing, and degree-showing*

We have seen that according to Austin all utterances within the fact-stating type of discourse have a side concerned with their force. The force has various aspects to it, two of which will interest us in particular: First, we have not understood the utterance aright, unless we take it to be in the descriptive, reporting business and not (say) in the advisory one (though it of course occasionally can do both duties). Secondly, even when that is settled, we may wonder whether it is a piece of information, or a very probable tenet, or just a guess.

In fact, argues Austin (*Words*.Ch.11), our actual utterances within the fact-stating type of discourse are illocutionary not only in a constative way; they are also often tinged with features of other discourses. Do we not sometimes ask 'Is that a *fair* statement?' Are the good reasons and the good evidence for that utterance worlds apart from the good reasons and evidence for warning and judging, which obviously are not constative acts? 'When a constative is confronted with the facts, we in fact appraise it in ways involving the employment of a vast array of terms which overlap with those that we use in the appraisal of performatives. In real life, as opposed to the simple situations envisaged in logical theory, one cannot always answer in a simple manner whether it is true or false.'

If this is so, whence do we get our philosophical opinion of statements and propositions? Well, answers Austin (p. 144f),

we abstract from the illocutionary (let alone the perlocutionary) aspects of the speech act and we concentrate on the locutionary: moreover, we use an over-simplified notion of correspondence with the facts—over-simplified because essentially it brings in the illocutionary aspect. We aim at the ideal of what would be right to say in all circumstances, for any purpose, to any audience, &c. Perhaps this is sometimes realised.

Here 'illocutionary aspect of the speech act' hovers between 'aspect of the force of the speech act' and 'aspect of the performatoriness of the speech act'; for he immediately adds that with the 'performative utterance' 'we attend as much as possible to the illocutionary force', and illustrates this by 'the issuing of simple executive orders'. But a constative is certainly not performatory. The constative neustic is force-showing. Austin ought to have held that in discussions of truth, we abstract from (not the constative, but) the degree-showing force—we do not consider other constatives than those which fully commit the speaker.

II. TWO KINDS OF FORCE-SHOWING

Within the sphere concerned with the force of an utterance, I have already drawn a rough distinction between phrases showing to what discourse an utterance belongs, and phrases showing how far the speaker wants to be committed to the usual implications of a certain discourse. Phrases of the first sort are to be called *discourse-marking expressions*; phrases of the latter sort *degree-showing expressions*. I shall now discuss a few examples of both sorts and also show that the classification is not exhaustive. What I say in this section is but loosely related to Austin's writings, but I hope to show how he came to conflate performatoriness and force and to say the bewildering things he did about the analogy between 'I know' and 'I promise'.

6. Discourse-marking expressions

The expressions I discuss in this paragraph will be concerned (6.1) with promising and (6.2) with fact-stating.

6.1. Promising

To attach 'I promise' to an utterance is, in non-parasitical situations, to tell the audience that the speaker shoulders the responsibilities of a promise-giver. Since he by employing it takes on these responsibilities, the expression conforms to both the Force Thesis and the Performative Thesis. To take the use of the phrase a paradigm of a performatory employment of a form of words is therefore risky: it easily involves a confusion of performatoriness and force. I want to show that they can be kept apart even in this case. Let us begin with the first of these functions.

6.11. The performatoriness of saying 'I promise'

What are the responsibilities of a promisor? A preliminary answer is: to carry out what he promises to do. This obligation is built into the notion of promising. Of course a man may promise without acting upon it; but imagine that nobody ever carried out or tried to carry out his promises! Then the action performed by uttering the words 'I promise' would not be promising; these men would not have our notion of promising. Promising is designed to be done by persons who act upon their words. A man who does not understand that a promise commits the speaker to a certain future behaviour is perhaps morally deficient and certainly mentally deficient—he does not understand his mother tongue. To the question 'Why should a (= any) promise be kept?', the basic answer is, that a form of words which does not oblige the speaker to act upon it is not a promise. It is, as Prichard himself recognizes, puzzling to say that promising

> can only exist among individuals between whom there has already been something which looks at first like an agreement to keep agreements, but is really an agreement not to use certain noises except in a certain way, the agreement nevertheless being one which, unlike ordinary agreements, does not require the use of language.[9]

It is less bewildering to say the training required to master the meaning of such phrases as 'I promise' and 'on my honour' has to include a training not to use them, and being prepared to condemn the employment of them, in other cases than those where the speaker regulates his subsequent behaviour in accordance with their supplementation.

A philosopher who wonders why promises should be kept is hardly satisfied with this type of answers. He does not want a conceptual investigation but rather an explanation of why we have the concepts we have. What is the point of having the institution of promising? What roles do promise-making and promise-receiving play in our lives? To answer these questions is to move closer to an elucidation of the responsibilities of the promisor.

The institution of promising. Studies of the institution of promising have usually been conducted from the speaker's point of view, almost neglecting the role of the addressee. The great innovation of von Wright's powerful paper 'On promises' is that the promisee is moved to the centre of the picture. *He* prompts the speaker to promise; and it is primarily to his, the promise-taker's, benefit that the institution exists. The role of the promisee explains why our institution has the features it has. As listed by von Wright,

[9] H. A. Prichard, *Moral Obligation*, p. 179.

they are (*a*) that the promisor and the promisee are human beings, (*b*) that the thing promised is something in the future which the speaker is able to do, (*c*) that there are certain forms of words characteristic (though not necessary) for promising, (*d*) that the promisor in making the promise puts himself under an obligation which the promisee has a right to demand he shall fulfil, and (*e*) that the promisee thinks that the thing promised is to his interest.

Granted that the promisee is the main agent in making the institution of promising what it is, the factors may be patterned thus.[10] We have seen that all linguistic communication relies on the tacit convention that the addressee can, in general, rely on the speaker's words. Having received a promise, I bank on it and arrange my plans according to it. If you let me down, it may have serious consequences for me—but also for you. Not only can I revenge myself, sometimes even by the aid of the law; but you may, by breaking your word, risk the penalty of never being trusted again. The excommunication from participation in the institution of promising deprives you of the possibility of giving promises, of being trusted; and to most individuals it is a severe punishment. It may be made still more severe by depriving you of the opportunity of receiving promises; and for man, depending on his fellow-creatures, that would be unbearable. The promisee therefore has powerful weapons to force the promisor to keep his word. In this way the institution of promising is perpetuated. But here it is vital that the promisee is an intelligent being—a being who understands that it is to his interest that promises are given and who can see to it that promise-breaking is (at least very often) followed by sanctions. This may explain why promises to oneself are felt to be less binding than promises to others. Nor is it an accident that it is doubtful whether you can promise your donkey a carrot—the fact that the animal cannot demand the carrot is, I think, not wholly irrelevant to the question whether your utterance has given it the right to demand it.

That the institution of promising exists primarily for the addressee's benefit also elucidates why there are certain forms of

---

[10] What follows is suggested by and draws heavily on von Wright's mimeographed contribution to the symposium on performatives but contains embellishments which may not be acceptable to him. He has published a second version of his paper in *Theoria* 28, 1962.

words characteristic for promising—it is of course of the utmost importance for him to know whether he can bank on the speaker's words, confidently expecting the action to be done.

He obviously cannot rely on them if the thing promised lies beyond the speaker's powers. If the inability is very evident, the promise is often discounted as a joke. Not even the most literal-minded girl claims that the man dancing attendance on her has promised her to take down the moon or make her Queen of Russia.

If the promisee is the driving force behind the institution, there is small wonder that 'I promise you a sound hiding' is no promise; or that we hesitate to say that a father has *promised* his daughter to send her to a nunnery if she does not want to go—even when we think that her refusal is due to incapacity to recognize what is good for her. When the addressee does not want the act to be done, the speaker's words do not constitute a promise.

Since I know of no other elucidation of promising which makes so good sense of all these factors, I shall assume with von Wright that the addressee is the main factor behind the whole institution.

If the philosopher still insists, 'Why do we have promises?', what are we to do? Let him imagine that we, weak human beings, relying for our very existence on cooperation with our fellows, could not give or receive promises, could not trust others to do what they said they would do, etc. Let him spell out the details of that life—ugly, brutish, and short; and he would have the answer. We have the institutions we have because we are the men we are and live in the world we do. By imagining what life would be like without the institutions, philosophy brings out the importance of such platitudes.

The obligations of a promisor. We may now discuss the obligations of a promisor, obligations which determine the discourse-implications of the phrase 'I promise':

A promise-giver puts himself under the obligation to undertake to bring the world into conformity with his words (or his thought, since what is promised may be specified by the context). He gives it to be understood that he is able to perform the action and that it is to the addressee's advantage. By his words he has also given the promisee a right to demand that the action be carried out.— I repeat that it is not necessary that a certain promisor intends to do what he says he will do, or that he actually carries it out. What *is* necessary to save the point of promising is that promisors *in general* have the appropriate intentions, and that they indulge in the appropriate subsequent behaviour.

By saying 'I promise' the speaker has shouldered the responsibilities of a promisor. His word is his bond and constitutes the promise. Hence, to use the phrase in that way is to do a performatory act.

6.12. *The force-showing function of saying* '*I promise*'

I am not entitled to signal that my utterance is a promise unless I shoulder or have shouldered the responsibilities of a promisor; so correct force-indication requires a performatory act. A promise has not come off unless the audience takes it as a promise; so a successful performatory act requires force-indication. 'I promise' performs both these functions at the same time; but they can be kept apart.

'*I promise*' *and* '*on my honour*'. One form of words used for removing force-ambiguities from 'I shall come' is 'on my honour': the device makes it clear that the discourse-implications of the utterance are those of a promise. Then 'I promise on my honour to come' ought to be redundant, like 'They arrived one after the other in succession'; and that suggestion is, I think, repulsive to most people. Let us therefore assume, as a matter of our sense of language, that 'I promise on my honour' is not redundant. We have then either to reject the view that both 'on my honour' and 'I promise' are force-showing, or to explain how they can be combined without any resulting redundancy. Since it is intuitively certain that the two expressions are force-showing, we have to study the second alternative. I can think of three suggestions:

(*a*) 'I promise on my honour' emphasizes the promise, like the importance of remembering is stressed in the advertisement slogan, 'Don't forget to remember to buy A'. I.e., 'I promise on my honour' has about the same function as 'I do indeed promise'.

(*b*) In 'I promise on my honour', the last three words give a further specification of the speaker's commitments within the institution of promising. A Victorian gambler who could not pay his losses might have said 'I promise on my honour to pay' in order to convey that his debt of honour would be settled before he paid his tailor, for example.

But how does (*a*) differ from (*b*)? Does the gambler not just convey that his promise will be kept even in the face of competing promises? I do not think so. In (*b*) a certain status is tacitly implied and put at stake. By a breach of promise the speaker incurs the risk of sanctions aimed at that status. I have made my gambler a Victorian, since Victorian society was a pronounced class-society, where certain distinctive obligations were tied to one's status and where it was very important to have high status. The gambler's 'on my honour' would there be taken as short for 'on my honour *as a gentleman*', and the addition of that phrase to the simple 'I promise' was significant in two intimately related ways. First, in Victorian society with its strict code of honour a person breaking promises given as a gentleman might be taken to have forfeited his status as a gentleman; and that would be a much severer punishment than being treated as a person who, although a gentleman, could not be relied on. Secondly, the loss of the status of gentleman would be all the more likely for our gambler in the case of promise-breaking, since one of the distinctive obligations tied up with that status was that of paying one's gambling-debts without failure.

(*c*) 'I promise' is both performatory and force-showing; it does two jobs simultaneously. 'On my honour' may occasionally acquire a performatory tinge but is essentially force-indicating. When the two expressions are combined, the work is divided up between them: 'I promise' functions performatorily and 'on my honour' shows the force. I.e., by saying 'I promise' the speaker performs the act of promising; by saying 'on my honour' he signals that the supplementation of the phrase is to be taken as a promise. An effect of the combination is also that the speaker emphasizes his promise.

Suggestion (*c*) may seem exceedingly improbable. It is essential to a promise that the addressee understands it as a promise; so why should anyone stress separately that the utterance has the force of a promise? Well, to say 'I promise to do it' is to create a promise (except when the present tense is habitual, as in 'I (always) promise brunettes everything'—where the utterance is disqualified as a performative). To say 'I shall do it on my honour' is, on the other hand, not to create a promise; it may be to repeat an old one. In the latter case it does not, however, say something like 'I promised I would do it'; for if it did, there would be no stultification in continuing 'but I am not going to'. 'I promised I would do it' reports that the speaker at some time in the past created a promise but does not by itself give us any hint as to whether he still feels himself bound by it; 'I shall do it on my honour' says nothing about the creation of a promise but just signals that the promisory obligations are tied to the supplementation. It may sometimes be clear that the speaker who says 'on my honour' is not just signalling this but also creating a promise; but that seems to be an occasional employment, not a standard one.

I suggest, then, that 'on my honour' has the force-showing function as its main function, whilst 'I promise' has it as an effect of its performatory job. If so, the division of work is not strange, and the combination 'I promise on my honour' may spring from a desire to convey not just that certain discourse-implications hold but that they are created by that very utterance. The two functions normally catered for by 'I promise' are thus marked out separately.

All three suggestions may account for the non-repetitional character of 'I promise on my honour'; but (c) is perhaps the best of them. For it is intuitively clear that 'I do indeed promise' does not empty the content of 'I promise on my honour', whilst (c) takes care of the emphatic element and also of something else. And (b) is at home in a society with few and sharply divided classes, arranged in a hierarchy. A man who pledged his status there really risked something which for him and his fellows was of more value than just his standing as an honest man. That society is moribund; and although 'on my honour' also is old-fashioned, I think we only occasionally take 'I promise on my honour' in the vein required by it.

6.13. *The interplay between the two functions*

The point that 'I promise' serves not only to create promises but also to remove force-ambiguities is perhaps obscured by the fact that the force-showing function seems to be built into the performatory one. One of the felicity-conditions of the performative 'I promise' (A.1; possibly also B.1) involves that the addressee

Q

hears and understands the phrase. Understanding it involves knowing the discourse-implications characteristic of promising. Consequently the performative is not felicitous, unless the addressee has been given to understand that the supplementation is to be taken in a certain vein. Hence the performatory function of 'I promise' normally caters also for the force-showing one. Nevertheless they can be separated. Suppose I say 'I shall come tomorrow' in a context which makes other interpretations than the promisory one far-fetched: then no doubt I have promised. I become anxious that I have not been understood, so I add 'I promise'. It would then be odd to say that in uttering the formula I brought the promise into being; it was already there, and all I did was to remove certain force-ambiguities from my previous utterance. This is, I think, a clear case of a purely force-showing use of 'I promise'; though my discussion of 'I promise' and 'on my honour' indicates that the former phrase is not normally employed for a merely force-showing job.

6.2. Fact-stating

A study of the functions of force-showing devices must proceed by examination of examples. I have discussed the discourse-marking job of two expressions signalling the promisory discourse, 'I promise' and 'on my honour'; and I have also tried to indicate what the promisory implications are. Phrases marking other kinds of discourses can be investigated along similar lines. There seems, however, to be at least one type of discourse without clearly discourse-signalling phrases—viz. the constative one.

Suppose that our conclusions about truth and its vehicle have been to the point. Then it is probable that the force-showing devices of the constative discourse are among the phrases explicitly concerned with the fit of words to the world or with the arguments of that relation. We may then hope to find a constative-marking element among such adverbial phrases as 'in fact', 'as a matter of fact', 'actually' and 'literally', or in such P-radicals as 'I state', 'I assert' and 'I maintain'. But all these expressions also go together with non-constative utterances.

Consider the adverbial phrases. They sometimes have a constative function. 'He is a hero' is, I suppose, a judgment with at least a commending and a 'descriptive' element. Nobody is a hero unless he has done his duty or more than his duty in situations where fear would lead most of us not to do it. But the very same behaviour could be described in other terms. That the man is called a hero and not (say) a daredevil indicates that the speaker looks favourably upon him, and this 'expression' of an attitude may perhaps also be included in the 'descriptive' component. (Note the strangeness of 'He's a hero, but I dislike him and his actions'.) The commending ingredient is, however, usually the dominating one. The effect of adding one of our adverbial phrases to the utterance is, I think, that the 'descriptive' factors come to the fore. There is a cool, matter-of-fact air about 'Actually he's a hero'. The utterance stresses that he conforms to certain standards more than it commends him or them: though that appearance may be more influential than utterances signalling an attitude-advocating force.

At the repair shop I am told 'As a matter of fact your car will be ready tomorrow, sir'. Is that a promise or a forecast? The question is inappropriate when the speaker is the man allotted to do the job at the car. For if *he* is prognosticating, the truth-value of his utterance depends on future actions for which he is responsible. Hence he is committing himself to a certain future behaviour, and his forecast shades off into a promise. This is a feature of all utterances about a speaker's own future voluntary actions. It is always an insult to ask such a speaker whether he is making a promise; for in this type of case the difference between constating and promising is non-existent.

But suppose that the speaker is employed at the reception service. Had he uttered 'Your car will be ready tomorrow, sir', his utterance would have been force-ambiguous, but in its present form it is clearly a forecast. If I say 'Do you promise?', I ask him to perform a *new* act and not how he intended his utterance to be taken.

Even if our adverbial phrases have a *tendency* to remove other forces than the constative one, they are pretty weak devices. They also have an emphatic job which sometimes is the only noticeable one. If I say 'As a matter of fact you are going to do it', I have usually not forecasted but given an emphatic order. And although 'That was, in fact, a spiteful thing to do' tends to convey that the action falls short of certain standards without blaming it, it often stresses how very blameworthy the deed was. The presence of the adverbial phrases is not enough to ascertain that the utterance is a constative.

The same conclusion holds good of 'I state', 'I assert' and 'I maintain'. They are certainly used to exclude non-constative forces from an utterance, but often they just signal that the speaker is firmly determined to defend a certain utterance, be it a constative, a value-judgment, or whatnot. 'I state that it is a good picture' only occasionally constates that the picture satisfies certain norms; more often than not it stridently commends the picture.

Why are there no discourse-marking expressions for constatives? Suppose there are no force-showing phrases for constatives. How are we to account for their absence? Can it be that constating is, in a way, very primitive? All it requires is (1) the ability to single out an item in the world and to predicate something of it as accurately as possible and (2) the convention that such a speech act is to be done only when the speaker knows or at least has good reason to believe that the item has the property signified.

The pragmatic implications of the constative are simply those of truthfulness and good information. The ability to do something, explicit consideration of what is to the addressee's advantake and so forth are irrelevant. To constate is in the ideal case to give a piece of information. Now language is mostly used for practical ends, so pieces of information are usually given with a view to influencing behaviour. They would not do so unless it was assumed that the speaker is speaking the truth; but what he is anxious to convey is how he wants the information to be taken —in what particular way he wishes to see it fit into the addressee's plans. A host of force-showing expressions are therefore invented to indicate the practical end of the communication: 'I warn', 'It is good that', 'I advise', and so on. Does 'disinterested' truth-telling, truth-telling that does not aim at goading or guiding behaviour, occur so seldom in ordinary life or in such characteristic circumstances that we have not bothered to coin a phrase for signalling it?

Be that as it may. For my present purpose it is enough if I have substantiated my claim that some force-showing phrases mark out a discourse, and if I have illustrated what marking out a discourse is like.

7. A new type of force-showing expressions

Contrast 'I promise' with 'I conclude'. To say 'I conclude that *p*' is to conclude that *p*, so the phrase can always be taken as a performatory device in Austin's sense (but not in the sense of *DP 2*). Nevertheless that interpretation is usually far-fetched: the audience does not want to know that the speaker is performing an act of inference, nor does he himself want to set out a piece of autobiography. The aim of the phrase is then the same as that of 'therefore' or 'hence'. The latter expressions are not performatory. They simply mark that *p* follows from something already said—that the speaker has no duty to back it up with new evidence. When 'I conclude' is used in that way, it is not performatory. In a genuine performative, the speaker cannot be ignored. There cannot be a promise without a promisor or an apology without someone who apologizes: promises and apologies are actions, and actions are performed by agents. But although there would be no use for 'hence' and 'therefore' unless there were people who inferred, these phrases only mark a logical relation between the conclusion and the premisses; they do not create it. The speaker does not by a fiat bring the relation into existence; rather he discovers it. So 'hence' and 'therefore' are clear examples of force-showing phrases without performatory elements; and 'I conclude' is an example of an expression which, in spite of its grammatical form, often has only a force-showing function. (Other inference-marking expressions are 'I deduce', 'I infer', 'it follows'. There seem to be differences between them in respects which may merit investigations.)

Inference-marking expressions neither assign an utterance to a certain type of discourse nor mark the extent to which the ordinary implications of that discourse hold. They mark logical relations. Hence there is no dichotomy between discourse-marking and degree-showing expressions, only a distinction. Yet the distinction seems sound, and I shall continue to employ it.

8. Degree-showing devices

For all I know, there may be degree-showing devices which are peculiar to a certain discourse. They may, for example, show that an utterance is not meant to be quite so definitely promisory as an ordinary promise, but they cannot be used for showing that an utterance is not quite so definitely binding in the constative way as an ordinary assertion. My examples will not, however, be of that sort. They are devices which a speaker uses for committing himself or avoiding to commit himself to all the implications of a discourse without signalling what the discourse is; its nature has to emerge from the context. The view I am going to advocate has found its clearest expression in J. O. Urmson's 'Parenthetical verbs'.

It often happens that we do not have satisfactory support for an utterance and that we want our audience to be aware of that fact. I am ransacking the drawers of my desk for the lease. Knowing my habits, my wife suspects that I have left it in a book. But she is not certain and does not want me to think she is. What is she to say? Well, she may try 'Didn't you leave it in a book?' or 'Perhaps you left it in a book' or 'I guess you left it in a book' or something of the sort. Her utterance 'I guess you left it in a book' does not purport to tell me something about her state of mind but only to give me a new idea of where to search for the paper. The phrase 'I guess' serves as a signal that she does not want me to take her utterance as a confident assertion. If her suggestion turns out to be wrong, I should be unreasonable if I reproached her as if she had stated that the lease was in a book; and I would be unreasonable precisely because the prefatory 'I guess' has made it clear, to everyone who hears her and knows the language, that she explicitly refused to assume the responsibilities of an assertor.

We may tie ourselves more or less firmly to an utterance. If it is clear to what discourse an utterance belongs and if it further contains no degree-showing device at all, then the speaker has made the standard commitments of that discourse; the utterance has its standard strength. To paraphrase Austin (1956a.138): the natural economy of language dictates that for the *standard* case of an utterance of a certain type of discourse no modifying expression is required. We cannot, however, assume that all utterances whose discourse is evident have their standard strength when no degree-showing device enters them. The force of an utterance may be shown by non-verbal means, like gestures and tones of voice; further, if everyone knows that a topic is notoriously difficult, there is no need for guarding expressions. What looks like a piece of information about occurrences in the remote future is normally taken as a surmise or a guess.

Let us disregard the non-linguistic, contextual ways of guarding an utterance. If I say 'There's a high wind', I have then stated that there is; I have shouldered the responsibilities of an assertor. Now I hesitate: perhaps the noise is not the wind in the trees but a distant aeroplane. To show that you ought not to rely on my words absolutely, I insert 'I believe', 'I think', 'it seems to me that', etc.; phrases implying that I have some though not sufficient backing. When I want to convey that I have still less to bank on, other expressions are at hand: 'I guess', 'as a surmise I should say' and so on. Finally, I may have no support at all for my view, although I see no obstacles to it. Here my signals are, e.g. 'possibly' and 'it may be the case that'. In this manner a scale is formed from 'categorical' utterances to 'problematic' ones. Step by step a 'categorical' utterance is carried to the point where it encounters a 'modal' concept, that of possibility.

8.1. 'I believe'

It would be superfluous to argue for the view that 'There's a high wind, I guess' is less committal than 'There's a high wind, I believe' and the latter utterance less committal than 'There's a high wind': everyone who knows English recognizes these facts. So it is incontestable that there is a scale of lesser and lesser commitments, and that its rungs are marked out by such phrases as 'I believe' and 'I guess'. Nevertheless most philosophers have strangely ignored the degree-showing employment of 'I believe'. Even Urmson who—together with Wittgenstein (*Philosophical Investigations*, II:x)—is the first philosopher to have drawn attention to it in my opinion errs in his attempts to relate it to other uses. It may therefore be worth our while to consider the force-showing employment of the phrase.

Consider, then, an aside by A. J. Ayer:[11]

You have no right to reproach me if I merely say that I believe [that *p*], though you may think the less of me if my belief appears to you irrational. If I tell you that I believe something which I do not, I am misinforming you only about my mental attitude.

[11] A. J. Ayer, *The Problem of Knowledge*, p. 17f (Pelican ed.)—The remark is dropped in a discussion of knowledge, not of belief.

This will no doubt do for some employments of 'I believe'; but imagine the following case. Planning to invest my money in shares I ask a business man what he believes about a certain stock. He answers, 'I believe they are going up'. Consequently I buy a considerable number of them. But they fall, and I learn that my advisor had thought they would. Accused of lying he retorts, 'I certainly hoodwinked you about my mental attitude, but that serves you right when you are rude enough to try and pry into my psychological make-up. And of course you can't reproach me with having misled you as to the shares: I ventured no opinion about them at all, did I?'

That defence is no good. Yet it would be proper if 'I believe' was always and exclusively used for psychological reports. The situation would have been the same even if he had originally answered 'I'm pretty sure (certain) that the shares will go up'. Consider how often questions beginning 'Do you believe . . . ?' or 'Are you certain (sure)'-utterances are answers to questions that are not about the speaker's state of mind. Is it not obvious that Ayer's account of believing that *p* leaves out the degree-showing use completely? And worse: that the employment thus ignored is a very common one?

The degree-showing and the delusional employment. Compare two situations. In the first I ask you, 'What time is it?' You make a gesture as if to consult your watch and then remember that it is out of order. Hesitatingly you reply 'About six, I believe'. In the second case I am a psychiatrist and you have consulted me about your delusions. I ask you what they are, and you answer, 'I believe that pink elephants are running after me'.

These are very different uses of 'I believe'. 'It's about six o'clock, I believe' is about the time, not about your state of mind; 'I believe that pink elephants are running after me' is not about elephants—since *ex hypothesi* you know they are delusions—but about your state of mind.

(*a*) Urmson has pointed out that in the first case I can say either 'I believe it is about six', 'It is, I believe, about six', or 'It is about six, I believe'. The patient who knows he suffers from a delusion can hardly use the two latter constructions. If he says 'Pink elephants are, I believe, running after me' or 'Pink elephants are running after me, I believe', his utterance would normally be taken not as a report about his state of mind but as a guarded claim that pink elephants are chasing him in space and time, not merely in his imagination.

(*b*) In the first case 'I believe' is, roughly speaking, replaceable by 'probably'. In the second case it is not—'Pink elephants are probably running after me' is a claim about the world, not about the speaker's state of mind.

(*c*) The patient could very well answer the psychiatrist by saying 'I can't help believing that pink elephants are running after me'. But 'I can't help believing it's about six' certainly doesn't answer the question 'What time is it?'

(*d*) 'I believe that pink elephants are running after me' can be telescoped into either 'I usually—though not necessarily at present—believe . . .' and 'At present I believe . . .'. Call them the iterative and the momentary interpretation. There is no iterative interpretation of 'It's about six o'clock, I believe'.

(*e*) In the clock case it makes no sense to say 'I believe falsely that . . .'; in the delusion case it does (in both interpretations). 'I believe falsely that pink elephants are running after me' is a way of saying that I realize I am the victim of a delusion. Wittgenstein was therefore only partly right in his remark 'If there were a verb meaning "to believe falsely", it would not have any significant first person present indicative' (*Ph. Inv.*, p. 190).

(*f*) A victim of a delusion may, I suppose, sometimes be uncertain whether he really thinks he is pursued by pink elephants. He can convey that by saying 'I probably believe . . .'. But nobody can answer 'What time is it?' by 'I probably believe it's six o'clock'—that retort is either a redundancy, like 'It's probably probable it's six o'clock', or an irrelevant piece of autobiography.

These points suffice to establish that 'I believe' has at least two different functions. In the clock case it is not autobiographical but serves only to show what degree of reliance the hearer is to place on the supplementation. In the delusion case its job is not to guard an utterance but to say that it is a piece of information about the speaker's state of mind.

A confusion of Moore's. Since the days of G. E. Moore's *Ethics*, philosophers have discussed why it will not do to say something of the form 'S is P, but I don't believe it'. A whole spectrum of answers have been produced, ranging from Moore's suggestion that the utterance is not out of order but merely surprising,[12] to the view (never expressed but clearly implicit in Urmson's 'Parenthetical verbs') that the utterance exhibits a form of self-contradiction. Our distinction between the delusional and the degree-showing use of 'I believe' is relevant here.

Using 'I believe' delusionally, we can truthfully say 'S is P, but I don't believe it'; so there is at least one use of the phrase for which Moore's suggestion is not so ridiculous as some philosophers want us to think. Nevertheless the utterance is self-stultifying and not just very surprising, when 'I believe' is employed as a degree-showing device. The stultification is about the same as that of 'S is P, but probably S is not P'; and then it is a form of self-contradiction. Two connected reasons against that view rest on a dubious assumption.

The first of them is that although S is P, someone may not believe it is. The disbeliever may be identical with the speaker. Hence 'S is P, but I don't believe it' may be true, and when it cannot be a self-contradiction (Moore, *loc. cit.*).—The second reason can be put thus: 'S is P, but I don't believe it' differs from 'S is P, but he does not believe it' or from 'S is P, but I didn't believe it' only in regard to the pronoun or tense. If you say 'S is P, but I don't believe it' and I, referring to you, say 'S is P, but you don't believe it', we have 'expressed the same proposition'. 'And how can the proposition expressed by one form of words be self-contradictory, if the same proposition, when expressed by another form of words, is clearly self-consistent?'[13]

Both arguments take it for granted that 'I believe' does the same type of job as 'he believes' or 'I believed'. But assume that 'I believe' is degree-showing, and a striking difference between it and 'believe'-phrases in other persons and tenses will leap to the eye. True, they can all be placed at the front, in the middle, or at the end of an utterance; but only the first person present indicative (singular or plural) is a force-device. My utterance 'Shakespeare died in 1617, I believe' is intended to be about Shakespeare's year of death; 'Shakespeare died in 1617, I believed (he believes)' is intended to say something about some-

---

[12] G. E. Moore, 'Russell's "Theory of description"', *The Philosophy of Bertrand Russell* (ed. A. Schilpp), p. 204.
[13] A. M. MacIver, 'Some questions about "know" and "think"', *Philosophy and Analysis* (ed. M. Macdonald), p. 91.

body's beliefs. If you inform me that Shakespeare died in 1616, I stand corrected in the first case but not in the second. 'He died in 1616, I believe' is a hesitant answer to the question 'When did Shakespeare die?'; 'He believes (I believed) he died in 1616' is an unguarded answer, and an unguarded answer to a totally different question, viz. (very roughly) 'What is his (What was previously my own) sincere answer to the question "When did Shakespeare die?"'. 'Shakespeare probably died in 1617, I believe' contains a redundancy; 'He believes (I previously believed) that Shakespeare probably died in 1617' does not. A 'believe'-phrase that is not couched in the first person present perfect indicative has not a degree-showing job.

If this is so, the two arguments against the contradiction thesis break down. The first of them requires that 'A believes that S is not P' and 'A is identical with me' together yield 'I believe that S is not P'. If this is to be an inference, 'believe' as it occurs in 'A believes' must be neutral as to person and tense; but then it is not degree-showing. Consequently it is not degree-showing in the conclusion either; and then the argument is irrelevant to the contradiction thesis. The second objection is ineffective in the same way. It is essential to it that 'believe' functions in the same way in the first person present simple indicative as it does in other persons and tenses; but if it does, it is not the force-showing 'I believe'. And only the force-showing phrase is relevant to the contradiction view.

'*He believes*'.* The person-and-tense neutral use of 'believe' which the two counter-arguments have drawn our attention to is of course not to be identified with an *oratio obliqua* report on a delusional employment. It is true it is *sometimes* such a report, e.g. 'She is, she believes, surrounded by blue devils'. It is then clear that she cannot help believing what she does believe, and it would be in questionable taste to ask 'What are her reasons?' 'Reason' has, after all, to do with 'rationale' and 'rational'; but her belief has no good rationale, and she is not rational. We have to search for the causes of her belief, not for her reasons for it. But most utterances of the form 'S is P, *x* believes' do not contain delusional uses of 'believe'. Your statement 'She believes that

*[Cf. M. J. Charlesworth: 'The parenthetical use of the verb "believe"'. *Mind* 74 (1965).]

smoking causes cancer of the lung' does not imply that she cannot help believing in and/or cannot give a good rationale of her belief.

Urmson has claimed that the use of 'believe' in other persons and tenses than the first person present simple indicative is derived from the degree-showing employment. His account is roughly that when you say 'Jones believes that X is at home', you are either (*a*) reporting in *oratio obliqua* Jones' warning use of the verb, or (*b*) stretching 'believe' to situations where Jones behaves in a way characteristic of people prepared to claim, guardedly or unguardedly, 'X is at home'—although Jones does not himself employ these words or words to that effect. Whether you employ the verb in the *oratio obliqua* sense or in the stretched way can be settled by the position of the clause 'Jones believes'. In the former case you may use whichever you like of the three constructions 'Jones believes that X is at home', 'X is, Jones believes, at home', and 'X is at home, Jones believes'. In the latter case you have not heard Jones say that he believes X is at home—you have, for example, only seen him knock at X's door. Then you can hardly use any other construction than the first. (Urmson, *op. cit.*, pp. 202-4.)

Neat though it is, Urmson's theory does not cover all the facts. Take the *oratio obliqua* case first. There your utterance implies 'the truth and reasonableness of the statement that Jones has made the statement that X is at home (Jones thereby implying its truth and reasonableness with the conventional warning signal about the evidential situation)' (p. 202). You have not claimed that X is at home. Consequently you are under no obligation to produce evidence that he is, nor are you to blame if he is not. You have only claimed to give a true and reasonable answer to the question 'Where, in Jones' opinion, is X to be found?'

So far, all is plain sailing. Urmson adds, however, that you are 'reporting Jones' parenthetical use of the verb' (p. 202); and that is wrong. Your utterance 'X is, Jones believes, at home' would certainly be careless if Jones had employed so strong warning devices as 'I guess' or 'I fancy'—then you ought to have said e.g. 'X is, Jones believes, *perhaps* at home'. But your utterance is strangely enough quite in order when Jones had no safeguard at all—when he said simply 'X is at home'. How are we to account for this? (i) Although he used no verbal warning device, he may have used non-verbal ones. (ii) Even if he has not, there is as a rule no need to convey that he did not guard himself. The principle of charity bids us to report refusals to stick one's neck out but not to report dauntless elongations of it. If we want to stress that Jones committed himself strongly, we may mark it by saying, e.g. 'X was, Jones asserted, at home'. So Urmson can perhaps, without detriment to his theory, retract the words that the *oratio obliqua* utterance reports a degree-showing use of 'I believe'.

Let us next turn to a case where *oratio obliqua* is ruled out (pp. 202–3):

Smith, who has discovered that there has been a sudden railway stoppage, sees Jones making his habitual morning dash to the station, and says, 'Jones believes that the trains are working'. This is a new, and, however important, derivative, use of the verb 'believe'. Note that in this context Smith could not say, 'The trains, Jones believes, are working'. Jones, who has probably not considered the matter at all, is behaving in the way that someone who was prepared to say either 'The trains are running' or 'I believe that the trains are running' would behave (no doubt he would be prepared to say one or other of these things if he considered the matter). We thus, in a perfectly intelligible way, extend our use of the verb 'to believe' to those situations in which a person behaves as a person who has considered the evidence and was willing to say 'I believe' would consistently behave.

The story, I take it, is this: The behaviour of individuals who after due consideration say 'S is (I believe) P' falls into certain characteristic patterns. (These will no doubt vary from situation to situation: Jones' belief that the train will leave in five minutes affects his actions differently, depending on whether he wants to catch the train or has decided to take a day off.) When somebody's behaviour conforms to such a pattern, we say that he believes that S is P, although he remains silent.

But why do we say it? Is it because we make an inference from analogy—'People who behave thus are usually willing to claim that S is P, so Jones probably will'? Or is it because it is conceptually impossible that someone whose behaviour in a certain situation really conforms to the pattern nevertheless disbelieves that S is P? These are utterly different types of explanations. According to the first, the resemblances between Jones' behaviour and that of someone who after due consideration of the evidence says 'S is (I believe' P' only *support the truth* of the assertion 'Jones believes that S is P'—the speaker can fall back on these resemblances if asked 'What's your evidence that Jones believes it?' According to the second, 'Jones behaves like a person who has considered the evidence and who is willing to say "S is (I believe) P"' is an *analysis* of 'Jones believes that S is P'. The claim that the degree-showing use of 'believe' is primary to the others makes it clear that Urmson advocates the latter type of explanation.

There is an obvious objection to Urmson's view. If 'Jones behaves like a person who after due consideration of the evidence is willing to say "S is (I believe) P"' really is the analysans of 'Jones believes that S is P', the utterance 'Jones believes that S is P, although he does not behave like a person who after due consideration of the evidence is willing to say "S is (I believe) P"' ought to be a contradiction; but it seems to be a perfectly intelligible utterance which cannot without investigations be dismissed as false. If Jones never said that S is P or uttered something presupposing it, and if he never exhibited a relevant pattern of behaviour, we could have no evidence for our assertion that he nevertheless believed that S is P, and so we should have no business to make it; but that is a different kettle of fish.

It is possible that the objection is less formidable than it looks. Consider the man who all his life behaved as if he believed that flowers feel but on his deathbed confessed it was all feigned.[14] *De mortuis nil nisi bonum*, but his disclaimer will not do—not because lifelong pretence requires superhuman perseverance but rather because the story for some reason does not make sense. There is, then, something unsatisfactory about the objection.

The psychological use of 'believe'. Let us start afresh. In ordinary life willingness to claim that S is P goes together with readiness to do certain actions and refrain from others. To be prepared to claim that a thunderstorm is on top of us goes together with such things as readiness to shut the windows, take in the washing and spread a tarpaulin over the stack of wood; whilst its jars with (say) setting out for a walk without an umbrella. These actions are performed against a background of the speaker's wishes and

[14] John Wisdom, *Other minds*, p. 7.

intentions: they are designed to stave off certain unpleasant consequences or take advantage of pleasant effects of an imminent thunderstorm. It would, I think, be superstitious to assume that the actions must be *caused* by a belief that there is going to be a thunderstorm. Often they are *constituents of* my belief: I may find I believe there is going to be a thunderstorm by catching myself performing the acts. Then it would be gratuitous to attribute them to my having entertained a proposition which I have not been aware of.

In the ordinary case there seem to be two sets of criteria for someone's belief that S is P, namely that, on a certain amount of evidence, he is willing to claim that S is P and that he is ready to act as if S were P. When 'believe' is governed by this double set of criteria, it is used *psychologically*. When the sets conflict with each other, the criteria from behaviour have the upper hand. He says he believes she is innocent, but his actions belie it. Loudly as Mrs Brown assures us that she believes that tomorrow will be the day of the Last Coming, our knowledge that she intends to spend next summer in Spain nevertheless rules out that she really believes what she claims to—although she may be quite sincere. You may be honestly mistaken as to your beliefs, not because you have not listened carefully enough to what you say in your heart but because you have not observed carefully enough what pattern your actions form.

It now seems as if it *is* self-contradictory to say 'Jones believes that S is P, although he doesn't say so, nor behaves like a person who after due consideration of the evidence is prepared to claim that S is P'—provided that his actions run counter to those we expect from someone willing to claim that S is P.

I have, however, ignored an obvious complication. A man may have ample reason to hide his beliefs. If he publicly confessed them, or revealed them in his actions, he would risk persecution. For this reason he may be afraid to occupy himself with them even in private. Then not merely the criteria of what he says but also the overwhelming amount of the criteria from behaviour speaks in favour of his *not* believing that S is P. Nonetheless he does believe it. He always has to pay heed to his actions and words; he always has to restrain himself. Were the risks absent, his behaviour and speech would change.

It is this kind of case which makes it plausible to say that although nobody has any evidence for saying that A believes that S is P but never reveals it in his speech or action, such an assertion nevertheless makes sense. But here there must be a reason for the concealment. When no conceivable reason can be found and the talk and behaviour camouflaging the belief bring down derision upon the agent, a deathbed confession that it was all feigned carries no conviction. The man who all his life behaved as if flowers feel could not, we rule, have indulged in such a pointless behaviour unless he in fact believed that they feel. Don Quixot could not—could never be allowed to — pass off all his fights against disguised magicians as an elaborate hoax. Our objection against Urmson's analysis of 'Jones believes that S is P' is valid only when a reason can be found for Jones' dissembling his belief.

There are certain beliefs which are based on evidence but which do not straddle preparedness to claim and preparedness to act. Beliefs about the past afford one type of example, and I suppose every one of us can list a number of beliefs he has which do not in the least involve any preparedness on his part to do anything except, perhaps, to state them and argue them. If they were taken to be basic we would have to ask why beliefs ever are reasons for actions. Since that question seems silly, it is better to treat them as derivatives from the psychological use than the other way round.

The psychological and the degree-showing use of 'I believe'. In the psychological use, a belief that S is P is something based on evidence and apt to change as new evidence crops up. It is not beyond the reach of rational argument, as the delusional belief. Both the psychological and the delusional use of 'believe' differ from the degree-showing one in that they can be used in grammatical forms other than the first person present simple active. Whilst the degree-showing employment simply serves to warn the listener that the utterance has less than its normal strength, the psychological one serves to tell us something about the subject's state of mind—viz. that he is ready to claim certain things and/or prepared to act in certain ways. The behaviour can *constitute* (part of) a psychological belief; a degree-showing use of 'believe' cannot be *constituted* of actions (barring the locutionary and force-showing acts) although it can be *replaced* by deeds, such as certain gestures. The psychological use is then not identical with either the delusional or the degree-showing one.

We do not master the degree-showing use until we know what it is to stand fully committed by our words. I presume that we have then already begun to understand such utterances as 'My boy, you believe sand is good for you, but it isn't' or 'Babies believe they can eat everything, but you are not a baby, are you?' We then know that certain patterns of behaviour in certain situations are criteria of certain beliefs; i.e., we have begun to grasp the essentials of *psychological* belief. If this was done at an age when we were hardly able to claim (guardedly or unguardedly) that, say, sand is edible, it seems plausible that the degree-showing use is an extension of the psychological one and not vice versa.

It is, however, risky to base claims to logical priority on claims to temporal priority. It is better to show that the suggestion that the psychological use is central, has a greater explanatory power than Urmson's hypothesis. The psychological 'believe' bridges the gap between the delusional and the degree-showing one. By making the readiness to claim and/or to act less and less impervious to new evidence and arguments, we step from a psychological belief to a delusional one. By stressing that the readiness to claim that S is P varies according to the speaker's backing and that it is sometimes convenient to have a verbal phrase for marking that the readiness is less than it could have been, we go from the psychological 'believe' to the degree-showing one. Urmson does not consider the delusional employment, except for a passing remark that it indicates a piece of 'psychological history' (*op. cit.*, p. 203); but if he were to explain it, he would have to give a similar account. Since he thinks that the psychological use is to be explained in terms of the degree-showing one, his account would be fairly complicated compared to mine.

You put down your book, rise, take your umbrella. Your dog tears upstairs and comes back with its leash. 'He believes I'm going out', you say. On the assumption that the behaviour a being in a certain situation indulges in is a criterion of its psychological belief, your saying is easy to explain. But how is Urmson to do it? By resorting to the anthropomorphism of 'The dog would after due consideration of the evidence claim that its master is going out' or 'The dog behaves as would a speaking dog which after due consideration of the evidence was willing to claim that its master was going out'? Less ridiculous answers are bound to be more complicated. It may of course be said that the dog does not believe anything; his behaviour is a conditioned reflex, and so on. This is a marginal case, far removed from the paradigm of a rational being who after due consideration is prepared to claim that I am going out and ready to act upon it. Nevertheless we *do* say that the dog has certain beliefs, and we say it because his actions form a peculiarly purposive pattern. An elucidation of the nature of belief is hard put to it to explain that use of language, if the degree-showing 'believe' is taken as the basic use.

'*S is P, but I don't believe it*' *again*. Earlier I dismissed two objections against the idea that 'S is P, but I don't believe it' is self-contradictory. They were based on the assumption that 'I believe' does the same duty as 'you believe' and 'I believed'; and that is not true of the degree-showing phrase. But what of the psychological phrase? Can I not psychologically believe something in exactly the way you believe it? Certainly I can; and then the two arguments seem valid: they show that the sentence 'S is P, but I don't psychologically believe it' can be used to make a true statement. But here I must enter two qualifications: in most contexts the psychological 'I believe' is otiose; and although our utterance can be *true*, it is always a self-frustrating thing to *say*.

The first point is this: Already in our discussion of serious talk we saw that a serious utterance entitles the audience to infer that the speaker holds the requisite psychological belief, and that it is necessary that speakers in general are not deceitful. Therefore it is otiose to preface a serious utterance by the phrase 'I (psychologically) believe'. The phrase has a job to do only in situations where we have said something which the addressee takes as a joke. It is then employed to rule out that possibility, thus reporting a psychological belief and *ipso facto* removing a force-ambiguity. It is also, of course, used in confessions, where I am not making claims about the world as much as recording what my claims are.

If psychological belief enters all serious speech, it must for all practical purposes except that of creating confusion be self-defeating to say 'S is P, but I don't (psychologically) believe it'. As a serious utterance, 'S is P' is issued with an implication that the speaker has a good backing and/or is willing to act as if S were P. To add 'but I don't psychologically believe it' is to retract the implication. The effect is that the utterance is withdrawn from the realm of serious utterances, having explicitly violated the fundamental rule of linguistic communication that a speaker is not to say something he cannot back up. But it is, of course, possible that S *is* P, although somebody does not have the requisite psychological belief. Hence 'S is P, but I don't psychologically believe it' can be used to make a true utterance but not to make a serious one.

'But can't I seriously say "I know she is dead, but I can't believe it"? There are good reasons to deny that "I believe" is used delusionally here, though it gives an autobiographical report; and if it is used psychologically, an utterance is *not* deprived of its seriousness when the speaker explicitly denies that he psychologically believes it.'

I agree that 'I cannot believe' here marks out a piece of autobiography which is hardly a piece of delusion; but I deny that it is a clear case of psychological belief. It is, I think, something between the two. What you mean when you say 'I know she's dead, but I can't believe it' is not that you are convinced she is alive. It is that you have not yet managed to grasp all the practical consequences of her death or to redirect your expectations and behaviour. You still catch yourself dialling her telephone number or looking forward to seeing her; but these tendencies are remnants of an old pattern which you deem to be no longer adequate. As soon as you are aware of them, you start effacing them. Normally you are successful, but in rare cases they resist your efforts. They have then become obsessional, and your utterance 'I can't believe she's dead' has changed its import—although you are aware she is dead you *cannot help* dialling her number, day after day, always hoping for a reply; i.e., you are confessing that you are under a delusion. Thus 'cannot believe' lies somewhere in the borderland between psychological and delusional beliefs; and then no counter-example is given.

'Probably' and the degree-showing 'I believe'. 'Probably' is a verbal, degree-showing device, roughly interchangeable with the

degree-showing 'I believe'. Why do we have two phrases with about the same function? The answer seems to be this:

If asked 'When did Shakespeare die?' I can answer 'In 1616, I believe' but hardly 'Probably in 1616'; if asked 'Who's the author of the *Eudemian Ethics*?' I can answer 'Probably Aristotle' but hardly 'Aristotle, I believe'—that would be to set myself up as an authority on Greek scholarship. 'I believe' serves to indicate that the speaker's reason for refraining from an unguarded utterance is that he personally does not have sufficient evidence; whilst 'probably' indicates that authorities disagree, so that the lack of certainty is not due to the speaker's personal deficiencies (his poor memory, etc.). For this reason 'I believe' has an autobiographical ring absent from 'probably'.

Austin on 'I believe'. In a passing remark, Austin reveals that he is aware that phrases beginning 'I think that . . .' are usually not intended to say something about the speaker's state of mind (*Words*.90). But he was never happy about 'I believe'. 'S is P, but I don't believe it' is not a contradiction (1940.32; *Words*.49; 'What I do as a philosopher'); and his short discussion of the difficulty in *Words*.Ch.4 pivots upon the consideration that when the speaker does not believe his own utterance 'S is P', it is not sincere, a fact which is reported by 'I don't believe it'. That is, he seems to say that the utterance can be true but nevertheless remains self-defeating (cf. 1940.31–2). He had, then, the psychological sense in mind most of the time. But in his list of expositives 'believe' occurs, though with a query; and this is an indication that he had detected the force-showing function—he can hardly have held that the phrase is performatory!

8.2. 'Problematic' devices

Let us now turn to utterances taking 'may' as their auxiliary or containing such words as 'possible' and 'possibly'. Confident assertions as well as more hedged ones, such as those containing 'probably' and 'I believe', imply that the speaker commits himself. His commitments decrease the closer we come to the 'may' and 'possible' utterances. There he does not want to stake anything at all. Hence 'S may and may not be P' is not a contradiction, though 'S is and is not P (, I believe, etc.)' is. All he claims when saying 'S may be P' is that what he knows does not rule it out that S is P; or, in the case of 'may and may not', that he does not know whether it is ruled out. In refusing to rule it out he also insists that, in spite of his lack of evidence that S is P, the question whether it is is worth settling; we cannot in good conscience just dismiss it.

This raising of a question, with the implied claim that its answer is relevant to a problem at hand, is the invariable and characteristic function of 'problematic' utterances. The reasons supporting the refusal to rule something out vary, however, from situation to situation. Sometimes they are just that the utterance embodies no self-contradiction; but that is unusual. If an editorial says that it is possible that Mao-tse-Tung's regime is tottering, it has to back it up in other ways than by arguing that 'Mao-tse-Tung's regime is tottering' is not self-contradictory; we expect, e.g., the claim that a government of an agrarian country is faced with difficulties after a series of bad harvests.

Notice also that it would be absurd to take 'not self-contradictory' as a minimum sense of 'possible'. Even if something is possible only because it is not self-contradictory, 'because' marks a reason and not a rule of meaning: 'S being P involves no self-contradiction and is hence possible' is no tautology—it does not mean 'S being P involves no self-contradiction and is not self-contradictory'. 'Possible' is a device giving the listener to understand that a suggestion is not to be ruled out without further ado; it gives the utterance that force. It is *not* a device telling the listener on what grounds he is to retain the suggestion—that has to be told separately. Force-showing is not stating. All this has been clearly argued in S. Toulmin's *The Uses of Argument*, Ch.2.

8.3. *The scale of degree-showing devices*

I have suggested that utterances of a certain discourse can be ordered in a scale with verbally and non-verbally unguarded utterances at the top and utterances merely suggesting a possibility at the bottom. Our assessments of constatives as true or false are best at home with utterances high up the scale and all at sea with 'problematic' utterances. If you say 'Charles I may have died a natural death' you are no doubt wrong; but it goes against the grain to assess your utterance as *just* false. It did not set out to be unquestionably true but only to suggest a possibility. Guesses are not much better off. They are assessed as correct or incorrect, but hardly as true or false. When we reach 'I believe'-utterances we are on firmer ground: If I say 'You find this boring, I believe' you are as apt to reply 'That is true' as 'That's right'.

It is not difficult to account for these linguistic facts. An utterance is true because the speaker has used a certain sentence with a certain sense and a certain reference in such a way that it fits the facts. By uttering it he has also committed himself in a certain manner. He has pragmatically implied that he has evidence for his view. The degree-showing phrases serve to lessen his commitments, to diminish his stake. The less risk he runs, the less he is blamed when wrong and praised when right; and assessing an utterance as true or false is not just to comment upon its relation to the world but also to bestow praise or blame upon the utterer.

In defence of the thesis that 'statements about the future' are not related to the world in the way statements about the present or the past are, it has been urged we do not assess the former as true or false.[15] But is not this because most of our so-called statements about the future are *not* statements but conjectures and guesses? Utterances about the future which have good backing and which are offered and taken as statements are by no means always assessed as merely correct or incorrect, right or wrong, but also as true or false—thus, it is true that I shall die some day.

*A model of degree-showing devices.** A model may, perhaps, shed more light over the function of degree-showing devices. In Ch. 3:12 we saw that the statement that S is P may be rendered as a combination of neustic and phrastic: 'I constate/that S is P'. Let us now symbolize how the degree-showing devices weaken the normal strength of the discourse-implications. The 'normal strength' is the degree of commitments usually carried by a confident and (verbally and non-verbally) unguarded statement. Let us arbitrarily assign the value 5 to this degree, whilst a 'may'-utterance, being non-committal, has the value O. We then get the following transformations:

---

[15] Gilbert Ryle, *Dilemmas*, Ch. 2.

*[But cf Ch. E. Caton, 'On the general structure of the epistemic qualifications of things said in English'. *Foundations of Language* 2 (1966).]

'S is P' 'I constate$_5$/that S is P'
'S is, I believe, P' 'I constate$_3$/that S is P'
'S is, I guess, P' 'I constate$_1$/that S is P'
'S may be P' 'I constate$_0$/that S is P'.

A new kind of logical conflict. Return for a moment to 'S is P, but I don't believe it'. Assume that 'believe' has the degree-showing sense. 'S is P' is, I suppose, a confident constative; hence it is to be rendered 'I constate$_5$/that S is P'. The grammatical appearance of 'I don't believe that S is P' may tempt us to the formalization 'Not-(I constate$_3$)/that S is P'; but the slightest acquaintance with its use shows that such a rendering would be mistaken. 'I don't believe that that colour suits you' means the same as 'That colour doesn't, I believe, suit you'; it is a guarded claim that it does not suit you. The correct schematization is 'I constate$_3$/that S is not P'. Hence the conjunction 'S is P, but I don't believe it' is to be rendered
(1) I constate$_5$/that S is P & I constate$_3$/that S is not P.
This is not a paradigmatic contradiction, for when logicians offer us 'S is P & S is not P' as a standard form of a contradiction, they clearly think of something like
(2) I constate$_5$/that S is P & I constate$_5$/that S is not P,
i.e., they assume that the neustics (= the discourse-implications) have the same strength in the two utterances. In an orthodox contradiction

(a) a phrastic is conjuncted with its own negation;
(b) the neustics are of the same type (usually 'I constate') and
(c) have the same strength (usually the degree five).

In (1) the first two conditions hold good but not the third. The resemblances to an ordinary contradiction are in my opinion enough to entitle us to call (1) a contradiction; but the terminological question is of small importance. What matters is that we see what is wrong with (1) and how that sort of failure resembles and differs from the one exemplified by (2).

8.4. *'I know'*

If there is a group of verbal devices—'may', 'possibly' and so forth—which serve to signal that a line of thought deserves further consideration, ought there not to exist devices showing that other contentions do not deserve attention and are to be ruled out? I shall argue that 'I know' is a case in point, and that Austin in all probability held that view. My main debts are, however, to Urmson,[16] White,[17] and Arner.[18]

Outside philosophical seminars, such utterances as 'I know I have two hands' or 'I know I'm in pain' are apt to provoke ridicule. They sound as if someone had doubted that the speaker has two hands or that he is in pain, and that is usually not the case. Usually both my audience and I can see my hands, there is no suggestion that anything is wrong with my eyes, that the light is unreliable, that I have had my hands amputated, etc. Since the hands are available for our five senses and no source of doubt has been suggested, it is silly to demand further evidence that I have two hands: here they are, as plain as the nose in your face. What better proof can be given of the existence of A than A itself? If *it* does not convince you, what does? Not only is the demand for *more* evidence silly; so also is the idea that my two hands are *evidence* that I have two hands: the existence of A is not evidence of itself. But that does not mean that I have no backing for my claim. On the contrary, my backing is too good to be mere evidence. (Cf 1946.73–6; *S&S*.115–16.)

So when no doubts are suggested and the demand for evidence is silly, 'I know'-phrases are inept. Suppose, however, that I am coming to after a motor accident. My eyes trick me, my swaddled arms hurt, and I cannot see my hands. You are in another bed, with your eyes bandaged; and you say you have heard that my hands have been amputated. Fighting down my panic I try to find out. I gather evidence and attempt to settle the different kinds of doubts assailing me. Finally I find that there was nothing to them; I cannot see how my claim to have two hands is to be invalidated. Then 'I know I have two hands' is in place. The prefatory 'I know' is tied to situations where doubts are envisaged and evidence is relevant. *By using it I give it to be understood that my backing is conclusive, that there is no substance to the doubts.*

That my backing is conclusive means no more than that I, the speaker, cannot see how it can fail to show beyond reasonable doubt that my utterance is true, and that I therefore offer it as

---

[16] Urmson, *op. cit.*
[17] Alan R. White, 'On claiming to know'. *Ph.R.* 66 (1957).
[18] Douglas Arner, 'On knowing', *Ph.R.* 68 (1959).

absolutely reliable. It does *not* mean that I signal that my support will, when set out in full, entail the claim—that my backing covers the claim one hundred per cent. The evidence may be conclusive without attaining that amount. When several witnesses have seen the prisoner at the bar stab the woman, when his finger-prints are on the knife, and when he also confesses the deed, we all agree that the evidence is conclusive. But the claim that he did the deed cannot be deduced from it; it is always possible—but oh, how improbable!—that it was a *Doppelgänger* with exactly the same finger-prints, and that the prisoner's story was a free invention. Similarly, when I claim that I do not just guess or believe but actually know that the sun will rise tomorrow, I signal that my evidence is conclusive but not that it covers my claim one hundred per cent. The function of 'I know' in 'I know that S is P' is to signal, in situations where doubts have arisen, that the speaker has conclusive evidence that S is P and hence that the addressee can safely disregard any suggestion to the effect that S is not P. The enormous practical importance of force-showing devices of this kind is plain.

My account may tempt you to object as follows: 'Assume I *think* I have conclusive evidence for the claim that S is P, and that I want to convey it to you. I say "I know that S is P". If your description of the force-showing use of "I know" is satisfactory, I have employed the phrase correctly. But suppose that S is not P. Then I cannot know that S is P; and consequently I have operated incorrectly with the phrase in "I know that S is P".'

The dilemma is not serious. We have to distinguish claiming to know from knowing. In saying 'I know' I lay a claim to know. That claim is reasonable (though perhaps false) if I am sure that S is P and think I have conclusive evidence for my view. When these conditions are fulfilled, I have used the phrase correctly for making a reasonable claim. But in saying 'I cannot know that S is P, if S is not P' I judge not the reasonableness but the validity of my claim to know that S is P. I have stated a necessary condition for the correct employment of the phrase for making a valid claim. Then the dilemma is illusory; for I can, of course, use a phrase correctly in the sense of satisfying the conditions for making a reasonable claim, without using it correctly in the sense of satisfying the conditions for making a valid claim.

'I know' and certainty. Nobody is entitled to say that he knows that S is P, unless he is sure it is: 'I know that S is P, but I'm not sure.' is self-stultifying. The reason is easily seen. A speaker who issues a serious utterance must psychologically believe he can back it up (or must, in case of insincerity, pose as if he did). When he wants to commit himself unguardedly to a serious utterance, the psychological belief must be whole-hearted (or, in case of insincerity, seem to be so). To confess that he is not sure is to retract the force of his 'I know'-utterance—it no longer rules out other suggestions.

But although the claim to know requires that the speaker is sure, 'I know' is not interchangeable with 'I'm sure'. If it were, 'I'm sure S is P, but I don't know it is' would be nonsense. A reasonable claim to know that S is P requires more than being sure; and I have argued that the additional element is that the speaker thinks he has conclusive evidence that S is P. Because he does not see how, in view of the evidence at his disposal, S can fail to be P, he uses 'I know' to rule out that alternative. In doing so he shoulders greater responsibilities than he would if he merely had said unguardedly 'S is P'. The latter utterance gives the hearer to understand that the speaker has good backing, but it does not signal that the evidence is conclusive. I take this to be the point of Austin's thesis that saying 'I know' is to take a plunge beyond saying simply 'S is P', since in the former case 'I *give others my word:* I *give others my authority for saying* that "S is P"' (1946.67).

Troublesome cases. A person knows that S is P only if his claim is (*a*) reasonable and (*b*) valid.—(*a*) If you say 'I know that S is P' without being sure and/or without being able to give grounds for your certainty, *you* don't know, are not entitled to say *you* know; and this is so whether or not S is in fact P.—(*b*) A person whose claim to know that S is P is reasonable nevertheless does not know it is unless S is in fact P—his claim is invalid in spite of its reasonableness. Yet we are ill at ease when faced with an eminently reasonable claim. We are even prepared to say that the doctrine of the four temperaments was part of ancient medical knowledge. Although this is an inverted comma sense, it is not the nasty one exemplified by the remark 'So, you "know" that Thales was a disciple of Anaximander's, do you?' Rather it is a honorary title given to claims backed up with reasons which to all the best-informed persons of that time must have seemed to put the matter beyond reasonable doubt.

Troubles arise when a claim is valid and we, but not the speaker, hold it to be reasonable. S is P, you are sure it is, but your backing is not in your opinion conclusive, so you refuse to claim to know. Yet *we* think your backing is conclusive. Do you know or don't you?

Again S is P, you are inclined to believe it is but you are not sure, and your backing is not what you deem conclusive, though we hold it is. Do you know or don't you?

These marginal cases are important only by setting off the paradigm; by noticing why we hesitate to say you know, we spotlight the ordinary conditions of knowing.

'*I know*' and '*he knows*'. A claimant is not his own judge and does not simultaneously stake a claim and pass a verdict on it. To say 'I know' is to claim that something is valid but not to assess it as valid. But saying 'he knows' or 'I knew' is both to report that a claim has been made and to assess it as valid. It is to report a claim, for if you show that the referent is (was) not sure that S is P or that his reasons for claiming it do (did) not seem conclusive to him, then the utterance 'He knows (I knew) that S is P' is false. And it is to assess a claim as valid, for if I say 'He knows (I knew) that S is P', I cannot afterwards slink off murmuring '*I* never claimed that S is P; I just reported that he knows (I knew) it'. In reporting that someone knows that S is P, I have committed myself unguardedly to the view that S *is* P.

In the first person present, 'know' operates to make a claim, and in other persons and tenses it works as a combination of report and verdict. But 'he knows' does not always report a claim. There is, for instance, the case where the referent never says he knows, but acts as a person who is confident he has conclusive evidence that S is P. Our assertion 'He knows that S is P' can then reasonably be taken as a combination of a claim on his behalf that S is P and an assessment of it as true. For reasons analogous to those given against Urmson's analysis of 'he believes' in terms of 'I believe' it cannot, however, *mean* 'He acts as a person who is confident', etc. I am inclined to think that 'knowing that S is P' straddles being sure, possessing what one thinks to be conclusive evidence, and correspondence between claim and the world; that oddities abound when any of these conditions are neglected; and that the force-showing 'I know' can be explained by means of the second of them. These surmises would, I guess, be borne out by a study of other employments of 'I know', e.g. those of admitting a difficulty, commiserating, agreeing and conceding.

The importance of the force-showing use. Whatever the true, unifying account of the different uses of 'know', the force-showing employment is practically important. In all conversations it is a great help to have a phrase signalling that on the speaker's evidence all suggestions except one can be dismissed—although the evidence does not cover the claim completely. The practical significance is by itself enough to justify an investigation of the force-showing function. It is also so common and so neglected that we may suspect that, unobserved, it has tangled some of the traditional threads in the problem(s) of knowledge. But a study of it is not a study of the *validity* conditions of claims to knowledge. It is a study of a new, hitherto neglected aspect of such claims, viz. how we try to get across to the listener that our words have their full force and commit us to the full degree. Austin, Urmson, White, and Arner are of course aware of the novelty of their undertaking, but critics have not always seen that their victims are not concerned with the traditional question of validity conditions.

9. Austin on 'I know'

I shall now argue that Austin held that 'I know' is force-showing, and I shall then relate his account to the one now given.

Austin on the force-showing 'I know'. What evidence is there that Austin was interested in the force-showing use of 'I know'? 'Know' is mentioned only in passing in the list of expositives (*Words*.161). His 1946 remarks on the resemblances between 'I know' and 'I promise' are, however, best understood if we assume he had the force-showing use in mind. (Since he did not distinguish the Performative Thesis from the Force Thesis, I doubt that his account can be made wholly satisfactory on any interpretation.) That unguarded assertions 'imply' that the speaker knows or at least believes they are true (1946.45) is, I think, another way of saying that they commit the speaker to at least the same degree as they would when guarded with 'I believe' or 'probably' and possibly to the same degree as they would when prefaced with 'I know'. It would be ridiculous to maintain that 'I believe' is a performative; so why hold that 'I know' is? That the latter is tied up with the speaker's degree of commitment is seen from Austin's remarks that when I employ it I bind myself and give others my word (1946.67), that the right to say 'I know' is transmissible, and that, by using the phrase lightly, I may be responsible for getting you into trouble (1946.68). They also indicate that the expression is used to guide my audience as to the force of my utterance.

'I know' does not signify that the speaker is in a certain state of mind (1946.67): the belief that it does exemplifies the descriptive fallacy, the fallacy of assuming that all language is purely descriptive. Austin tries to expose the flaw (1946.71):

Utterance of obvious ritual phrases, in the appropriate circumstances, is not *describing* the action we are doing, but *doing* it ('I do'): in other cases it functions, like tone and expression, or again like punctuation and mood, as an intimation that we are employing language in some special way ('I warn', 'I ask', 'I define').

The former part of the quotation has received its share of attention and contributed to creating the idea that 'I know' according to Austin is a performative. But let us also remember that he says that 'utterance of obvious ritual phrases' (and 1946.70 makes it exceedingly probable that he counted 'I know' as such a phrase) in other cases functions like tone and expression or punctuation and mood. The exclamation mark in 'You go nowhere!' 'intimates' that the utterance has the force of an order; the phrase 'I order that' performs the same duty. So some ritual phrases 'intimate' the force of an utterance—i.e., the sort and/or degree of discourse-implications of an utterance and the responsibilities the speaker shoulders. Why should not 'I know' belong there? All the phrases to which it is compared—'I promise', 'I give my word', 'I guarantee', 'I swear'—are discourse-marking and/or degree-showing devices, even if they *also* are performatory.

It is ludicrous to maintain that to say 'I know' is to know in a way even faintly resemblant to that in which to say 'I promise' is to promise. Yet Austin must have held that view if he meant that his parallel between 'I know' and 'I promise' is a parallel in performatory function. If we assume he wanted to make a comparison not of performatory but of force-showing function, his view is no longer silly. When you say 'I promise', you signal to the addressee that you shoulder certain responsibilities and give him rights to lean on you in certain respects; when you say 'I know', you also signal to the addressee that you shoulder certain responsibilities and give him rights to lean on you in certain respects. This much they have in common, though the responsibilities and rights are very different. On this interpretation Austin has drawn an apt and elucidating parallel.

I have, however, left out certain puzzling features. Austin notices that both 'I know' and 'I promise' are in place only in certain 'appropriate circumstances', but this notion soon becomes all-inclusive. 'I know' is in place only when the speaker is sure, has good evidence and is not mistaken, and 'I promise' is in place only when he has the ability, intends to do the action and in fact performs it; and a failure in any of these respects makes the invocation equally inept. In this early paper Austin sees no important difference between making an honest and reasonable but invalid claim to know that S is P and promising without intending to perform—

the essential factors are (a) You said you knew: you said you promised (b) You were mistaken: you didn't perform. The hesitancy concerns only the precise way in which we are to round on the original 'I know' or 'I promise'. [1946.70–1].

To defend this he is driven to the extreme of saying that a false promise is no promise, a claim he withdraws in *Words*.

The previous discussion of 'I promise' and 'I know' shows what has gone wrong, and I shall not repeat myself. What we now ought to notice is that Austin nowhere in all this says anything supporting the contention that 'I know' is a performative.*

*[Neither S. Davis in '"I know" as an explicit performative' (*Theoria* 30, 1964), nor M. Wright in '"I know" and performative utterances' (*AJP* 43, 1965) does, I think, anything to show that Austin thought of 'I know' as a performatory device.]

He does not allow that you can know that Shakespeare died in 1616 unless Shakespeare did die in 1616, and this is nothing you can create by an act of will. But your performance of promising is something you can create by an act of will. Hence the parallel between 'I know' and 'I promise' is pointless as a comparison of their performatory functions, for on Austin's own showing 'I know' is no performative.

Here I rest my case that Austin thought of 'I know' as a force-showing device.

Final remarks. There are several differences between Austin's view and the one given in §8.4. Urmson has set out the case for the evidence-showing role of 'I know' more clearly than Austin; White has explicitly drawn the distinction between claiming to know and knowing; Arner has made the immensely important point that 'I know' has a conclusive function that does not imply that the speaker poses as having evidence which covers the claim completely. Austin's is a first rough sketch of something which others afterwards have drawn more faithfully. But he is the first philosopher who discerned the performatory and the force-showing functions and began to explore them; he has given the impetus to this form of research.

Postscript

I. A RECONSIDERATION OF THE LOCUTIONARY/ILLOCUTIONARY DISTINCTION

Both the locutionary and the illocutionary dimension of an utterance are within or very close to the region explored in theories of meaning (cf. *Words*.148). Let us begin an inquiry into these dimensions by considering a 'nonnatural' sense, or family of senses, of the verb 'mean'.

1. *Nonnatural meaning introduced*

In his essay 'Meaning' (*Ph.R.* 66, 1957), H. P. Grice distinguishes two senses or two families of senses of 'mean'. He does so by contrasting

(1) 'Those spots mean measles'

to

(2) 'Those three rings on the bell (of the bus) mean that the bus is full.'

Grice asks us to consider the following differences:

(i) I cannot say 'Those spots mean measles, but he has not got the measles.' I can say 'Those three rings mean that the bus is full, but it isn't full.'

(ii) I cannot argue from (1) to any conclusion about 'what is meant by those spots'. I can argue from (2) to some conclusion about 'what is meant by those three rings'.

(iii) I cannot argue from (1) to any conclusion to the effect that someone meant by those spots so-and-so. I can argue from (2) to the conclusion that the conductor meant or should have meant so-and-so by the three rings.

(iv) We can reword (2), but not (1), by a phrase in inverted commas after 'mean': 'Those three rings mean "The bus is

LOCUTIONARY/ILLOCUTIONARY DISTINCTION 257

full"' but not 'Those spots mean "Measles" or "He has got the measles".'

(v) We can reword (1), but not (2), with a phrase beginning 'The fact that'. 'The fact that he has those spots means that he has got the measles' is a restatement of (1). 'The fact that the bell has been rung three times means that the bus is full' is not even an approximate reformulation of (2).

'Mean' is used 'naturally' in (1) and 'nonnaturally' in (2). Grice uses 'mean $_{NN}$' as shorthand for 'mean nonnaturally'.[1]

2. The vehicle of meaning $_{NN}$

What kinds of thing mean $_{NN}$? Grice does not discuss the question except for a passing comment that he calls 'any candidate for meaning $_{NN}$' an utterance, since this word has a 'convenient act-object ambiguity' (*op. cit.*, p. 380). But his examples of things that mean $_{NN}$ are the three rings on the bell of the bus, a certain remark, and the act of drawing a scabrous picture and showing it. It is, I think, clear that the rings and the remark cannot be just a jumble of noises, and that the drawing cannot be just a squiggle. Looked at in that way they would perhaps mean naturally, be signs *of* something or other; but they would not mean $_{NN}$. To mean $_{NN}$ they must at least be regarded as something *produced by human beings*. But this is by no means all; there is a whole series of requirements.

---

[1] 'Mean' covers two Swedish verbs, 'betyda' and 'mena', corresponding to the German 'bedeuten' and 'meinen'. 'Mena', like 'meinen' and the Anglo-Saxon 'mænan', signifies *purpose*, says A. Gardiner in *A Theory of Speech and Language*, §31. It is human beings who *menar*. Grice's third point comes out nicely in Swedish: it is simply gibberish to argue from (1) to any conclusion about 'vad som menas med fläckarna' (for if this locution makes sense, it means that somebody has used the spots in order to convey something); but it makes perfect sense to argue from (2) to something about 'vad som menas med de tre ringningarna'.

Although somebody *menar* something with his words and signals, these themselves do not *mena*. They *betyder* (with direct object). Grice's non-natural sense cannot therefore be rendered with 'mena'. Nevertheless his distinction seems to be borne out by the differences between, not 'mena' and 'betyda', but derivatives from them, *viz.* 'ha mening' and 'ha betydelse'. Spots as well as rings may both *betyda* and *ha betydelse*. But the spots cannot 'ha meningen mässling' nor 'ha meningen "mässling"' nor 'ha meningen "Han har fått mässling"', whereas the corresponding constructions about the rings make perfect sense.

S

These requirements have been discussed by Grice in 'Meaning', by P. F. Strawson in 'Intention and convention in speech acts' (*Symp*), and by John R. Searle in 'What is a speech act?' (*Philosophy in America*, ed. Max Black). These writers seem, however, to discuss partly different matters. Strawson's main concern is meaning NN in a budding or even a preverbal language. Searle concentrates on meaning NN in an established language. Grice shifts back and forth. The notion of meaning NN that he singles out—the one given in the previous section—is a notion of meaning NN in an established language. But he tries to analyse it with a combination of conditions saying something about intentions of speakers. These conditions are, I shall argue, relevant (but certainly not sufficient) for an analysis of meaning NN in an early stage in the development of language. But they will not do for the stage he has singled out, as Ziff has shown in his devastating attack.[2]

2.1. Meaning NN in a preverbal language

Strawson's example. Consider an example which Strawson gave in an early version of 'Intention and convention . . .', read to Filosofiska föreningen at Göteborg University in April, 1963:

Savage S and savage A do not speak the same language. One day when A is out, a lion appears at his hut. Its traces are washed away by the rain. S wishes to warn A. He possesses a lion's paw which he can use for making traces in the sand. If he does so when A is not there, he has not *told* him about the lion, since A will take the indentations as signs, possibly forged ones, *of* a lion rather than as a message that a lion has been there.

Since S wants to get into touch with A, he makes the traces in A's presence, accompanying his performance with an exaggerated facial expression of fear. Then S has, in a single performance, told A that there are lions about and also warned him of them.

Here is a germ of a language. For the success of the performance gives a presumption of subsequent success, if the same performance is repeated with the same purpose and is directed to an audience who witnessed and understood its original employment. Although there have been no rules or conventions governing S's and A's doings, gestures, etc., S may now try to lay down

[2] Paul Ziff: 'On H. P. Grice's account of meaning'. *Analysis* 28 (1967).

LOCUTIONARY/ILLOCUTIONARY DISTINCTION 259

at least the analogue of a linguistic rule by deciding to go through the performance with the lion's paw in this manner only for the purpose of warning against lions.[3]

Strawson's example analysed. An analysis of Strawson's example must, I think, stress the following factors which together provide an elucidation of both *what* is meant $_{NN}$ and *how* meaning $_{NN}$ is brought about:

(1) Traces of lions are signs of lions, i.e., do 'naturally' bring about an idea of lions.

(2) To make imitation traces of lions in somebody's presence is therefore to bring about, in him, an idea of lions.

(3) To be aware that somebody is present at one's making traces of lions and that he is paying attention is to be aware that one's making traces of lions most probably brings about, in that person, an idea of lions.

(4) To make it clear to someone that one is aware of his presence at one's making traces of lions is to make it clear to him that one is aware that one most probably brings about an idea of lions in him.

(5) To make traces of lions while aware of someone's presence at one's production is to know that he knows (provided he is not blind, etc.) that the traces are not made by lions.

(6) To make it clear to someone that one is aware of his presence at one's making traces of lions is to make it clear to him that one is aware that he knows that the traces are not made by lions.

(7) To make it clear to someone that one is aware of his presence at one's making traces of lions is therefore to make it clear to him that one is aware

(7.1) that one most probably brings about an idea of lions in him, and

(7.2) that he knows that the traces are not made by lions.

(8) To make it clear that one is aware of (7.1) and (7.2) is to make it clear to the addressee that one most probably *intends* (7.1) and (7.2), i.e., that one most probably *intends* to bring about an idea of lions in him and *intends* him to know that the traces are not made by lions.

At this stage it is clear that S tries to establish a communication

[3] Being based on notes made at the lecture, this summary may contain grave omissions and misleading insertions.

situation between him and A. Suppose that he manages to get across that he intends (7.1) and (7.2). Then

(9) A understands that by making traces of lions S most probably want to convey something about A: by bringing about in A the idea of lions (as an idea brought about by S) S wants to convey something about lions.

(10) Unless something more than an idea of lions is communicated, A does not know what to do with that idea. Does S want him to join a hunt for lions? Or ask him to beware of lions? Or inform him that there are lions about? What does S want to convey *about* lions? Since there is not much point in conveying just the idea of lions, A assumes that also other parts of S's action are *communicatively relevant*—are designed so to supplement the idea of lions that something is communicated *about* lions. I.e., A assumes that S wants to convey a complete thought.

(11) S makes it clear to A which parts of his, S's, actions are communicatively relevant. He does so e.g. by repeating them or by using illusion-cancelling tricks such as interrupting his anxious behaviour, grinning, and then resuming the expression of exaggerated fear.

(12) A takes the sham fear as communicately relevant, like the traces of lions. An argument analogous to (1)–(9) shows that A then understands that S intends to bring about the *idea* of fear in A.

(13) By S's action (his use of the paw and his dumb show) the *ideas* of lions and of fear are brought about in A as a complete and ordered whole. The action by which the idea of fear is conveyed is, however, secondary to the action by which the idea of lions is conveyed. The former action is the style or manner in which the latter action is done; and although all actions must be done in some style or other they do not have to be done in this particular style. So if the manner is shown to be communicatively relevant, A will take the idea of fear as a sort of information about the idea conveyed in the primary action. He will see that the message has lions as its subject-matter but that its point is to convey that lions are something to be afraid of.

Comments. We expect ourselves and our fellow-men to act rationally. Normally we assume that someone who goes through S's movements has a point which may be worth looking for.

(i) The savages are agents in a world incessantly demanding decisions and actions, so they are likely to assume not merely that S's action has a point but also that this point is practical—that he aims at something more than the goal of just making himself understood. They assume that S wants A to do something *because of* A's grasp of S's complete thought. This something is presumably something like A's being on his guard or his taking precautions.

S could not reasonably hope for this effect of A's understanding the message unless A *believes* S—believes both that there are lions about and that they are dangerous. So the principles of serious speech are presupposed even in this primitive speech situation.

(ii) What has the germ of meaning $_{NN}$ is not an idea by itself but an ordered combination of ideas, a thought. It is a complete unit of communication. It singles out something and says something about what is thus singled out.

Like Austin I shall not discuss the question what such an order of ideas or concepts is like. See, however, L. Jonathan Cohen's 'Do illocutionary forces exist?' and my 'Meaning and illocutionary force', both of them included in *Symp*.

(iii) The vehicle of the germ of meaning $_{NN}$ is not traces together with a pantomime but on S's part the *production*-of-the-traces-in-a-certain-manner and on A's part the knowledge or belief that the traces are humanly produced.

This is why we can step from the truth of 'Those three rings mean that the bus is full' to an argument about what is meant (purported, intended) with the three rings. For although the vehicle of meaning $_{NN}$ in an established language is no longer the *production* in a certain manner of certain noises and marks, there is an important connexion with human beings and (institutionalized) intentions.

(iv) In (13) it was said that any production of something is done in some style or other and that in the preverbal situation it is the *style* in which S makes the traces that shows how the idea of lions is to be supplemented into a complete thought. In that primitive situation style and production together create the complete message: *A frightful situation—lions are about!*[4]

[4] I owe this way of making the point to a suggestion made by James Rachels.

The style may, however, be modified in important ways. If S directs all his gestures towards himself, he is probably trying to convey his own feelings. If he directs some of his gestures towards A, obviously indicating that he wants A to take part of the anxiety, he may be trying to caution A against lions or to frighten A of lions—A can no longer take him to convey just an autobiographical piece of information.

The preverbal language of S is, however, meagre in comparison to an established one. Cautioning and frightening cannot yet be kept apart. But in an established language there is a barrier between the former ('illocutionary') act and the latter ('perlocutionary') act.

2.2. Meaning $_{NN}$ in a budding language

The emergence of conventions. Suppose that S knows that he has managed to get across what he wanted to communicate.

He may then see that he is likely to reach the same successful result if he repeats the same performance with the same purpose and with A as his addressee. He may also understand that if he repeats the same performance to A but *not* with the same purpose and if A later on grasps that he did not have the same purpose, then one can hardly expect that A will, without further ado, take yet another repetition of the performance as conveying the same thought as on the original occasion. If S wants to facilitate communication with A, he had better take his success as a reason to repeat the performance to A only when S wants to convey the original thought. S has to regulate his own action. This is the first step towards the creation of linguistic rules.

S's success may, however, encourage him to try and warn A of wild elephants by going through the original performance in the same manner, but this time with an elephant's foot instead of a lion's paw. An analogue to (1)–(9) of 2.1 makes it probable that A recognizes that S has tried to evoke the idea of elephants. Since the rest of the performance is like the one A first grasped, A is likely to understand S's whole piece of communication. For reasons just given, S will go through the performance with the elephant's foot only when he wants to convey the thought of danger of elephants, or of the advisability of taking precautions because of elephants.

S may also attempt to exploit his original success in another way. He may go through the movements with the lion's paw but abstain from feigning fear. Instead he stabs at imaginary beasts, shouts with joy, and beckons A to fetch a spear and join a hunt. By the conditions (1)–(9) S has then communicated the idea of lions to A. By (10) and (11) the two communicants are agreed as to what other parts of S's action are communicatively relevant. By a process analogous to the one outlined in (12) and (13) A is given to understand that he is invited and perhaps encouraged to go hunting. If S wants to make communication easy, he will henceforward direct any repetition of his performance in the new manner to A only when he wants to achieve this kind of uptake.

The emergence of linguistic conventions. (i) Consider a community whose members originally attempted to make people take precautions against lions by making traces with a lion's paw in front of their addressees in a manner indicating exaggerated fear. They hit upon the expedient of grunting instead of making the traces.

Suppose now that a speaker grunts in the appropriate manner, goes hunting, and returns with a slain beast which is not a lion. He makes it clear that this is the animal he intended to signify. Imagine that his addressees shake their heads, draw a picture of lions, point at it and grunt, and that they then point at his prey and emit another sound. This could be an attempt at correcting his language—an attempt at teaching him to what kind of animal a certain noise is assigned as a classificatory label.

What is communicated is a complete thought. Assume that the thought is of the time-honoured subject/predicate pattern. The performance gives the subject part, the manner of performing the predicate part. (For my present purpose the snags of this oversimplified account do not matter.) It would be inconvenient if the addressee always had to look at the speaker to see what he predicated of lions when grunting; we may expect that different conventionalized manners get different noises attached to them as words. Henceforward, a juxtaposition of a grunt and a wail (say) will do the same duty as S's original production of traces in a manner indicating exaggerated fear. The manner of producing the piece of communication has become absorbed into what is produced; but in an established language it will return, in another form and with another function.

(ii) What does the wail signify? In the prelinguistic situation it is impossible to distinguish (a) what S wants to communicate from (b) what he wants A to do as a result of A's having grasped what S wants to communicate. There is no notion of a standard uptake of a certain performance and *a fortiori* no notion of intending to bring about a standard uptake. Consequently there is no notion of a distinction between (a) and (b). But the situation changes radically as soon as the communicative performance becomes rule-governed.

Let a speaker give the appropriate kind of grunt and the appropriate kind of wail but immediately begin to press spears into the hands of his listeners and beckon them to join him in a hunt for lions. Some addressees remonstrate by repeating his juxtaposition of grunt and wail and then proceed by pretending to run away or to cow. They do so in a manner which makes it fairly clear that they are not afraid of lions; they just object to his linguistic performance when he continues it by exhorting them not to react with fear. Their objections is conceptual. This string of noises is in their language to be used only when a speaker wants a reaction incompatible with the one that the organizer obviously hopes for. Other listeners, however, do not make this kind of objection. They carefully test the edge of their spearhead and look wary. They take him to invite them on a hunt for dangerous lions, not to invite them on a hunt for lions which he tries to make them afraid of.

Earlier, warning had not been kept apart from attempting to get people to take precautions. From now on, the language-users are aware of a lack of articulation. If they want to remove it, they are faced with a choice. Either they allow that the wail is intended to be taken as the objectors did; and then the speaker is inconsistent when he exhorts them not to be afraid. Or they rule that the speaker's wail is not primarily designed to induce fear; and then he may very well go on in the way described. If they make the latter choice, they soon see the need for distinguishing what the speaker intends to communicate from what he intends his audience to do as an effect of its (the audience's) understanding of what he communicates. They will say that a speaker who grunts and wails intends to communicate only that lions are dangerous or that he warns against lions; but that the point of this kind of communication sometimes is to frighten the addressees.

If the wail is interpreted in this way, a distinction arises between two main sorts of effects which a speaker may hope for when communicating something:
    (a) the efforts he obtains just in virtue of the fact that the noises or scratches he produces are conventionally accepted (as means of bringing about a certain idea);
and
    (b) the effects he obtains because of (but not as a logical consequent from) his having reached effects of type (a).

Effects of type (b) may be brought about in other ways than by means of effects of type (a). I may frighten you or make you take precautions without communicating anything. Effects of type (a) differ from effects of type (b) by depending entirely on the existence of conventions of language and also, in a more established language than the one now under consideration, on conventions of speech. Someone who knows these conventions and produces his piece of communication in accordance with them and as being in accordance with them cannot fail to bring about these effects in anyone who perceives what he does and knows the conventions. But a speaker may obtain these results and yet fail to obtain some result of type (b) for the sake of which he brought them about.

2.3. Meaning $_{NN}$ in an established language

Meaning $_{NN}$ and conventions. What has meaning $_{NN}$ is a complete thought. In an established language its vehicle is roughly a sentence-in-use and not words or phrases.

This may seem upside down. Do not sentences-in-use mean $_{NN}$ only because they are built up of words or phrases with meaning $_{NN}$?

Well, the 'meaning $_{NN}$' of the latter is perhaps elicited from the meaning $_{NN}$ of the former. Anyone who masters a language L knows what a given sentence of L means, since he knows the linguistic and grammatical rules of L; but it may be that it is only because he grasps the meaning $_{NN}$ of the sentence as a whole that he can eliminate, as irrelevant, linguistic rules which in other contexts govern some of the words in the sentence. Nobody who knows both German and English thinks, even for a moment, that 'Sie sind ein deutscher Offizier' means the same as the gibberish 'They are a German officer.'

Every instance of 'Sie sind ein deutscher Offizier' is, to any German-speaking person who receives or utters it, something meaning $_{NN}$ that the addressee is a German (military or marine) officer. There is a presumption that the instance does not merely happen to be in accordance with the rules of German but also is uttered *in* German. Taken in this way every instance of 'Sie sind ein deutscher Offizier' brings about, in virtue of the established conventions of German, the thought that the addressee is a German officer. These conventions also require that anyone who utters the sentence as a German sentence intends to bring about this thought in his addressees. He can fail to reach the goal intended only if the addressees are ignorant of German or mishear (misread, etc.) his words.

The intention to bring about the thought which the sentence-in-use means $_{NN}$ is an intention which the speaker has *qua* language-user, not or not only *qua* private gentleman. He may be an Englishman who wanted to say 'Sie sind ein deutscher Beamte' but did not find the right translation of the English word 'officer' in this context. Whatever he wanted to say, what his words in fact mean $_{NN}$ is that the addressee is a German military or marine officer, not that he holds a civil or public office.

In a preverbal language 'x means $_{NN}$ something' and 'The speaker S means $_{NN}$ something with x' are intimately connected. *Pace* Grice (*op. cit.*, p. 385) they are not, however, even roughly equivalent. For communication involves both a speaker (with certain intentions, etc.) and a listener (with a certain grasp of what the speaker intends, etc.); and x's meaning $_{NN}$ can be elucidated only in terms of an interchange between these two communicants. Grice's analysis concentrates on the speaker and forgets the addressee. Yet 'x means $_{NN}$ something' does, at least in the preverbal language in which one person is *the* speaker and the other *the* addressee, entail 'S means $_{NN}$ something with x', although the converse does not hold.

In an established language there is still a connexion between 'x means $_{NN}$ something' and '*Somebody* means $_{NN}$ something with x', as Grice points out (*op. cit.*). We cannot, however, go

LOCUTIONARY/ILLOCUTIONARY DISTINCTION 267

directly from 'x means $_{NN}$ so-and-so' to 'The current speaker, Mr A, means $_{NN}$ so-and-so with x.' For if most persons are in the habit of meaning $_{NN}$-that-p with x, then it will normally be taken for granted that even the next speaker who uses x does the same. When this assumption has become ingrained, we can argue from someone's production of x to what he *should* have meant $_{NN}$ with x, whether he did so or not. Even if *he* did not mean $_{NN}$ that p with x, x itself means $_{NN}$ that p. The standard meaning $_{NN}$ of x becomes explicable in terms of most language-users' intentions and understanding of intentions in connexion with most productions of x. The current speaker's and the current addressee's intentions and understanding are no longer decisive for x's meaning $_{NN}$.

It is therefore not surprising that strings of sounds with no meaning $_{NN}$ may in an established language all the same satisfy all the conditions of Grice's analysans of meaning $_{NN}$ in a budding or preverbal language; or that strings of sounds that in an established language have meaning $_{NN}$ may fail to satisfy these conditions. This does not show that an analysis of meaning $_{NN}$ in terms of intentions is totally on the wrong lines. All it shows is that there is not much hope for such an analysis of meaning $_{NN}$ in an established language.

What e.g. 'Sie sind ein deutscher Offizier' means $_{NN}$ is something which every German-speaking person knows as soon as he hears or sees the *sentence* and knows what its referring expressions refer to. He knows this in virtue of his mastery of the conventions of the German language, although he may be ignorant of the actual speech situation in which the words occur and of the style (tone of voice, etc.) in which they are uttered. Meaning $_{NN}$ is, in an established language, tied to the conventions of language and not to the conventions of speech. It is misleading to say as I did in the opening paragraph of 2.3 that its vehicle is a sentence-in-use; for use may include style. The vehicle is a sentence-cum-reference, rather than an instance of such a sentence uttered in a certain style in a given speech situation.

Meaning $_{NN}$ and conventions of speech. Two instances of the same sentence-cum-reference may be issued in very different styles. I may say '1227 will be a square' as a forecast; but if I am in a position to determine the form of 1227 I may also say it as a promise. The styles belong to the performing, to sentences as issued in particular speech situations, to speech. They do not alter the content of the performance, but they give it a certain tinge. Together with the features of the situations in which they occur they give the audience a clue as to how what is said (the sentence-cum-reference) is to be taken and/or to what degree it is to be so taken.

As a consequence, they give the audience a clue as to in what respects and/or to what degree the speaker stands committed to back up the correctness and relevance of his words. Although the manner of issuing a piece of communication has had this commissive duty also in a preverbal and a budding language, it had to be obscure there, for reasons given in 2.1 and 2.2. The poverty of means of expressions made communicants concentrate on meaning $_{NN}$, more or less presuming that attempts at communication occur only when the speaker wants to commit himself in respects which the situation makes obvious. Subtle variations in kinds and degrees of commitment could hardly be conveyed until linguistic conventions had liberated the style of uttering something from its predicative function and until those communicative effects that on p. 265 were called effects of type (a) were firmly distinguished from communicative effects of type (b).

Certain styles of uttering a sentence (e.g. an assertive tone of voice or an interrogative intonation contour) have in an established language become recognized ways of *letting the addressee know* (as distinct from merely dropping him a hint as to) in what respects and to what degree the speaker answers for what he says. The more a style becomes the conventionally established one for making overt a certain commitment in one's words, the more it demands everyone who knows this convention to take the styled issuing of a sentence (a sentence which the recipient may not understand) as something committing the speaker to such-and-such a thing. Since the style is conventionalized, the speaker is not free to use it as he pleases—unless he wants to be misunderstood. The more established the convention is, the more plausible it becomes to say that the style itself carries the obligation. If the current speaker uses it for entering other obligations, he abuses it.

A mechanism analogous to the one that out of meaning $_{NN}$ in a preverbal or budding language created what we ordinarily refer to as the meaning of words has, by means of an interchange between normal speaker-intentions and normal uptake of these intentions, turned the style into something with a fixed significance.

This may tempt us to count, in an established language, the significance in question as a kind of meaning $_{NN}$, or at least to take the sentence-cum-reference-*cum-style* as the vehicle of meaning $_{NN}$.

But it is, I think, wise to resist the temptation. Whenever something is said there is, I believe, a distinction to be drawn between a topic-directed dimension and an audience-directed dimension of the words uttered. The former dimension corresponds roughly to what Austin called the locutionary act and the latter to what he called the illocutionary act. The topic-directed dimension gives or creates the topic of the utterance and does so in virtue of the conventions of *language*. It is concerned with the content of what is said and not with the saying of it. The audience-directed dimension is concerned with guiding the audience as to how what is said in the topic-directed respect is to be taken. This guidance is done by considering the datable and clockable saying of what is said—the tone of voice, the intonation contour, etc. The conventions brought into play here are more concerned with *speech* than with language. If we want the meaning $_{NN}$ of words to be something that is relatively stable in the flux of linguistic intercourse, the significance given by the audience-guiding conventions ought to be excluded from the notion of meaning $_{NN}$.[5]

3. *Meaning $_{NN}$ and the locutionary/illocutionary distinction*

I shall now argue that Austin's distinction between the locutionary and the illocutionary 'act' is an attempt to do justice to our feeling that the style of a linguistic performance is intimately connected with the meaning $_{NN}$ of that performance but is not itself a constituent part or factor of that meaning.

A survey of Austin's account. Locutionarity and illocutionarity are, according to my reading of Austin, two dimensions of or

[5] In 'Meaning and illocutionary force', I have discussed the notions of topic-direction and audience-direction, their connexion with Austin's ideas of locutionarity and illocutionarity, and the reasons why it is inadvisable to include illocutionary force or conventions of audience-direction in the notion of meaning.

abstractions from the semantic result of the performance of any ordinary, unobjectionable speech act. A locutionary act is the act *of* saying something. Questions of what he calls 'sense and 'reference' pertain to and exhaust its semantic result, the locution.

An illocutionary act is the act performed *in* saying something. You may know both the sense and the reference of the utterance 'We shall come tomorrow' and yet be uncertain of what is done *in* the utterance. Does the speaker intend to ask a question, to promise, to threaten, or what? Has his utterance the force of a question, a promise, a threat, or what? Ought his utterance to be taken as a question, a promise, a threat or what? When you know the answer to these questions you know what illocutionary act is performed.

If I understand rightly, Austin maintains that the locutionary and the illocutionary 'act' have two intimately connected things in common: (i) They are up to the speaker, in the sense that the *current* addressee's response does not enter the definition of the 'acts'. (ii) They are essentially conventional, in the sense that they demand that any recipient who knows the language should be able to decide, by hearing what the speaker said, what locutionary and illocutionary act is performed (with reservations for ambiguities of different kinds). I.e., both the locutionary and the illocutionary 'act' demand that there is *a* kind of response, viz. that of grasping what is meant $_{NN}$ and what the style of production commits one to; but this response is not necessarily a response of the *current* addressee.

The perlocutionary 'act' is partially defined in terms of the *current* audience and its reaction, a reaction which is not or not merely the uptake of the rule-governed meaning $_{NN}$ or the rule-governed style of the utterance.

The locutionary dimension of my utterance 'The ice over there is thin' is on Austin's view exhausted by the meaning (which equals the 'sense' and 'reference') of my words.[6] Their meaning is determined by the conventions of language; their reference by the referential conventions of language together with the non-linguistic situation in which they are brought into

---

[6] For problems in this equivalence, see L. J. Cohen: 'Do illocutionary forces exist?', my 'Meaning and illocutionary force' and Cohen's note on my paper, all in *Symp.*

play in this particular case. Hence, the locutionary dimension is essentially conventional, governed by the rules of language. Linguistic conventions cannot obtain unless a number of language-users keep to them. The fact that some listeners do not understand a given utterance does not necessarily imply that the speaker has failed to say something with a certain meaning. He *has* been successful if his utterance is understood by those who master the conventions of the language he speaks and who know the situation in which he uttered the words. This shows not only that locutionarity is conventional but also, as the other side of the same coin, that when a language is established, the act of saying something *with sense and reference*—i.e., the locutionary act—is up to the speaker.

Austin insists that when I say 'The ice over there is thin', I do not merely say something with a certain meaning, i.e., sense and reference; I also e.g. inform you or warn you. Informing and warning exemplify phenomena within the illocutionary dimension. They are neither consequences of the locutionary 'act' nor additional references to some of its consequences; they have another status (*Words.*113).

My utterance may also alarm you or convince you; but alarming and convincing are perlocutionary and not illocutionary phenomena. For they essentially involve a reaction on the part of the (current) audience, a reaction going beyond that of merely grasping certain conventions of speech and language. The perlocutionary reaction is a further reaction, perhaps caused by but not conceptually dependent on the audience's grasp of these conventions. If my words do not cause you to be afraid or to accept my view, I have not alarmed you or convinced you. At most I have attempted to do these things. But even if my words do not cause you to accept my view or to be afraid, they do constitute a piece of information or a warning; they are not merely attempts at these things.

Critics of Austin have remarked that the point just made is true only when 'inform' and 'warn' are used in their standard way. (i) Occasionally they may be used to include that non-locutionary and non-illocutionary audience-response for the sake of which the illocutionary act of warning was performed: 'I tried in vain to warn him.' (ii) In the passive voice, 'inform' and 'warn' may get a special employment. They may signify that someone has grasped something which was not intended. In that case the construction 'He was informed (warned) by her' is not a recasting of the standard active voice construction 'She informed (warned) him': she did not intend to do it; he drew his own conclusion from clues which she gave him unwittingly—in her actions, tone of voice, etc.[7] But neither (i) nor (ii) blurs Austin's contention. There remains a sense in which a speaker *has* warned his addressees when he has uttered 'The ice over there is thin' in a manner which to anyone who masters the conventions of speech makes it undisputable that he is warning. For this sense it is irrelevant whether the *current* addressee takes precautions because of the warning. It does not even matter whether he understands it.

There is an intimate connexion between the locutionary and the illocutionary 'act'. In an established language, both are brought about in virtue of the (normal) audience's knowledge of linguistic conventions or at least, in the case of certain illocutionary acts, in virtue of the (normal) audience's knowledge of conventions that may be turned linguistic. Thus, the utterance 'The ice over there is thin' is expansible. By adding such clauses as 'I warn you that' or 'I inform you that' (i.e., the 'P-radicals' of Ch.5:3) we can make its illocutionary element explicit (cf. *Words*.103).

Austin is cryptic about the relation between the locutionary and the illocutionary 'act'. 'An effect must be achieved on the audience if the illocutionary act is to be carried out', he says (*Words*.115–16). 'Generally the effect amounts to bringing about the understanding of the meaning and of the force of the locution'. W. P. Alston is no doubt a reliable interpreter when he says, in his *Philosophy of Language*, p. 36: 'An illocutionary act . . . requires a locutionary act as a base'. (Cf. e.g. *Words*.98–9, 115–16, 132.) But Alston seems to take this exegesis as a reason for holding that the locutionary 'act' enters the illocutionary one in the sense that a correct understanding of the latter also must include a correct understanding of the former. This is, I believe, exegetically wrong. When 'The bull is dangerous' and 'Passengers are warned to cross the track by the bridge only' are intended as warnings and understood as so intended, they have the same illocutionary force but are totally different locutionary

---

[7] I owe the observation to Per Lindström.

'acts'. An illocutionary 'act' *presupposes* a locutionary one to operate upon, but the latter does not become a part of the former. Alston's tenet (*loc. cit.*) that 'the fact that two sentences are commonly used to perform the same illocutionary act . . . is sufficient to give them the same meaning' is, I think, a far cry from Austin's view—and can hardly be correct, for reasons given by D. Holdcroft in 'Meaning and illocutionary acts', *Ratio* 4 (1964).

Illocutionary force and illocutionary intention. In *Words*.98–9 Austin treats the questions
 (1) Does the speaker intend to advise?,
 (2) Has the utterance the force of a piece of advice?, and
 (3) Ought the utterance to be taken as a piece of advice?
as if they were three ways of posing the same problem, viz. Does the speaker perform the illocutionary act of advising?

In my opinion, (1)–(3) pose different problems. I would take (1) as a question about the *current* speaker's intentions in issuing the utterance, (2) as a question about the *standard intention* of most speakers in issuing such an utterance in that manner and those circumstances, and (3) as a question about the *standard uptake* of an utterance of that kind issued in that manner in those circumstances. The three problems are interwoven but not identical. A good, though not a decisive, reason for holding that the utterance is to be taken as advice is that the current speaker did so intend it. A good, though not a decisive, reason for holding that the current speaker intended the utterance as advice is that most speakers do intend to advise in issuing an utterance of that type in this manner in these circumstances. And so forth.

Strawson seems to hold that Austin defines 'illocutionary force' in terms of the *current* speaker's intentions in issuing the utterance; and that he defines the illocutionary 'act' in terms of that intention together with its correct understanding by the current audience (cf. 'Intention and convention . . .), *Symp*, p. 390f). But it is fairly clear, I think, that although there certainly is a trend in this direction in *Words*, another and stronger trend is that an utterance may occasionally have a certain force whatever the speaker intended (e.g. *Words*.33). It is, e.g., liable to have a construction as to its illocutionary force put on it by judges (*Words*.115n, also 121). More weighty than these passages (which may be taken as stylistic quirks) is that the whole effect of stressing the conventionality of the illocutionary 'acts' is to minimize the importance of the current speaker and the current audience. Illocutionary force becomes next of kin to meaning, in Austin's sense of 'meaning'. In an established language it would be disastrous to define these relatives in terms of the current speaker's intentions and the current addressee's (or recipient's) understanding of these intentions, as Searle makes very clear in 'What is a speech act?', pp. 228–31.

Meaning $_{NN}$/style versus locutionarity/illocutionarity. I trust that not much argument is needed to show how the locutionary and the illocutionary 'act' are connected with meaning $_{NN}$ and style.

In a locution we say something about something. It is topic-directed. In an illocution we make it clear to an addressee (roughly) how we want him to look at the locution, e.g. as fitting into his actions, plans, or intellectual life. It is audience-directed. Already this fact may make us suspect that illocutions are tied more to speech than to language.

In an investigation of the locutionary dimension we are concerned with a certain abstraction from the result of a total speech act, viz. a sentence-cum-reference. Our task is to elucidate it by eliciting conventions of *language*. These conventions cannot be defined in terms of any of the current speaker's intentions and the current audience's understanding of these intentions but are nevertheless connected with them, as I tried to show on pp. 265–9.

In an investigation of the illocutionary dimension we are considering another abstraction from the result of a total speech act, viz. not what is said but the saying of it. We are studying how the manner of issuing the locution allocates what is said to a certain discourse or modifies the commitments within a given discourse. A given locution may, taken in isolation, belong to several types of discourse or need qualification as to degree of commitment within a given type of discourse; but the utter*ing* of it often gives the audience to understand how it is to be taken. The more or less conventionalized manner of issuing something belongs to *speech* rather than to language.

The illocutionary intention of a speaker S is S's intention that the addressee, A, shall take the locution (issued by S with the intention that A shall recognize it) as belonging to a certain type of discourse, and consequently as committing the speaker to have a characteristic sort of support for the truth (etc.) of his locution. But when there arise conventions for making this intention overt, the illocutionary force of uttering something in a certain manner gets detached from the current speaker and the current audience and must be defined in terms of the *standard* illocutionary intention in issuing a locution in that manner, together with the *standard* uptake of the intention.

In an established language, the locutionary and the illocutionary dimension of an utterance involve an intellectual response from any recipient who knows the conventions of the language in question together with the conventions of speech. This intellectual response is simply the grasping of the standard topic-directed intention and the standard audience-directed intention with which the utterance is issued. When a speaker by his words performs a perlocutionary act, he does so by getting his audience to do something as a result of its having grasped his locutionary and/or illocutionary intention. The effect is obtained by means of the principles of serious speech. The principle of relevance to the addressee and the principle of trustworthiness make the addressees take the utterance as relevant to their reaction. The effect is not, in contradistinction to the audience-reactions involved in the locutionary and the illocutionary acts, brought about by the speaker's conveying his intention to bring it about.

I have argued—though not in Austin's terminology—that in a preverbal language the locutionary and the illocutionary audience-reactions cannot be distinguished from the perlocutionary ones, and that the distinction can hardly be made in a budding language. Searle has complained (*op. cit.*, p. 229) that Grice fails to distinguish perlocutionary from illocutionary effects; and it seems to me that the central part of Strawson's 'Intentions and conventions . . .' (pp. 396–400) is vitiated by the same flaw. The conflation is hardly surprising, since Grice sometimes and Strawson most of the time take a budding language as their model of our everyday language.

4. *Illocutionary devices*

In any language, the locution is tied to a whole sentence-cum-reference or its analogue; and the illocution to the manner of issuing instances of whole sentences-cum-reference or their analogues. Locutionarity and illocutionarity (or in the parlance of Sect. 1, meaning NN and style) may therefore be regarded as two dimensions of (or two kinds of abstractions from) the semantic result of whole acts of communication, and not as dimensions of (or abstracts from) the semantic result of having uttered certain words that are mere constituents of such acts.

Purely illocutionary devices. From sentences-cum-reference the meaning NN of which we know we can elicit what contribution or set of contributions a certain word W standardly gives to their meaning NN. This standard contribution may be called W's meaning NN in a transferred sense; or it may be called W's locutionary sense.

Such words and phrases as 'probably' and 'on my honour' always make explicit the style of an uttering of a sentence-cum-reference. Their one function, in any context, is to announce the illocutionary force of the utterance to which they are joined. Call them *purely illocutionary devices*.

Someone may see a sentence in which one of the purely illocutionary devices is inserted. He does not know anything about the situation in which the sentence was scribbled down. Yet his knowledge of the rules of language give him a better understanding of what the utterance is meant to convey than he would have had if the device had been left out. Suppose that the vocabulary of S_0 is enlarged with 'probably'. To say '1227 is probably a square' is not to predicate more things or a more specific thing of 1227 than that it is a square. 'Probably' has no classificatory or individuating job. It announces that the speaker wants his addressees to know that he has not quite committed himself to 1227 being a square—that he wants them to take his assertion with a grain of salt. Any English-speaking person knows that this is the job of 'probably'. So the phrase contributes to the intelligibility of the inscription or utterance, is normally designed to do so, and normally has that effect. Does it come sufficiently close to words with locutionary sense to be acknowledged as having such a sense?

No. The purely illocutionary devices do not contribute to what a *sentence* (-cum-reference) says. They neither refer nor classify. They do quite another job, viz. that of making overt to the audience what kind or degree of support the *issuing* of the sentence (-cum-reference) standardly commits the speaker to have for the correctness of what he says. They do not have locutionary sense; but we may perhaps call them words with an illocutionary sense (in analogy to words with a locutionary sense).

An apparent contradiction. There is an apparent conflict between *Words*.94 and *Words*.134. In the former place the locutionary 'act' is partly defined in terms of the noises uttered. Hence, I do different locutionary (type) 'acts' when I say '1227 is probably a square' and, in a hesitant tone of voice, '1227 is a square'. But the drift of *Words*.134 is that the two utterances are used to do the very same 'act' (which seems to entail the same locutionary 'act').

In my example (which differs from Austin's own in a way which will soon be discussed), the contradiction can be explained away. For in the situation imagined, the only difference between '1227 is probably a square' and '1227 is a square' (said hesitantly) is that the former contains a parenthetical insertion of a locutionarily empty phrase—i.e., a phrase with no locutionary sense;[8] and the only function of this phrase is to make verbally explicit an illocutionary intention which is brought out by other means in the other utterance.

[8] Hence it is misleading to say that '1227 is a square' and '1227 is probably a square' are *just* rhetically equivalent. Austin does not exemplify rhetical equivalence; but 'I am ill' (said by me) and 'You are ill' (said by you of me) will probably do. For when used with the same 'sense and reference' two different phemes constitute rhetically equivalent 'acts' (*Words*.97). But the important difference between '1227 is a square' (said hesitantly) and '1227 is probably a square' is not that they contain phrases which, though having the same locutionary sense, are phatically different. The trouble is that the phrase making one utterance phatically different from the other does not function locutionarily at all.

(Austin's notion of rhetical equivalence is not free from difficulties even on the merely locutionary side. Are (1) 'The author of *A Farewell to Arms* committed suicide' and (2) 'The author of *The Old Man and the Sea* committed suicide' rhetically equivalent? The subject expression picks out Hemingway, and the predicate expressions do both say the same thing about him; so if two utterances are rhetically equivalent when the referring expressions have the same referents and the predicate expressions make the same predication, then (1) and (2) are rhetically equivalent. But their referring expressions also have sense and contain sub-references, and these are not the same as (1) and (2); so if it is demanded that rhetically equivalent utterances have the same sense and the same sub-references also in their subject expressions, (1) and (2) are not rhetically equivalent.)

The explanation works well when the only phatic difference between the utterances is that one of them contains a purely illocutionary device. But there are phrases that only occasionally do duty as illocutionary devices. In 'I think that 1227 is a square' and '1227 is probably a square' the phrases 'I think' and 'probably' do about the same job. But 'probably' can, whenever it appears, be defined only in terms of its illocutionary function. The words 'I think', on the other hand, occur in many contexts in which they must be defined in terms of their contributions to the locutionary dimension of an utterance. How can we be sure that the phrase 'I think' does not bring also its merely locutionarily explicable contribution into contexts where it works as an illocutionary device? Are 'I think that 1227 is a square', '1227 is probably a square', and the hesitant '1227 is a square' really performances of the same locutionary 'act'?

Take whole utterances—whole stretches of speech from silence to silence—as the basic unit of analysis. We can then easily single out one use of 'I think (that)' in which the phrase serves as a parenthetic clause. This is the use in which we can say, indifferently, '1227 is, I think, a square', 'I think that 1227 is a square', and '1227 is a square, I think.' They differ in emphasis only. Adverbs and adverbial phrases cannot normally be shuffled around the utterance in this way (cf. 1956a.147). For they usually modify just a part of the utterance, and their position indicates what part. Hence the meaning of the utterances changes when the adverbs are moved. The movability of the parenthetic 'I think (that)' indicates that it modifies the whole utterance and not a part inside it. Adopting a term from J. O. Urmson's 'Parenthetical verbs', I shall call the movable 'I think (that)' a *parenthetic insertion*. In this use it is not employed to give autobiographical reports; it is interchangeable with such an adverbial illocutionary device as 'probably'. The 'parenthetic' 'I think (that)' may therefore reasonably be counted as illocutionary. It is not regarded as contributing to the *locutionary* dimension of the utterance but just as making the illocutionary force explicit. (Cf. 5:8.)

The same explanation works with Austin's actual pair of examples, 'He did not' and 'I state that he did not'. They are indeed used to make 'the very same statement' if in a given context they single out the same man, predicate the same thing about him, and have the same illocutionary force. In spite of *Words*.94, the fact that they are built up of different words does not warrant us to say that they are locutionarily different. For 'I state (that)' occurs as a parenthetically inserted and merely illocutionary device. Hence, I do not do different locutionary (type) 'acts' in uttering 'He did not' and 'I state that he did not.'

II. ARCHETYPICAL PERFORMATIVES

5. *Archetypical performatives*

Hume's discussion 'Of the obligation of promises' in *A Treatise of Human Nature*, Bk. III, Pt. ii, Sect. 5, comes close to a discovery of the performatory function. Austin's thoughts about performatives were nursed by reflections on Prichard's ideas of the obligation to keep promises. In 'Other minds' the form of words typically used in promising is the clearest example he gives of a performatory formula. It is also clearly to be seen in *Words*. The utterance 'I promise to do so-and-so' is one of the classic examples of explicit performatives, and promising is one of the classic examples of performatory actions.

This is a pity. Take Austin's general characterization of a classic explicit performative. Demand that the performative be an apparently descriptive utterance in the first person present indicative active, an utterance that is a constituent of a ceremonial procedure and whose point is not to *describe* but to *effect* the action. Then promises and the phrase 'I promise to do so-and-so' are *not* clear cases of performatory actions and performatory formulae. On the contrary they entice us to confuse performatoriness with illocutionarity.

At least a few of Austin's verdictives and a good many of his exercitives come closer to his general (though no doubt schematic) characterization of performatives. In acquitting, convicting, appointing, demoting, excommunicating, naming, or pardoning somebody; or again in annulling, repealing, or vetoing something —in all such cases I am usually acting in an official capacity. There is an institutionalized procedure in which an utterance containing the appropriate P-radical is a constitutive part. In the right circumstances an issuing of the utterance is a performance of the act. If I have the appropriate capacity and in the right circumstances say to you, 'I acquit (appoint, excommunicate) you', you are acquitted (appointed, excommunicated).

I shall call performatives of this sort *archetypical* performatives. They have three characteristics:

5.1. Archetypical performatives are accomplished. With the utterance of the words the action is performed in its entirety. This may be brought out by a number of contrasts:

(i) In the right circumstances I say to you, 'I promise to do so' or 'I advise you to do so.' You are thereby promised or advised. But something has gone very wrong if I utter the words and then forget about it. My use of them commits me to do something in the future or to take responsibility if the course advised takes a bad turn. My action does not just consist in uttering the words but in shouldering obligations for the future by doing so.

Archetypical performatives are different. Their performer shoulders no obligations for the future. He has as it were pressed a button in a social machine. Thenceforward the machine works without his interference—or if it does not work, it is not necessarily his business to put it aright. Of course it would be odd if I demoted you but did nothing to prevent you from keeping your former rank; but the explanation is not that I, in demoting you, have undertaken to look to it that you really are reduced to a lower rank (in the way a commitment to stand by one's words is built into the notion of promising). The oddness is due to a general principle of rationality bidding an agent to act to a purpose. It has nothing to do with demoting. It has to do with the general unreasonableness of doing something and then undoing it. In most cases of the performatives to be discussed the man who gives the verdict or exercises his powers is, however, not identical with the man appointed to look to it that certain consequences ensue.

(ii) I may promise or advise for foolish reasons. If I usually do so I am bad at promising or advising. But even if I usually acquit (etc.) for foolish reasons I am not bad at acquitting. The complaint is not, as in promising or advising, that I bungle the act; it is that I am only too successful—I have done the deed although I ought not to have done it.

(iii) The main purpose of my promise or advice is not achieved unless you take me seriously. The main purpose of my acquitting (etc.) is achieved even if you, my grammatical addressee, do not take me seriously. The effectiveness of the performatory formula is, in the latter case, independent of the grammatical addressee's uptake. In promising and advising there has to be an addressee. In archetypical performatives he hardly exists, except in a grammatical sense. Think of the 'addressee's' role in the naming of a ship or the baptism of an infant! The performative is, so to speak, directed to the society at large.

5.2. *Archetypical performatives are alinguistic.* Acquittals (etc.) resemble ordinary actions more than promises, warnings, and advice do. As utterances conforming to a certain syntax and a certain grammar all performatives are conventional, but in widely different ways. Some demand for their effectiveness the existence of very specified, formal procedures. Others rely on a fairly unspecific set of informal felicity-conditions. The more formal a performative is, the less does the meaning of its P-radical contribute to its effectiveness; what is important is only the *making* of certain noises (which may have no sense). The less the meaning of a P-radical matters and the more momentous the issuing of the P-radical is, the further the performative moves away from an ordinary linguistic utterance and the more it approaches an action. Austin's pet performatives—promises, warnings, etc.—are fairly informal, compared to the archetypical ones.

(i) Acquittals, demotions, excommunications and so on all demand that the appropriate P-radical is produced. Promises, warnings, etc., can be given without the use of any P-radical. I am not wedded unless the appropriate authority has uttered the classic wedding formula; but I may be promised something without help of the classic promisory formula and even without help of any paraphrase of it.

This difference between archetypical performatives on the one hand and promises, etc., on the other remains even when the utterances have vestiges of P-radicals. 'I *shall* pay you back tomorrow' and 'I give you my word I shall pay you back tomorrow' are promises just as much as 'I promise I shall pay you back tomorrow.' In the classic promisory formula the P-radical can be replaced with synonyms or near-synonyms, and the use of the new formulae will remain promisory in all situations where the use of the original formula is promisory. But it is at least doubtful whether an appropriate authority which says 'I decide that you are not guilty' or 'I order that from now on you are not an officer any more' has really thereby managed to acquit or demote in all situations where he could have done so by the use of the appropriate classic performatives. The sense of his utterance can easily be rendered by a classic performative. But the fact that he has not employed the standard formulation affects the success of his deed.

(ii) If the accepted procedure for demoting somebody was to rip off his medals in silence, the action would be a non-verbal equivalent to the one in which the performative 'I demote you' enters.

Compare this possible world to one in which promising is done by putting one's hand to one's heart. The gesture is by itself *not* a non-verbal equivalent to the deed performed by uttering a performative of the form 'I promise you to do so-and-so'. Promising, warning, and advising are *ancillary* acts, saying how a piece of communication is to be taken. I do not promise you (period) or warn you (period) or advise you (period). My act must have a content, otherwise nothing would be promised, warned, or recommended. But I acquit you (period) or demote you (period) or excommunicate you (period). These acts stand on their own feet.

Promising and its fellows as well as acquitting and its fellows are done on certain presuppositions. Acquittals presuppose (the suspicion of) an offence, demotions presuppose that the delinquent does not have the lowest rank, and excommunications presuppose that the offender is a member of the Church (say). Promising presupposes that the content is to the addressee's interest and would not come about without the promisor's agency. When the presuppositions are mistaken, the performance is e.g. unnecessary (there was no offence nor any suspicion of it; the thing promised would have come about without the promisor's help) or ought not to have been done (you were convicted although you were innocent; you were promised something which in fact was to your disadvantage). But archetypical performatives are not open to the infelicity that affects promising (etc.)-without-content.

(iii) Archetypical performatives do not have much to do with ordinary linguistic communication. The action done by means of formal performatives consists in carrying through a distinctive *ceremony*, conventionally accepted as giving a certain social result. When certain words are esssential to the ceremony, what matters is that they are *issued* and not that they make sense. They are regarded as sound-patterns characteristic of the proceeding and not as words. Hence an expression in such a formula cannot simply be replaced with a synonym. The new string of sounds will not have the same effect as the old one. It *says* the same, but what is said does not count.

Let a convention bid the performer of a demotion to do nothing except addressing the delinquent with the noises 'Hickory dickory dock.' To pronounce this rigmarole is, in the right circumstances, to demote—just as 'I demote you' is in our world. It is the right phrase for demoting. It does not follow that it is a meaningful sentence—let alone a phrase—in the language.

Promising is different. We may imagine a world in which otherwise English-speaking persons paradigmatically promised by canting 'Inny minny moo'. It is the right phrase for promising. Thereby, I think, it ceases to be gibberish and becomes a significant phrase. It is a distinct sound-pattern with an established linguistic use, and this qualifies it as a word or a phrase. 'Hickory dickory dock' would be a complete sentence, not a phrase in a sentence; but for reasons given in (ii) 'Inny minny moo' would be a phrase in a sentence or at least demand contextual supplementation of a sentence—otherwise it would lack content. It could not stand on its own but only be a constituent of the linguistic meaning of the utterance to which it belongs.

'Hickory dickory dock' could, and could only, stand on its own. The uttering of it in isolation would in the right circumstances be an act of demotion. The noises would not be a constituent of the linguistic meaning of an utterance. Nor would their alleged meaning (if any) be constituted of ingredients recognized as words and phrases. This may be enough to explain the feeling that they would not acquire meaning by being the noises conventionally employed to demote somebody, but that 'Inny minny moo' would acquire meaning by being the noise conventionally employed for promising.

(iv) The same verb often occurs both in the P-radical of a

performative and in the third person present indicative active. When this is so, we are entitled to say 'He x-es' only because the man referred to has said 'I x' or used a phrase synonymous to it or performed a ceremony that is a non-verbal equivalent to it. The third person use is quotative, reporting the performatory one. (*Pace Words*.155 this rules out e.g. 'I choose' from the class of standardly performative radicals. We cannot reasonably maintain that we are entitled to use 'He chooses' *only* because he has used 'I choose' or some synonymous expression or gone through a ceremony nonverbally equivalent to it.)

Call the verb of the P-radical of an archetypical performative 'x'. Let 'y' stand for the verb of the P-radical of a 'performative' of the 'promise' group. I suggest that the relations between 'I x' and 'He x-es' is less intimate than that between 'I y' and 'He y-s'. The fact that the same verb has both a performatory and a quotative duty is almost due to chance when the verb is 'x' but not when it is 'y'.

Language works according to a principle of laziness. It seeks to combine a minimum of vocabulary with a maximum of expressiveness. If no risk of confusion is imminent, it is handy to let the same verb do duty both in the performance of a deed and in a description of that performance. This is why 'x' often has both a performatory and a quotative function. The two uses have no core of meaning in common. To acquit is no more to describe the acquitting than to swim is to describe the swimming. In its performatory function the verb is, as we have seen, an ingredient of a sound-pattern more than something thought of as having meaning. It is singled out as a verb since *this* archetypical performative happens to be made up of noises which also occur as words in a language. In the performative they do not, however, work as words—they cannot be replaced with synonyms, and so forth.

The 'y' group is different. Its members are ancillary to locutionary acts. In y-ing I always y something; what I say has a locutionary intelligible content (given in words or supplied by the context). Without this content it would be pointless. The P-radical is designed with a view just to making the audience understand in what way the content is to be taken. The fact that they are standarly intended to be recognized as contributions to the uptake of the content of an utterance distinguishes them from archetypical P-radicals. They are, in fact, illocutionary devices. The use of them is intended to make the audience recognize that the speaker commits himself in certain ways. Since language could not persist without such commitments on the part of the speakers, there is a close connexion between the principles of serious speech and their specifications. Any two illocutionary devices are interchangeable within a language L if they are governed by the same specificatory convention. The sound-pattern is, as in the case of ordinary words, less important than the rules governing the use of the sound-patterns: replacement with synonyms is allowed, etc. The two employments of the 'y' verbs have one characteristic in common: they mark that the man in y-ing has committed himself in a certain way to the content of his deed. As far as I can see, there is no parallel in the two employments of the 'x' verbs.

5.3. Archetypical performatives are essentially neither locutionary nor illocutionary. Take them as paradigms of performatives, and performatoriness will be very different indeed from illocutionarity.

(i) If it is true that what matters in archetypical performatives is that certain sound-patterns are issued and that their sense or senselessness is not pertinent, then these performatives do not satisfy Austin's definition of the locutionary 'act'. They are phones but neither phemes nor rhemes.

(ii) Austin claims that 'whenever I "say" anything (except perhaps a mere exclamation like "damn" or "ouch") I shall be performing both locutionary and illocutionary acts' (*Words*.132). But if (i) is true, then someone uttering an archetypical performative does *not* perform anything with a locutionary side to it. Now Austin characterizes the illocutionary 'act' as something making clear how a locutionary 'act' is to be taken (e.g. *Words*.98–9). In that case, how can an illocutionary 'act' be performed without a locutionary 'act'? Archetypical performatives are neither locutionary nor illocutionary.

(iii) Strawson gives a shrewd turn to Austin's notion of illocutionarity by claiming that both such acts as warning and such acts as demoting are illocutionary since they are intended to be understood. When understanding is secured, an audience-intended intention is recognized, and recognized as intended to be recognized. Hence performatives are illocutionary. (See 'Intention and convention ...', pp. 398–400.)

Strawson's suggestion conflates two different kinds of intention, viz. on the one hand the intentions to make the audience aware in what way the speaker wants to stand committed in his words, and on the other hand the intentions to make the audience aware that the ceremony performed is bringing about a certain result conventionally and immediately. The first type of intention singles out intentions of serious speech. These are, as we saw in Ch. 3, necessary for the existence of language but not part of it. The second type of intention is concerned with intentions not tied to language at all. They are essentially concerned with non-linguistic matters, with sound-patterns and performance-patterns. Since Austin certainly thought of his doctrine of illocutionary force as a contribution to what is generally labelled the theory of meaning (cf. *Words*.148), he cannot consistently have maintained that intentions of the second type are illocutionary. In a discussion of Austin's distinction between locutionarity and illocutionarity Strawson's suggestion can be ignored.

6. *Archetypical performatives and promises*

In the last chapters of *Words* Austin seems to give up his idea of a distinguishable group of performatives. He seems to argue in favour of the view that all serious speech is performatory.

If he did do this, he committed a bad mistake. All serious speech is illocutionary, and therefore no linguistic utterance can be archetypically performatory. Pending one-word sentences, no utterance can reasonably count as linguistic unless it is (a) built up of entities governed by certain accepted rules, (b) these entities are strung together in a way that makes grammatical sense, and (c) the utterance is issued with the intention of saying something that makes sense. An archetypical performative does not satisfy these minimum requirements. Acquittals and excommunications certainly contain strings of noises that are constitutive parts of them and look like linguistic entities; but since these strings do not usually allow of substitutions of synonyms for synonyms (etc.) they function as sound-patterns and not as linguistic entities.

If this is right, performatoriness and illocutionarity are indeed very different, but my attempts to account for the dissimilarities in *LIA* were mistaken. If it be conceded that in order to be true an utterance must at least make sense and that an archetypical performative has neither a locutionary nor an illocutionary side to it, then there is no need to argue at length that such performatives can have no truth-value and, *a fortiori*, that definitions of them in terms of how they cause their own truth must be mistaken (pp. 202–6). Moreover, in my efforts to point to a rift between the Force Thesis and the Performative Thesis I singled out behabitives as particularly clear examples of performatives. No doubt some of them are kindred to archetypical performatives. But compare them to 'I acquit you' and you will see that Austin's list of verdictives and exercitives offers much better examples. But be careful: his assemblages of P-radicals are surprisingly mixed bunches.

Archetypical performatives and semiperformatives. As serious speakers we constantly perform acts going beyond those of uttering mere rhemes: we shoulder certain discourse implied responsibilities for what we say. This tempts Austin, at the end of *Words*, to make *all* serious utterances performatory. Thereby 'the descriptive value of the term [sc. 'performatory'] has been eroded by a typically philosophical inflation' (Cohen, *op. cit.*, p. 438). Take 'I acquit you' and its fellows as clear cases of performatives, and all inclination to succumb to Austin's temptation disappears. Units of linguistic communication are, above all, units that make sense. Although their primary business is to be true if they are constatives, wise if they are counsels, etc., a necessary prerequisite for this business is that they are issued as meaningful utterances and are taken as so issued. It is, however, typical for archetypical performatives that they are *not* thought of as linguistic. Consequently the agent does not shoulder, and is not taken as shouldering, responsibilities for what he *says*. He does not *say* anything. His sounds are not meant NN either in the preverbal or in a more established language.

By the words 'S will be a P' the serious speaker may enter either the responsibilities of a prognosticator or the responsibilities of a promisor. The first of these two kinds of responsibility is tied to a spectator, the second to an agent. There is a wide gulf between them. In shouldering the responsibilities of making the world conform to one's words one does do something in a far more fully fledged though intuitive sense of 'do' than in taking the responsibilities for one's present words' conformity to a future state of the world. *Qua* essentially linguistic, a promise-giving cannot be an archetypical performative. Yet it comes close to archetypical performatives: in it the speaker undertakes to use his agent-powers in certain ways. Could it not reasonably be called a semiperformative?

In Ch.3:8 I called the undertaking to use one's agent-powers to a certain purpose a performatory (and not merely a semi-performatory) act; and I discussed two definitions of performative in terms of such an act. Thereby I committed the very fallacy I was at pains to point out: I confused performatoriness with illocutionarity. By promising I shoulder responsibilities to bring about the things mentioned in the content of my promise. By excommunicating I shoulder no responsibilities to cut someone off from the sacraments: I actually cut him off. I launch a campaign and do not merely declare my intention to launch it.

To issue an archetypical performative is not to bring about one's committing oneself to do something; it is the doing of that something. But to issue a promisory formula is to bring about one's committing oneself to do something; it is not the doing of the something.

As Austin detected in the last chapters of *Words*, there is no sense of 'bringing about' in which the man who seriously says 'I promise to do it' has brought about more things than the man who seriously says 'I warn you that the bull is dangerous' or 'I state that she shot him.' By their words they have shouldered various obligations but not made the words effective. Since the obligations of a promisor, but not those of a Cassandra or a witness, are obligations to make the world conform to the words, promising is tied to actions in another and more intimate way than warning and stating are. But it remains a taking on of responsibilities for an action and not the doing of the action. Like warning or stating or assuming or advising or exhorting it is an illocutionary act. But its obligations differ from these other acts in being practical—i.e., in being obligations to make the world conform to the words. Hence it comes closer to actions than stating etc. do. Obligations of promising also differ from other practical illocutionary obligations in the respect that their fulfilment is implied to be entirely up to the speaker who undertakes to work till he has fulfilled them.

A linguistic oddity. I hold, then, that serious utterances of the form 'I promise to do so-and-so' are too unlike archetypical performatives and too like ordinary linguistic utterances to be called performatives. But there is at least one further resemblance between promises and archetypical performatives.

Degree-showing devices such as 'probably' and 'possibly' cannot be inserted in archetypical performatives without destroying their characteristic function. 'Perhaps I acquit you' or 'Perhaps I excommunicate you' are not utterances which can reasonably be used to acquit or to excommunicate. For, first, since the official who performs the ceremonial acts does not shoulder the responsibility in uttering the formulae, he does not shoulder it to any extent. Secondly, even if he had, 'perhaps' would be out of order, since the string of sounds he has uttered is not judged meaningful or meaningless.

At least *prima facie* we might expect that in all force-showing illocutionary acts the speaker shoulders more or less of the ordinary responsibility. Promising, advising, and other illocutionary acts of the practical sort cannot, however, be qualified by the ordinary degree-showing devices. If President Nixon says 'I probably promise to order cease-fire' or 'I probably advise the Congress to take this line' he has not made a weak promise to order cease-fire or given a feeble piece of advice. He has at best made a half-hearted and grammatically faulty promise-cum-forecast that he later on will promise or advise.

This resemblance between archetypical performatives and illocutionary utterances of the practical sort is superficial. The performatives cannot be weakened at all. The illocutionary utterances can be weakened, but not with 'probably' and 'possibly'. 'I as good as promise to order cease-fire' and 'Perhaps I ought to advise you to take this line' are, to my mind, a weak promise and a hesitant piece of advice.

The fact that archetypical performatives cannot be weakened by *any* kind of illocutionary device is, as Beata Agrell has pointed out to me, a support of the claim that they do not have any locutionary dimension: there is nothing for the illocutionary devices to operate upon. And the perplexing fact that 'perhaps' and 'possibly' cannot qualify promises and other 'practical' illocutions (an oddity that is mirrored in several languages) is perhaps explicable in a way which does not make it a mere quirk. But the suggestive remarks which Jan Andersson has made towards a solution of the problem would take this Postscript too far afield.

Bibliography

A. COLLECTIONS

Aesthetics and Language. Ed. W. Elton. Oxford, 1954.
British Philosophy in the Mid-Century. Ed. C. A. Mace. London, 1957.
Essays in Conceptual Analysis. [ECA] Ed. A. G. N. Flew. London, 1956.
Logic and Language. [L&L, I] Ed. A. G. N. Flew. Oxford, 1952.
Philosophy and Analysis. Ed. M. Macdonald. Oxford, 1954.
Philosophy and Ordinary Language. Ed. Ch. E. Caton. Urbana, 1963.
Philosophy in America. Ed. M. Black. London, 1965.
Semantics and the Philosophy of Language. Ed. L. Linsky. Urbana, 1952.
Symposium on J. L. Austin. [Symp.] Ed. K. T. Fann. London, 1969.
The Philosophy of G. E. Moore. Ed. A. Schilpp. 2nd ed. New York, 1952.
The Philosophy of Bertrand Russell. Ed. A. Schilpp. 3rd ed. New York, 1951.

B. ARTICLES AND BOOKS

Albritton, R: 'On Wittgenstein's use of the term "criterion"'. *J.Ph.* 56 (1959).
Alston, W. P: *Philosophy of Language.* Englewood Cliffs, N. J., 1964.
Ambrose, A: 'Austin's Philosophical Papers'. *Ph.* 38 (1963).
Anscombe, G. E. M: *Intention.* Oxford, 1957.
Anscombe, G. E. M: 'Pretending'. *PASS* 32 (1958).
Arner, D: 'On knowing'. *Ph.R.* 68 (1959).
Ayer, A. J: *Language, Truth & Logic.* London, 1936.
Ayer, A. J: *Philosophical Essays.* London, 1954.
Ayer, A. J: *The Problem of Knowledge.* Pelican ed. Harmondsworth, Middlesex, 1956.
Barnes, W. H. F: 'Knowing'. *Ph.R.* 72 (1963).

Bennett, J: ' "Real" '. *Symp.*
Braithwaite, R. B: Review of Hare's *The Language of Morals. Mind* 63 (1954).
Brown, R: Joint review of *Words* and *LIA. AJP* 41 (1963).
Caton, Ch. E: 'On the general structure of the epistemic qualification of things said in English'. *Foundations of Language* 2 (1966).
Cavell, S: 'Austin at criticism'. *Symp.*
Charlesworth, M. J: 'The parenthetical use of the verb "believe" '. *Mind* 74 (1965).
Chisholm, R. M: 'J. L. Austin's Philosophical Papers'. *Symp.*
Cohen, L. J: 'Do illocutionary forces exist?'. *Symp.*
Cook, J. W: 'Wittgenstein on privacy'. *Ph.R.* 74 (1965).
Cousin, D. R: 'How not to talk'. *Analysis* 15 (1954/55).
Cox, J. W. R: 'Fitting and matching'. *Analysis* 16 (1955/56).
Cox, J. W. R: Review of *LIA.Ph.Q.* 16 (1966).
Danto, A. C: 'A note on expressions of the referring sort'. *Mind* 67 (1958).
Davis, S: ' "I know" as an explicit performative'. *Theoria* 30 (1964).
Frege, G: *The Foundations of Arithmetic.* Oxford, 1953.
Furberg, M: 'Mr Halldén on essence statements'. *Theoria* 27 (1961).
Furberg, M: 'Meaning and illocutionary force'. *Symp.*
Gardiner, A. H: *A Theory of Speech and Language.* 2nd ed. Oxford, 1951.
Gellner, E: *Words and Things.* London, 1959.
Grant, C. K: 'Pragmatic implication'. *Ph.* 33 (1958).
Grice, H. P: 'Meaning'. *Ph.R.* 66 (1957).
Griffiths, L: 'The logic of Austin's locutionary subdivision'. *Theoria* 35 (1969).
Hall, R: 'Excluders'. *Analysis* 20 (1959/60).
Halldén, S: *True Love, True Humour and True Religion.* Lund and Copenhagen, 1960.
Halldén, S: 'A reply to Mr. Furberg'. *Theoria* 27 (1961).
Hampshire, S: 'J. L. Austin'. *Symp.*
Hanson, N. R: *Patterns of Discovery.* Cambridge, 1958.
Hare, R. M: 'Imperative sentences'. *Mind* 58 (1949).
Hare, R. M: *The Language of Morals.* Oxford, 1952.
Hare, R. M: Review of E. W. Hall's *What Is Value? Mind* 63 (1954).
Hartnack, J: *Filosofiske essays.* Copenhagen, 1957.
Hartnack, J: 'The performative use of sentences' (mimeographed). Published in *Theoria* 29 (1963).
Hedenius, I: 'Performativer' (mimeographed). An English version in *Theoria* 29 (1963).

BIBLIOGRAPHY

Holdcroft, D: 'Meaning and illocutionary acts'. *Ratio* 4 (1964).
Hume, D: *A Treatise of Human Nature*.
Husserl, E: *Logische Untersuchungen*, II:1. Halle a.d.S., 1913.
Hägerström, A: *Religionsfilosofi*. Stockholm, 1949.
Hägerström, A: *Socialfilosofiska uppsatser*. Stockholm, 1939.
MacIver, A. M: 'Some questions about "know" and "think"'. *Philosophy and Analysis*.
Malcolm, N: 'Wittgenstein's *Philosophical Investigations*'. *Ph.R.* 63 (1954).
Mayo, B: 'The varieties of imperatives'. *PASS* 31 (1957).
Mitchell, B: 'The varieties of imperatives'. *PASS* 31 (1957).
Moore, G. E: *The Commonplace Book*. London, 1962.
Moore, G. E: *Ethics*. London, no date.
Moore, G. E: *Philosophical Papers*. London, 1959.
Moore, G. E: *Philosophical Studies*. London, 1922.
Moore, G. E: 'A reply to my critics'. *The Philosophy of G. E. Moore*.
Moore, G. E: 'Russell's "Theory of Descriptions"'. *The Philosophy of Bertrand Russell*.
Moore, G. E: *Some Main Problems of Philosophy*. London 1953.
Naess, A: 'Towards a theory of interpretation and preciseness'. *Semantics and the Philosophy of Language*.
Naess, A: *Interpretation and Preciseness*. Oslo, 1953.
New, C. G: 'A plea for linguistics'. *Symp.*
Nordenstam, T: 'On Austin's theory of speech-acts'. *Mind* 75 (1966).
Nowell-Smith, P. H: 'Contextual implication and ethical theory'. *PASS* 36 (1962).
Nowell-Smith, P. H: *Ethics*. Pelican ed. Harmondsworth, Middlesex, 1954.
Passmore, J: *A Hundred Years of Philosophy*. London, 1957.
Peirce, C. S: *Collected Papers*, V. Cambridge (Mass.), 1934.
Prichard, H. A: *Knowledge and Perception*. Oxford, 1950.
Prichard, H. A: *Moral Obligation*. Oxford, 1949.
Russell, B: *My Philosophical Development*. London, 1959.
Russell, B: *Portraits from Memory*. London, 1956.
Russell, B: *The Problems of Philosophy*. London, no date.
Ryle, G: *The Concept of Mind*. London, 1949.
Ryle, G: *Dilemmas*. Cambridge, 1956.
Ryle, G: 'Feelings'. *Aesthetics and Language*.
Ryle, G: 'Ordinary language'. *Ph.R.* 62 (1953).
Ryle, G: 'Philosophical arguments'. Oxford, 1945.
Ryle, G: Review of Carnap's *Meaning and Necessity*. *Ph.* 24 (1949).
Ryle, G: 'The Theory of Meaning'. *British Philosophy in the Mid-Century*.

Ryle, G: 'Systematically misleading expressions'. *L&L*, I.
Samek, R: 'Performative utterances and the concept of contract'. *AJP* 43 (1965).
Saussure, F. de: *Cours de linguistique générale*. Paris, 1955.
Searle, J. R: 'What is a speech act?'. *Philosophy in America*.
Searle, J. R: Review of *LIA*. *Ph.R.* 75 (1966).
Scriven, M: 'The logic of criteria'. *J.Ph.* 56 (1959).
Segelberg, I: *Studier över medvetandet och jagidén*. Stockholm, 1953.
Shorter, J. M: 'Facts, logical atomism and reducibility'. *AJP* 40 (1962).
Stenius, E: *Wittgenstein's* 'Tractatus'. Oxford, 1960.
Stevenson, Ch. L: *Ethics and Language*. New Haven, 1944.
Strawson, P. F: 'Identifying reference and truth-value'. *Theoria* 30 (1964).
Strawson, P. F: *Individuals*. London, 1959.
Strawson, P. F: 'Intention and convention in speech acts'. *Symp*.
Strawson, P. F: *Introduction to Logical Theory*. London, 1952.
Strawson, P. F: 'On referring'. *ECA*.
Strawson, P. F: 'A reply to Mr. Sellars'. *Ph.R.* 63 (1954).
Strawson, P. F: 'Singular terms and predication'. *J.Ph.* 57 (1961).
Strawson, P. F: 'Truth' I. *Philosophy and Analysis*.
Strawson, P. F: 'Truth' II. *PASS* 24 (1950).
Strawson, P. F: 'Truth: a reconsideration of Austin's views'. *Ph.Q.* 15 (1965).
Tarski, A: 'The semantic conception of truth'. *Semantics and the Philosophy of Language*.
Toulmin, S: *The Place of Reason in Ethics*. Cambridge, 1953.
Toulmin, S: *The Uses of Argument*. Cambridge, 1958.
Urmson, J. O: 'John Langshaw Austin'. *Analysis* 20 (1960).
Urmson, J. O: 'Austin's Philosophy'. *Symp*.
Urmson, J. O: 'On grading'. *ECA*.
Urmson, J. O: 'Parenthetical verbs'. *ECA*.
Urmson, J. O. & Warnock, G. J: 'J. L. Austin'. *Symp*.
Vendler, Z: *Linguistics in Philosophy*. Ithaca, N.Y., 1967.
Waismann, F: 'Verifiability'. *L&L*, I.
Warnock, G. J: *English Philosophy Since 1900*. London, 1958.
Warnock, G. J. & Urmson, J. O. See Urmson.
Wennerberg, Hj.: *The Pragmatism of C. S. Peirce*. Lund and Copenhagen, 1962.
White, A. R: *G. E. Moore*. Oxford, 1958.
White, A. R: 'On claiming to know'. *Ph.R.* 66 (1957).
White, A. R: 'The "meaning" of Russell's Theory of Descriptions'. *Analysis* 20 (1959/60).

White, A. R: Review of Austin's *Philosophical Papers*. *Philosophical Books* 3 (1962).
White, A. R: Review of *LIA*. *Mind* 74 (1965).
Whorf, B. L: *Language, Thought and Reality*. New York, 1959.
Wilson, J. C: *Statement and Inference*. Oxford, 1926.
Wilson, P: 'Austin on knowing'. *Inquiry* 3 (1960).
Wisdom, J: *Other Minds*. Oxford, 1952.
Wisdom, J: *Philosophy and Psycho-Analysis*. Oxford, 1953.
Wittgenstein, L: *The Brown and the Blue Books*. Oxford, 1958.
Wittgenstein, L: *Philosophical Investigations*. Oxford, 1953.
Wittgenstein, L: *Tractatus Logico-Philosophicus*. 2nd English ed. London, 1961.
Wright, G. H. von: 'On promises' (mimeographed; reprinted in *Theoria* 28 (1962).
Wright, M: ' "I know" and performative utterances'. *AJP* 43 (1965).
Ziff, P: 'On H. P. Grice's account of meaning'. *Analysis* 28 (1967).

(The following abbreviations have been used:
AJP for *The Australasian Journal of Philosophy*,
J.Ph. for *The Journal of Philosophy*,
PASS for *Proceedings of the Aristotelian Society, Suppl. Volume*,
Ph. for *Philosophy*,
Ph.Q. for *The Philosophical Quarterly*, and
Ph.R. for *The Philosophical Review*.)

Index

aberration, 77–80
abuse, 198
adapter-word, 16, 60–70, 171
Agrell, 289
Albritton, 72n
Alston, 272–3
Ambrose, 24n, 31n
Andersson, 290
Anscombe, 23, 104n
apposition usage, 141f
Aristotle, 15, 16, 44, 51, 79, 122
Arner, 248, 252, 255
Ayer, 7, 137, 191n, 231f

backing, conclusiveness of, 248ff
backing, reliability of, 174, 182–5, 249, 251f
backing, sufficiency of, 174–82, 250f
Barnes, 195–6
'basic proposition', 77–80, 181–2
behabitive, 215–16, 287
belief, 231–44
Bennett, 60n
Braithwaite, 114n
Broad, 51
Brown, 201n

Caton, 246n
Cavell, 31n
Charlesworth, 235n
Chisholm, 59n, 81n
Cohen, 261, 270n, 287
commissive, 215
concept, 3–27
constative, 37, 75, 116f, 158–73, 201–6, 217–18, 226–8
contradiction, 204f, 247

convention, classificatory, 58, 76–80
convention, horizontal, 70f
convention, individuating, 58
convention, vertical, 33, 58, 71–4
Cook, 18n
Cousin, 58
Cox, 83–4, 86, 213n
criterion, 72, 187–91
criteria-delimitation, 51, 72f, 175–177, 189

Danto, 155
Davis, 254n
degree-showing expression, 219, 229–55
discourse, 99–107
discourse-implication, see implication
discourse-marking expression, 219–228

entailment, 70f, 167
etiolation, 97–8, 199
excluder, 62–5
exercitive, 215, 279, 287
expositive, 215

fact, 136–55
fit, 163–6, 168–71
fit, direction of, 82–8
force, illocutionary, 7, 56, 89–117, 134, 206–55, 263–90
Force Thesis, 192, 206–19
force-ambiguity, 207f, 212
Frege, 6, 36

Gardiner, 6, 52, 57, 257n

INDEX

Gellner, 35n, 43–6
Grant, 95, 97f, 102
Grice, 256–8, 266–7, 275
Griffiths, 57n

Hall, 63
Halldén, 44n, 66–9, 173
Hampshire, 31n, 36–7, 46n, 49n, 50, 52n, 56
Hanson, 39n
Hare, 25, 113f
Hartnack, 150n, 192n, 194n, 202
Hedenius, 192n, 193n, 202–6
Holdcroft, 273
Hume, 20f, 25f, 279
Husserl, 113f
Hägerström, 27n, 210

illocutionary act, 89–115, 192–290
illocutionary force, see force
implication, discourse, 99–101
implication, pragmatic, 94–107
inference-marking expression, 229
I-word, 75

Kant, 33n, 107, 205

language, science of, 47–50, 107f
Lindström, 272n
Locke, 79
locutionary act, 56–88, 108–15, 203, 256–79

MacIver, 234n
Malcolm, 72n
match, onus of, 82–8
Mayo, 114n
meaning, name theory of, 5, 9–31, 59, 65
meaning $_{NN}$, 256–79
misfire, 198, 202
Mitchell, 114n
Moore, 2–31, 38, 45, 55, 65, 74n, 94, 186n, 233f

Naess, 50n
neustic, 114–15, 208, 218, 246–7
New, 27n

Nowell-Smith, 25, 93, 96
Nordenstam, 213n, 216n

open texture, 33, 34, 71–4

Passmore, 47n
Peirce, 107n
performative, 37, 106–7, 127f, 192–206, 212–18, 279–90
performative, archetypical, 280–90
performative, explicit, 193–200
performative, implicit, 211f
performative, primary, 211f
Performative Thesis, 192, 200–23, 225f
perlocutionary act, 109–11, 263–5, 269–75
pheme, 57f, 75, 87, 111, 121, 134, 203, 277f, 285
phenomenology, linguistic, 23, 31–47
phone, 56ff, 111, 285
phrastic, 113–15, 246–7
Plato, 17, 18, 59, 63n
P-radical, 206–7, 208, 214–17, 226, 272, 279–90
preciseness, 163, 168–71
presumption, 73–4, 177–80
'presupposition' 119, 121, 155–8
'problematic' device, 205, 244f
promising, 106f, 200, 210, 212, 219–226, 227, 279–90
Prichard, 51, 52, 220, 279
proposition, 27f, 30f, 218

quasi-contraction, 61–2, 68ff
quasi-extension, 61–2, 69f

Rachels, 261n
referring, 76–9, 121f, 156–8, 171–3
Reid, 34n
relevance (to the addressee), 93ff
rheme, 57f, 75, 87, 111, 121, 122, 134, 207, 277f, 285, 287
roughness, 166–8
Russell, 1n, 12–15, 17f, 29, 155
Ryle, 23, 25f, 28, 52, 53n, 246n

Samek, 193n

Sapir, 27
Saussure, de, 57
schematization, 168
Scriven, 72n
Schopenhauer, 15n
Searle, 116n, 213n, 214n, 258, 274, 275
Segelberg, 137, 144f, 168
Shorter, 143n
statement, ideal, 169f
Stenius, 114
Stevenson, 67, 126
Strawson, 71n, 117–60, 166, 187, 188, 258–9, 273–4, 275, 285f
supplementation: see P–radical

Tarski, 117, 121, 122
Toulmin, 25, 192n, 245
truth, ideal, 170–3
T–word, 75

universal, 9–19
Urmson, 25, 31n, 36n, 37, 38n, 192n, 230, 231, 232, 234, 236–42, 248, 251, 252, 255, 278

verdictive, 215, 279, 287
Vendler, 145n
vocable, 58

Waismann, 33n, 74
Warnock, 36n, 37, 88n
Wennerberg, 107n
White, 2n, 4f, 13n, 26n, 30, 144, 248, 252, 255
Whorf, 27
Wilson, J. C., 51, 52
Wilson, P., 73, 177f, 180–1
Wisdom, 39n, 51, 238n
Wittgenstein, 2, 15, 18n, 23, 24n, 29, 34, 35n, 39n, 49, 50–5, 77, 108, 146, 160, 231, 233
Wright, M., 254n
Wright, G. H. von, 192n, 202, 220–222

Ziff, 258